Hiking
Wyoming's
Wind River Range

Ron Adkison

FALCONGUIDES ®

GUILFORD, CONNECTICUT
HELENA, MONTANA

AN IMPRINT OF THE GLOBE PEQUOT PRESS

FALCONGUIDES®

All black-and-white photos by Ron Adkison.
Cover photo of Indian Basin and Fremont Peak by Fred Pflughoft

Library of Congress Catologing-in-Publication Data

Adkison, Ron.
    Hiking Wyoming's Wind River Range / by Ron Adkison.
        p.   cm.
    ISBN-13: 978-1-56044-402-2
    1. Hiking—Wyoming—Wind River Range—Guidebooks.
2. Mountaineering—Wyoming—Wind River Range—Guidebooks. 3. Wind
River Range (Wyo.)—Guidebooks. 4. n-us-wy I. Title.
GV199.42W82W5617 1996
917.87—dc20   96-9104
                                                                                CIP

♻ Text pages printed on recycled paper.
Printed in the United States of America
First Edition/Eighth Printing

CONTENTS

CONTENTS

CONTENTS

ACKNOWLEDGMENTS

Writing this guidebook to the Wind River Range has fulfilled a dream I've had for more than fourteen years, when I first began exploring these wonderful mountains. From the initial planning stages through the final printout of the manuscript, this project has been an immensely rewarding and unforgettable experience. But without the help and support of numerous people, this book still would be just a dream.

Special thanks go to Randall Green at Falcon Press, who has supported and steadfastly stood behind this project since its inception.

And without Cindy Stein, Eric Sandeno, and Mary Skinner at the Pinedale Ranger District, who shared their documents and vast knowledge of the Bridger Wilderness, this book would be incomplete at best.

Countless others, both on the trail and in ranger district offices, shared their knowledge and insights, and they, perhaps unknowingly, contributed enormously to this book.

ABOUT THE AUTHOR

Ron Adkison, an avid hiker and backpacker, began his outdoor explorations at age 6. Since that time, he has logged more than 5,000 trail miles in ten western states. When he's not on the trail, Ron is managing a remote ranch in the mountains of southwestern Montana, with the help of his wife and two children, where they raise sheep and llamas.

Ron shares his love for the backcountry in this, his fifth guidebook.

OVERVIEW MAP

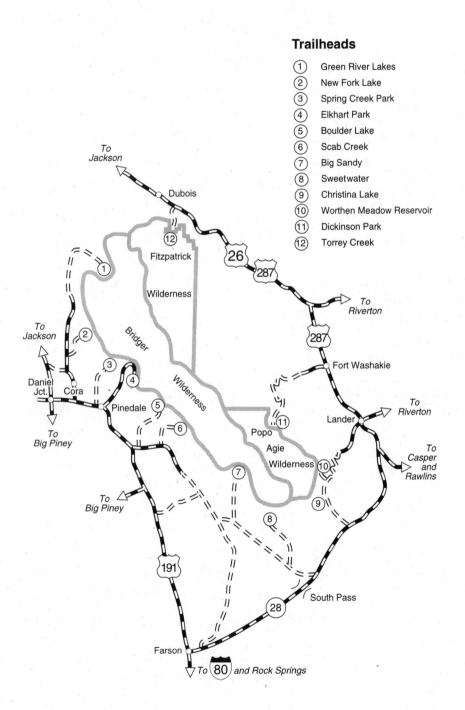

Trailheads

1. Green River Lakes
2. New Fork Lake
3. Spring Creek Park
4. Elkhart Park
5. Boulder Lake
6. Scab Creek
7. Big Sandy
8. Sweetwater
9. Christina Lake
10. Worthen Meadow Reservoir
11. Dickinson Park
12. Torrey Creek

USGS TOPOGRAPHIC MAPS

Index to USGS 7.5 Minute Quadrangles

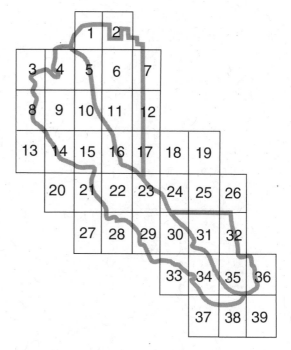

1 Simpson Lake
2 Torrey Lake
3 Big Sheep Mountain
4 Green River Lakes
5 Downs Mountain
6 Ink Wells
7 Hays Park
8 Kendall Mountain
9 Squaretop Mountain
10 Gannett Peak
11 Fremont Peak North
12 Bob Lakes
13 New Fork Lakes
14 Fremont Lake North
15 Bridger Lakes
16 Fremont Peak South
17 Alpine Lake
18 Paradise Basin
19 St. Lawrence Basin
20 Fremont Lake South
21 Fayette Lake
22 Horseshoe Lake
23 Halls Mountain
24 Roberts Mountain
25 Washakie Park
26 Moccasin Lake
27 Boulder Lake
28 Scab Creek
29 Raid Lake
30 Mount Bonneville
31 Lizard Head Peak
32 Dickinson Park
33 Big Sandy Opening
34 Temple Peak
35 Sweetwater Gap
36 Cony Mountain
37 Jensen Meadows
38 Sweetwater Needles
39 Christina Lake

LEGEND

State or Other Principal Road	(000)	Marsh	
Forest Road	0000	Campground	▲
Paved Road		Bridge	
Gravel Road		Cabins/Buildings	■
Unimproved Road	= = = = = = = ▷	Peak/Elevation	9,782 ft.
Trailhead/Parking	◯ Ⓟ	Falls	
Main Trail(s)		Pass/Saddle	) (
Climbing Route		Snowfield	
Alternate/ Secondary Trails/ Cross-Country Trails		Cliffs	
River/Creek		Gate	
Lake		Map Orientation	N
Ditch		Scale	0 0.5 1 Miles
Spring			
Continental Divide			

Mount Bonneville and South Fork Boulder Creek from the Dream Lake Trail.

INTRODUCTION

Rising abruptly from the sagebrush-clad hills of South Pass in west-central Wyoming, the stony battlements of the Wind River Range pierce the sky with 12,000- and 13,000-foot summits for some 90 miles northwest to Union Pass. Here the range abandons its lofty prominences and meanders northwest in a series of progressively lower timberline hills for another 20 miles to Togwotee (pronounced To-gu-tee) Pass, where the range merges with the volcanic Absaroka Range.

The Wind River Range encompasses an area of 2.25 million acres, and stretches 110 miles between South Pass and Togwotee Pass. It also helps form a triple divide, shedding water to three major western rivers: the Gros Ventre (a Snake River tributary), the Green (a Colorado River tributary), and the Wind (a Yellowstone River tributary) rivers.

From the Green River Basin on the west, to the Wind River Valley on the east, the range averages 35 to 40 miles wide. It is the largest fault block range in the Rocky Mountain chain, with some of the greatest vertical displacement on Earth.

Much of the Wind Rivers' crest forms the Continental Divide, capped by a succession of broad summits, alpine plateaus, and needlelike spires (forty-eight of which exceed 12,500 feet in elevation). The range reaches its apex atop 13,804-foot Gannett Peak, the loftiest summit in Wyoming.

From the divide, broad alpine plateaus, deep canyons, and long hogback ridges of sedimentary rocks slope eastward into the semi-arid expanse of the Wind River Valley near the towns of Dubois and Lander. The western flanks of the range rise steadily from the upper Green River Basin, near the towns of Farson, Boulder, and Pinedale, to a broad, terracelike bench that occupies much of the range's west slopes from about 9,500 to 10,500 feet. Above that bench, U-shaped alpine valleys reach up to cirque basins carved into the high peaks of the Continental Divide.

Four wilderness areas embrace nearly one million acres of the Wind River backcountry. The 428,169-acre Bridger Wilderness, consistently one of the ten most heavily used wilderness areas in the nation, protects the bulk of the Wind Rivers' west slopes. The 191,103-acre Fitzpatrick Wilderness, the 180,387-acre Wind River Roadless Area (administered by the Wind River Indian Reservation), and the 101,991-acre Popo Agie (pronounced po-PO-zhia) Wilderness protect the high country east of the Continental Divide.

More than 2,000 high mountain lakes and countless tarns and ponds dot the backcountry, many of them brimming with a variety of trout species, making the Wind Rivers one of the finest backcountry fishing areas in the contiguous United States. The largest glaciers in the American Rockies cling to the flanks of the serrated 13,000-foot peaks in the northern reaches of the range, and smaller glaciers and permanent snowfields reside in sheltered recesses throughout the range.

The bulk of the Wind Rivers was carved and sculpted by three major glacial episodes, leaving behind extensive areas of ice-polished granitic bedrock. In spite of the dominance of bedrock in the backcountry, there are broad stretches of meadows and tundra rich with the fragrant and colorful blooms of myriad wildflowers.

The Wind Rivers are a mecca for backcountry travelers, with exceptional opportunities for wilderness rock climbing, mountaineering, off-trail exploration, and extended backcountry trail trips. There are also ample opportunities for trips by day hikers and families with children.

USING THIS BOOK

An almost unlimited variety of trips are available in the Wind Rivers, and every group entering the backcountry has different plans and expectations. This guidebook covers nearly all of the wilderness trails in the range and offers suggestions for extended trips. Ultimately, however, it is left to the reader to devise a trip that best suits his or her goals. This book, then, is but a stepping stone into the backcountry of the Wind River Range.

The trail descriptions in this guidebook are, for the most part, self-explanatory. A few points, however, require further discussion to help you get the most from each description.

An *extended* trip indicates a commitment of several days on the trail. If a trip is listed as a day hike or overnight trip, then the trip can be completed in one day, or can be taken at a slower pace, allowing for nights spent in the backcountry.

There are four types of trips described in the book. The *round trip,* where you travel in to a destination and return the same way; the *loop trip,* where you travel into the backcountry on one trail, and return on another; the *semi-loop* trip, where you retrace part of a trail after making a loop somewhere along the way; and the *one-way* trip. One-way trips as described in this guidebook usually lead you to a major trail junction in an area where you can establish a base camp. These trips offer the possibility of extending a trip by choosing from a variety of nearby trails.

Difficulty indicates the rigors of a particular trip, based on the probability that you will be covering the trail over several days time.

Traffic indicates the average level of use. *Heavy* traffic means you're likely to encounter 10 or more other groups on the trail each day. On trails with *Moderate* traffic, you may see 5 to 10 groups daily, and *Light* traffic indicates 5 groups or less per day on the trail. Trail traffic can be highly variable, and fluctuates daily. In the off-season (September), heavy traffic areas can become almost deserted.

Elevation gain and loss figures also help you to determine the rigors of a trail. On a loop or semi-loop trip, gain and loss figures show the *total* amount of up and down travel encountered on a trail. For round trips and one-way trips, elevation gain and loss figures show the one-way amount of up and down travel. For example, on a trail where you gain 1,500 feet and lose 1,000 feet while en route to your destination, you must the regain that 1,000 feet of lost elevation on your return trip to the trailhead.

Since most trails as described are multi-day trips, the *best day hike destination* offers suggestions for day trips along parts of certain trails.

Key points show cumulative mileage between prominent features and junctions.

Unnamed features mentioned in trail descriptions are referred to as "Lake 10,450," "Peak 11,860," "Point 12,246," or "Pass 10,850."

Some cross-country routes mentioned are classified as *class 2* and *class 3* routes. Class 2 routes are typically scrambles over rough terrain, involving occasional boulder-hopping and scrambling over steep and sometimes unstable slopes. You must use your hands at times to latch on to a handhold and to maintain balance.

Class 3 routes are more demanding, and entail rudimentary rock climbing skills where the use of handholds and footholds come into play. These routes often involve some exposure, and a fall can lead to serious injury.

MAPS

The maps in this book are designed to provide a general overview of trails. They are not intended for serious navigating in the backcountry.

Three kinds of maps are useful for navigation in the Wind Rivers. First, there are Forest Service maps, available at ranger district offices, which give you a general overview of the range, and they are particularly useful for finding trailheads. The map of the Pinedale Ranger District, including the Bridger Wilderness, shows contour lines (in meters) and all maintained trails.

The most popular maps with Wind River travelers are produced by Earthwalk Press. These useful maps are printed on tear-resistant, waterproof material, and are on a scale of 1:48,000 (1 inch = 1.25 miles). Most trails covered in this guidebook are shown on the two large maps that cover the Wind Rivers. The Northern Wind River Range Map shows the range from Elkhart Park north, and covers eighteen 7.5-minute USGS quads. The Southern Wind River Range Map shows the range from Pole Creek to Sweetwater Gap, but does not show the Sweetwater, Christina Lake, or Worthen Meadow Reservoir trailheads. This map covers fifteen 7.5-minute USGS quads. Be aware that in many places the trails are not accurately plotted on these maps, and some trails shown are unmaintained, abandoned, or are invisible on the ground. To add to the confusion of map users, trails are shown as dotted lines, and trailless routes are shown as dashed lines.

Earthwalk maps are available at outdoor shops and ranger district offices in Dubois, Lander, and Pinedale.

USGS 7.5-minute maps offer the most accurate representation of the landscape and trails in the Wind Rivers, and many seasoned veteran travelers prefer them. These maps are on a scale of 1:24,000 (1 mile = 2 5/8 inches), and to travel most of the trail trips covered in this guidebook, you need only carry two or three USGS quads.

Some of these maps are outdated and may not show some trails. Like Earthwalk maps, some trails shown on USGS quads may be impossible to locate on the ground.

USGS quads are available in outdoor shops and USFS stations in towns adjacent to the Wind Rivers, or you can order them directly from the USGS. Topographic quadrangles are available at a cost of $4.00 each, with a handling charge of $3.50 on all orders. USGS orders often take one to two months to process, so order your maps well in advance of your trip.

Send orders to: Distribution Branch, United States Geological Survey, Box 25286, Denver Federal Center, Denver, Colorado 80225.

BACKCOUNTRY TRAVEL

More than 900,000 acres of wilderness lands and 700 miles of trails creates a puzzling dilemma for many wilderness travelers, both novices and veterans alike: Where to go in the vast, high mountain landscape of the Wind Rivers?

A timberline campsite in the Wind River backcountry. Notice that the camp is located on a durable site, well away from the streambank and trail.

Well-known places such as Titcomb Basin and Big Sandy Lake attract a disproportionately large number of visitors, while lesser-known but equally attractive areas see few visitors.

Before embarking on your wilderness vacation in the Wind Rivers, first study topographic maps and the trail descriptions in this book, then decide where you intend to go *before* you leave home. Too many backpackers arrive in nearby towns such as Pinedale without a backcountry itinerary, and they end up crowding into ranger stations and local outdoor shops, and begin their lengthy interrogations with, "We want to go backpacking in the Wind Rivers, but we don't know where to go."

Preparation and advanced planning are the key to a successful and enjoyable trip in the Wind River backcountry. But along with the freedom this wilderness inspires goes a measure of responsibility for its preservation, and for your own personal safety.

WHAT IS WILDERNESS?

If you've ever been to places like Island Lake, Titcomb Basin, or Big Sandy Lake in the Bridger Wilderness, with their tent cities typical of the summer months, you may conclude that this is not "wilderness." People

Popo Agie Wilderness boundary.

Continental Divide peaks from a pass east of Lozier Lakes. Gannett Peak (highest in Wyoming) is at right center.

have different expectations of their wilderness experience; some find comfort among other travelers in the backcountry, while others seek out the most remote recesses in the range, far from colorful tents and neighboring campers.

At many trailheads you'll find large numbers of vehicles, but the backcountry landscape is vast and intricately dissected by creeks, ridges, domes, basins, and cirques. Such a landscape can absorb and dilute the number of visitors. Except at the most popular backcountry destinations, the wilderness lands of the Wind Rivers seldom seem crowded.

Novice backcountry travelers are visiting the Wind Rivers in increasing numbers each year, and some of them may be unaware of what defines wilderness. The Wilderness Act of 1964 was enacted "to assure that an increasing population, accompanied by expanding settlement and growing mechanization, does not occupy and modify all areas within the United States," and "to secure for the American people. . . the benefits of an enduring resource of wilderness."

The act defined wilderness as "an area where the earth and its community of life are untrammeled by man, where man himself is a visitor who does not remain."

In the Wind River wilderness, there are no roads, only trails; there are few signs and no developments of any kind, save for occasional bridges. Here natural processes continue unrestricted by human interference. Nature's schedule in the wilderness is tied to the rising and setting of the sun, and to the changing of the seasons, not to the time clock. Here you are on your own, free to travel wherever and whenever you choose. But you are also responsible for preserving the wilderness resource, not only in regard for the communities of plants and animals that reside there, but also for the next person on the trail and for future generations to enjoy as you did.

WILDERNESS REGULATIONS

To preserve the wilderness resource for both natural communities and to maintain the qualities of wilderness that visitors seek, the Bridger and Shoshone national forests have adopted the following regulations. Familiarize yourself with them *before* you venture out into the backcountry.

BRIDGER WILDERNESS

1) Group size is limited to 15 people and 25 pack and saddle stock.

2) Camping within 200 feet of any lake or maintained trail is prohibited. This includes tethering and picketing of stock. (All trails shown on the Pinedale District map of the Bridger National Forest are maintained trails.)

3) Organized groups, including scouts, church groups, school groups, etc., and visitors using pack and saddle stock (including llamas and goats), must obtain a visitor permit, available free of charge from the Pinedale District Office (see address below). Groups are advised to plan their trips in advance to avoid scheduling conflicts with other organized groups applying for permits.

Organized groups are encouraged to camp outside of the following areas to reduce physical and social impacts to resources and other visitors: Titcomb Basin, Island Lake, Seneca Lake, Hobbs Lake, Barbara Lake, Big Sandy Lake, Green River Lakes, and Slide Lake.

4) Campfires are allowed below timberline, using downed materials only.

5) The maximum length of stay is 16 days. After 16 days, campsites must be moved at least 1 mile from the original site. Visitors may not return to the original campsite for at least 5 days. Campsites may not be left unattended for more than a 24-hour period.

6) Bulk hay or straw is not permitted in the Bridger Wilderness.

7) Motorized and mechanized vehicles, including bicycles, chain saws, snowmachines, and carts, are prohibited (as they are in all national forest wilderness areas).

8) All unburned refuse must be packed out, not buried.

9) Grazing, picketing, and tethering of recreational stock must be at least 100 feet from streams and 200 feet from lakes, maintained trails, and other occupied campsites. Stock must be tied so as not to damage any tree, vegetation, or the soil.

POPO AGIE WILDERNESS

1) Camping within 200 feet of trails, lakes, and streams shown as a solid blue line on USGS topographic maps is prohibited.

2) A livestock use permit is required for recreational use of pack and saddle stock, including goats and llamas. The permit is available free of charge from the Washakie Ranger District office in Lander (see address below).

3) Shortcutting trails and switchbacks is prohibited.

4) Group size is limited to 20 people, and 30 head of transportation livestock.

5) Maximum length of stay at campsites is limited to 16 consecutive days between Memorial Day and Labor Day.

6) Camping at sites posted closed to camping is not permitted.

7) Camping, and building, maintaining, attending, or using a campfire within 0.25 mile of the shore of Lonesome Lake (in the Cirque of the Towers) is prohibited.

FITZPATRICK WILDERNESS

1) Campsites must be located at least 100 feet from trails, lakes, and streams shown as a solid blue line on USGS topographic maps.

2) Camping at sites posted closed to camping is not permitted.

3) Maximum group size is limited to 20 people, and 30 head of pack and saddle stock.

4) Only pelletized feed, processed grain, or weed seed-free hay certified by a federal, state, or county officer, is allowed in the wilderness.

5) Shortcutting switchbacks is prohibited.

6) Visitors are required to pack out all unburned refuse, and to dismantle camp structures including hitch rails, tent frames, picket pins, and fire rings, before leaving campsites.

7) Camping, leaving camping equipment, or otherwise occupying a single location for a period exceeding 16 consecutive days is prohibited. The term "location" means the occupied undeveloped campsite and the lands within a 5-mile radius of the campsite. After leaving a location, a minimum of 7 days is required before any group or person may reoccupy the original location.

8) Using a saddle, pack, or draft animal on maintained trails, unless the animal is being ridden or led by a rope, is prohibited, except where hazardous footing exists or where posted.

9) Possessing or using a wagon, cart, bicycle, or other vehicle, and motorized equipment, is prohibited. Persons using a non-motorized wheelchair as a necessary medical appliance are exempt from this prohibition.

10) Camping within 100 feet of any campsite signed, and assigned for outfitter permittee use during the permittee's scheduled use period, is prohibited.

11) Building, maintaining, or using a campfire, and overnight camping by

groups with transportation livestock, is prohibited between the confluence of Knoll Lake Creek and Dinwoody Creek (at the south end of Wilson Meadows), and the base of the Dinwoody Glacier, on the Glacier Trail.

WIND RIVER INDIAN RESERVATION

This guidebook does not cover trails in the Wind River Roadless Area on the Wind River Indian Reservation. Trails there are infrequently maintained, unsigned, and sometimes hard to follow. Several trailheads once open to the public are now closed, unless you hire an outfitter/guide licensed to operate on tribal lands.

Some travelers, however, cross over onto tribal lands from the Bridger and Popo Agie wilderness areas. Users of the Reservation are required to purchase a tribal fishing permit, which also serves as a trespass permit, allowing you to fish, hike, and camp on tribal lands. Permits are available at the Shoshone and Arapaho Tribal Fish and Game Office in Fort Washakie (14 miles north of Lander on U.S. Highway 287), and at various locations in Lander, Dubois, Riverton, and Pinedale.

For further information, contact:
Shoshone and Arapaho Tribes
Fish and Game Department
P.O. Box 217
Fort Washakie, Wyoming 82514
(307) 332-7207

For further information regarding the Bridger Wilderness, contact:
Bridger-Teton National Forest
Pinedale Ranger District
29 East Fremont Lake Road
P.O. Box 220
Pinedale, Wyoming 82941
(307) 367-4326

For further information regarding the Popo Agie Wilderness, contact:
Shoshone National Forest
Washakie Ranger District
33 East Main Street
Lander, Wyoming 82520
(307) 332-5460 or 332-9071

For further information regarding the Fitzpatrick Wilderness, contact:
Shoshone National Forest
Wind River Ranger District
1403 West Ramshorn
P.O. Box 186
Dubois, Wyoming 82513
(307) 455-2466

WHAT TO EXPECT ON WIND RIVER TRAILS

Hundreds of miles of backcountry trails in the Wind River Range offer relatively easy access into its remote interior. Some visitors never leave the trails during their travels, while others seek out tracts of trailless terrain. Nearly all of the trails in the national forest wilderness areas within the range are passable even to novice travelers, but most trails are rough and some are difficult to follow.

In the Bridger Wilderness most trails traverse the extensive benchland at mid-elevations. Ascents and descents there are relatively minor. Major canyons, typical of most mountain ranges, are noticeably absent in the Bridger, and the few canyons lie far below the bench, near the western foot of the range.

By contrast, the eastern slopes of the range are dissected by many long, deep canyons. Backcountry travel here is more rigorous, often involving lengthy ascents over high passes and plateaus, and arduous travel into and out of the prominent canyons.

Lower No Name Lake.

Trails are maintained as funding and personnel allow. There is a lack of an adequate number of backcountry rangers in most areas, so not all trails are frequently maintained. You may encounter down trees or rocks blocking some trails, signs missing at junctions, or unchecked erosion.

Signs are usually posted at junctions on maintained trails. In the Shoshone National Forest, signs usually give the trail's name. In the Bridger Wilderness, signs point to the nearest destination, likely a lake, pass, or trailhead. Signs showing mileage in the Bridger are being removed; it will be up to visitors to estimate distances between points. Place-name signs, such as at lakes and streams, are absent.

Most Wind River trails are easy to follow, and few trails have very steep grades. But most are rocky, which can slow your pace considerably. In the tundra above timberline, and in meadows and bogs, trails are often obscure. Cairns may indicate the route of an invisible trail; in other places you must navigate on your own, even though the trail may be considered maintained and is shown on maps.

The greatest obstacle to travel in the Wind Rivers is not a lack of signs or trail maintenance but a lack of bridged stream crossings. Bridges are found only where no safe crossing exists during periods of normal water flow. Fording streams is a part of the challenge of wilderness travel, but fords slow you down and can be dangerous and even impossible if runoff is high.

After snowmelt runoff subsides, most stream fords covered in this book are little more than a nuisance, though waters in some streams can be knee deep, and moss-covered rocks are slippery.

It is best to avoid fording streams in your boots; hiking with wet boots invites blisters. Many backpackers ford streams in camp shoes or sandals. A staff is helpful to maintain your balance.

Backpackers far outnumber users of pack and saddle stock on Wind River trails. Yet traveling on horseback is a traditional means of backcountry transportation, and stock parties who follow minimum impact guidelines may have little more impact on the wilderness than backpackers do. When sharing trails with stock parties, hikers can employ some basic trail courtesy to help avoid unnecessary conflicts.

Since it is difficult and sometimes dangerous for stock traffic to move off the trail, hikers should yield the right-of-way and stand well off the trail to allow stock parties to pass. Talk to the packer in a normal tone of voice to let the animals know you're there. If you're traveling with a dog, keep it under control when approaching stock parties; some horses are easily spooked by dogs. Llamas (used as pack animals) may also spook a horse.

Finally, bear in mind the high elevations of most of the Wind Rivers' trails, generally at or above 10,000 feet. Altitude sickness, characterized by symptoms of headache, shortness of breath, fatigue, nausea, lack of appetite, and insomnia, is the most common affliction of travelers in the Wind Rivers. If you live at a low elevation, spend a day or two in a local town or at the trailhead to acclimate to the reduced oxygen at higher elevations. Travel slowly during your first few days on the trail until your body adjusts.

SEASONS

Winter snowpack and early autumn storms dictate the open season for backcountry travel in the Wind Rivers. Summer weather also varies greatly from year to year, further influencing visitors' travel plans. For example, the summer of 1993 was abnormally wet and cold, with frequent snows above 10,000 feet. During the 1994 season, a light snowpack and warm early spring conditions allowed travelers to reach the high elevations of the range by mid to late June. And an unusually heavy snowpack in the spring of 1995 rendered much of the backcountry inaccessible until mid-July, with lingering snow and high stream flows throughout much of the summer.

In general, expect most trails to be open between early July and mid-September. The highest use period typically occurs between late July and mid-August. Wildflowers are in full bloom, stream flows have subsided, but mosquitos and biting flies are at their peak. In some years the mosquitos are so thick that some visitors use headnets on the trail and around camp.

During summer, afternoon thundershowers from the southwest are common, but sometimes showers move in after dark and can linger until sunrise. The passage of an occasional cold front from the northwest may bring a day or so of showery weather that often ends with vigorous thunderstorms followed by cooler, but dry weather. Snow is possible at any time. Daytime highs are typically in the 70s, and rarely in the 80s, with nighttime lows averaging in the 30s, though subfreezing temperatures are possible.

By late August, flowers wilt, bugs begin to disappear, meadows dry up, streams fall, and most visitors have left the backcountry and returned home. This is a fine time to visit the Wind Rivers. You may find normally busy places in the backcountry to be deserted after the end of August.

September may be the best month to visit the Wind Rivers. The weather can be stable for days at a time, with sunny, warm days, and clear and frosty nights. Temperatures average in the 50s and 60s during the day, and drop into the teens and 20s at night. After mid-September, days are often cold above 10,000 feet, and nights can bring hard freezes. The possibility of lengthy storms increases through the month, and travelers must be prepared for a foot or more of snow.

Hunting seasons for elk and deer begin as early as mid-September in the Bridger Wilderness, and begin by October 1 in the Popo Agie and Fitzpatrick wilderness areas. Until significant snow falls, causing the animals to gather and descend from high elevations, hunting pressure is low. To be safe, wear a blaze orange hat or vest while traveling during hunting seasons.

TRAILHEADS

The Wind River Range is far removed from major population centers, and only three sizable towns—Lander, Dubois, and Pinedale—are adjacent to the range. Most trailhead access roads begin near these towns, but the roads quickly leave civilization behind. Except for the road to Elkhart Park, near Pinedale, trailhead access roads are unpaved, and most are very rough but still passable to cars.

Some trailheads are as much as 40 miles from the nearest town and services. Be prepared for a variety of conditions and situations before driving to Wind River trailheads. Be sure you have a full tank of gas, good tires and at least one spare, and that your vehicle is in good condition. Carry extra food, clothing, and water. If your vehicle breaks down, keep in mind that assistance is several hours away at best.

There are no telephones at Wind River trailheads. Guard stations (which may or may not be staffed) and campground hosts at Elkhart Park and Green River Lakes can offer assistance. Cellular phone users should note that most trailheads are out of range for their phones.

FISHING

Many Wind Rivers visitors enjoy dangling a line while in the backcountry. But for some, fishing is the sole reason for visiting the range, and for good reason. Stocking programs that began in the 1930s have established vigorous populations of cutthroat, brook, golden, rainbow, and lake trout in nearly all sizable lakes and most streams in the range.

If you intend to fish in the national forest wilderness areas of the Wind Rivers (see above for Wind River Indian Reservation information), you must purchase a Wyoming state fishing license, available at many locations in nearby towns. Wyoming state fishing regulations apply—study them before entering the backcountry.

Fishing licenses are available to non-residents for 1 day, 5 days, 10 days, and for the entire season. Local outdoor shops in Pinedale, Dubois, and Lander are glad to share information on what spots are hot, and what flies and lures are working in backcountry lakes and streams.

Middle Lake in the Smith Lake basin.

SHEEP, CATTLE, AND THE WILDERNESS ACT

Sheep have been grazed in the southern half of what is now the Bridger Wilderness since the 1870s. The Congressional Grazing Guidelines attached to the Wilderness Act of 1964 allow "domestic livestock grazing to continue in national forest wilderness when such grazing was established prior to wilderness designation." Currently, cattle use parts of the Popo Agie and Bridger wildernesses, and sheep graze the high meadows of the southern Bridger Wilderness. The grazing season generally lasts from about early July until mid-September.

Many visitors to the Wind River backcountry oppose the grazing of sheep and cattle, feeling it interferes with their wilderness experience, and that it is inappropriate on wilderness lands. But the law is clear—grazing is an acceptable and legitimate use of certain parts of some wilderness areas as established by Congress.

If you would rather not encounter sheep or cattle on your wilderness trip, avoid the areas listed below. Sheep bands are constantly on the move, and it is difficult to determine where they will be on any given day. If you contact the Pinedale District office prior to your trip, they can inform you of the general location of sheep bands in the backcountry, and you can then plan your trip accordingly.

14

CATTLE

Cattle are likely to be seen along the lower reaches of the Middle Popo Agie River and near Dickinson Park within the Popo Agie Wilderness. In the Bridger Wilderness, expect to find cattle near the Sweetwater Trailhead, along the Scab Creek Trail to Lightning Lakes, and at Spring Creek Park.

SHEEP

Since sheep graze the high meadows of the southern Bridger Wilderness, range conditions determine where, when, and if sheep will be turned out on grazing allotments. Range conditions and pasture rotation are monitored by the Forest Service to minimize overgrazing and adverse impacts on vegetation. Nevertheless, lasting scars are evident in the denuded meadows of Fish Creek Park, on terraced hillsides around Dads and Marms lakes, and beside the East Fork River along the Fremont Trail, a traditional sheep driveway.

Sheep grazing allotments extend from Little Sandy Creek northwest to Hay Pass on the Continental Divide, north of North Fork Lake. Sheep are most commonly encountered from Big Sandy Opening north to Pyramid Lake, and to the meadows of the South Fork Boulder Creek near Raid and Dream lakes.

BACKCOUNTRY TRAVEL WITH CHILDREN

Traveling with children in the backcountry is one of the most rewarding and memorable experiences to be enjoyed as a family. It also offers a tremendous learning experience, giving children confidence and a growing awareness of the world around them.

It's important to choose a destination that is accessible to your kids, and you should set your goals with your youngest child's ability in mind. If you're carrying a young child in a kid-carrier backpack, then perhaps you can travel farther than if that child were walking. Some young children can travel farther under their own power. I once met a family with a 4-year-old girl at Pyramid Lake, more than 12 miles from the Big Sandy Trailhead. They made the trip there in three days, and the girl walked much of the way herself, taking frequent rest stops. The parents shared the burden of the child's gear.

As a general rule, children 2 to 4 years old can be expected to walk up to 2 miles per day, taking rest stops every 10 to 15 minutes. Children 5 to 7 years of age can usually hike up to 4 miles a day, and should rest every 30 to 45 minutes. Once children reach 8 to 9 years of age, they can be expected to cover up to 7 miles a day.

Consider spending a day or two at the trailhead to allow you and your child time to adjust to the reduced oxygen at the higher elevations of the

Wind Rivers. Limit the weight of your older child's pack to 20 percent of the child's body weight. Parents will have to carry much of the child's gear. Younger children over age 4 can carry a day pack, but parents should be prepared to carry the pack for a tired child.

Plan a short trip so the kids become accustomed to hiking at high elevations over rough trails. Kids can tire quickly and become easily distracted, so don't be surprised if you don't make it to your destination. Stay flexible and consider alternate turnaround points or campsites en route to your destination. Point out special sights, sounds, and smells along the way to help your children enjoy the trip and learn about what they see. Make the hike fun, help the kids to stay interested, and they will keep going.

Careful planning with an emphasis on safety will help make your trip an enjoyable one. Allow older children to carry their own packs, and perhaps bring a favorite toy or book along. These things, along with some equipment they can carry themselves, helps them to develop a sense of responsibility and to learn at an early age the advantages of packing light.

Kids may become bored once you reach camp, so a little extra effort may be required to keep them occupied. Have your children help with camp chores, setting up the tent, or gathering firewood. Imaginative games and special foods they don't see at home can make the trip a new and fun experience for kids.

Set up the tent at home and consider spending a night or two in it so your child can grow accustomed to your backcountry shelter. Some kids may become frightened by dark nights, so you might pack along a small flashlight to use as a nightlight. Kids seem to prefer rectangular, rather than mummy-style, sleeping bags that allow freedom of movement. And a cap for those cool nights will help keep your child warm.

Young skin is very sensitive to the sun and to insect bites. Apply sunscreen to your kids before and during the trip. Carry a good insect repellent, preferably a natural product, and apply it to your kids as necessary. Also, consider carrying a product that helps take the itch out of insect bites. A hat helps keep the bright sun out of sensitive young eyes. And rain gear is also an important consideration. Kids seem to have less tolerance to cold than adults, so ample warm clothing is important. If your campsite will be next to a lake or stream, careful supervision of your kids is a must. Consider bringing a life vest for your child.

Parents with very young children must, of course, carry plenty of diapers, and be sure to pack them out when they leave. Some children can get wet at night, so extra sleeping clothes are important. A waterproof pad between the child and the sleeping bag should keep the bag dry, an important consideration if you're staying out for more than one night. Lightweight and inexpensive dry baby foods (just add water) are an alternative to carrying baby food in jars.

Since children learn by example, day hiking and backpacking trips offer an excellent opportunity to teach children to tread lightly and to reduce their impacts on the wilderness.

Thus, important considerations to bear in mind when hiking with children are careful planning, with an emphasis on safety, and making the trip fun and interesting.

All or part of the following trails are suitable for family day hikes or overnight trips. Carefully read each hike description and prepare for any hazards that may be present. After each hike number are suggestions for destinations. Where *base camp* follows a destination, that site is suggested for an overnight stay.

1: Loop around lower Green River Lake; or a base camp anywhere between Green River Lakes and Beaver Park.

2: Clear Creek Falls, or Clear Creek Natural Bridge.

5: Upper end of New Fork Lakes; or a New Fork Park base camp.

6: Glimpse Lake or Trapper Lake base camp.

10: Eklund Lake or Barbara Lake base camp.

14: Miller Lake; or Miller Lake or Middle Sweeney Lake base camp.

17: Beaver ponds near Boulder Creek.

25: Meeks Lake; or Meeks Lake, Mirror Lake, Dads Lake, or Marms Lake base camp.

26: Big Sandy Lake base camp.

32: Lower or Upper Silas lakes base camp.

34: Sheep Bridge.

35: Smith, Cook, or Middle lakes base camp.

38: Lake Louise.

FOR YOUR SAFETY

Wilderness travelers must realize that help is far away in the Wind River backcountry. Patrols by wilderness rangers are infrequent on many trails, and unpredictable. Your safety is your responsibility; it depends on the good judgment of you and the members of your group. Common sense and an awareness of potential hazards and the ability to deal with them is your best insurance for a safe and enjoyable trip.

- A good first-aid kit and a working knowledge of its components and first-aid techniques is essential.
- Leave a detailed travel plan with a responsible person back home. If you fail to return at a predetermined time, have that person contact the ranger station nearest your travel area to begin search and rescue efforts.
- When traveling cross-country, observe landmarks and locate them on your topo map to stay oriented as you go. Much of the Wind River backcountry is open, allowing easy recognition of landmarks. Remember that the landscape can look quite different when you travel in opposite directions.

Cirque of the Towers; Lonesome Lake, with Pingora Peak at left.

- Proper equipment selection is important. Expect adverse weather conditions and be prepared with the proper equipment. Well-broken-in boots, a dependable waterproof tent with mosquito netting, warm clothing (layers of wool or synthetic garments that retain insulation when wet are best), rain gear, insect repellent, a filter for water purification, a signal mirror, sunglasses and sunscreen, a pocket knife, and plenty of food are basic items for any wilderness traveler.

- Choose a trip within the capabilities of the members of your group, and stay together when traveling.

- Never take unnecessary chances. Don't exceed your capabilities when scaling peaks or traveling off-trail. Remain flexible and alter your plans if swollen streams or snow blocks your route, or if someone in your group becomes ill.

- Don't underestimate the time and energy required for a trip in the high elevations and on the rough trails of the Wind Rivers. Allow ample time to reach your goal, and travel at the pace of the slowest member of your group.

- Seek shelter during thunderstorms, preferably in a low-lying area in a dense grove of small trees of uniform size. Avoid lakeshores, tall or solitary trees, high points and ridges, and overhangs at the base of cliffs during thunderstorms. Stay away from conductors such as metal tent poles and pack frames. Stock users should dismount and wait out the storm. Heart failure is possible in people struck by lightning. A working knowledge of CPR can save someone's life in the event of a lightning strike.

- Carry a good insect repellent. Products containing the ingredient DEET are most effective. If you prefer to use a natural product, those containing citronella work best. A mosquito headnet may be advisable to withstand the onslaught of mosquitos at certain times.

- Avoid hypothermia—the abnormal lowering of the body's internal temperature—by staying dry. Wet travelers at temperatures as mild as 50 degrees F. are at risk for developing hypothermia. Windy conditions can intensify its onset.

  Symptoms of hypothermia include shivering, slurred speech, fumbling hands, stumbling, and drowsiness. Immediate treatment is essential; hypothermia can be fatal if left untreated.

  Wet clothing should be removed from a hypothermia victim immediately. Warm drinks—but no caffeine or alcohol—should be given to warm the victim internally. External warming in a sleeping bag, preferably with body-to-body contact, should begin as soon as possible.

- Surface water is abundant in the Wind Rivers; you rarely need to pack water. But water supplies in the Wind River backcountry are known to contain bacteria and protozoans, including *Giardia lamblia,* that cause illness. Visitors should be sure to treat all water for drinking, and even brushing teeth, throughout the backcountry.

  Pump-type canister filters, such as Katadyn, First Need, Pur, Sweetwater, and MSR, are very effective at removing *Giardia* and other water-borne organisms, rendering water safe to drink. These filters are widely available at outdoor shops and can be purchased in towns adjacent to the Wind Rivers.

- Although you may not encounter black bears while in the Wind River backcountry, they are known to inhabit much of the range, mostly below timberline. They have become frequent visitors on nightly food raids in the Big Sandy Lake area, the Cirque of the Towers, and in popular lake basins near Dickinson Park.

Black bears are essentially herbivores in the Wind Rivers, and they typically avoid contact with humans. But bold bears habituated to human food may raid your camp, usually at night. If a bear goes after your food, don't attempt to stop it. To avoid serious injury, never try to recover your food from a bear.

Visiting bear country requires special precautions to ensure the protection of your food supply and to prevent bears from becoming habituated to human food. Habituated bears lose their fear of humans and become attracted to campsites. This disrupts their normal foraging habits, and the bears may not be prepared to survive the oncoming winter with adequate stores of fat.

There are several useful means of protecting your food. If you're camping at Big Sandy Lake, use one of the two bear-resistant food storage containers installed there by the Forest Service. Others may be installed in the future; check with the Pinedale District office.

Bear-resistant containers that you carry in your pack—tough plastic cylinders—can be used for food storage, but they should be hung by a rope as outlined below. These can be purchased at outdoor shops, but are quite expensive. They are also available at the Pinedale, Washakie, and Wind River District offices where, for a donation, you can use them for the duration of your trip.

Rock climbers are at an advantage, for they can hang their food on a boulder or rock wall, at least 15 feet off the ground, well out of the reach of bears.

Many people bear-bag their food, but this must be done properly. If you hang your food in a tree, and tie off the end of the rope to the trunk, an experienced bear can chew or claw through the rope and quickly consume your entire food supply.

To properly bear-bag your food, the counterbalance method of suspending your food works best. You will need about 50 feet of nylon cord and two stuffsacks. Put all of your food, including any other items with an odor that may attract bears (trash, toothpaste, soap, cookware, coffee, etc.) into two stuffsacks. One should be a little heavier than the other. Select a tree with long, heavy branches about 15 feet off the ground and at least 100 yards from your tent.

Tie one end of the rope to a rock and throw it over a suitable branch. Remove the rock and tie the heavier stuffsack to the end of the rope. Tie a loop to the rope so you can later retrieve your food. Pull the stuffsack up to the tree branch, then tie the other stuffsack, or a rock for a counterweight, onto the rope as high as you can reach. With a stick or walking staff, push the second stuffsack up until both are hanging an equal distance below the branch. Ideally, your food should be hanging about 5 feet below the tree branch, 10 feet from the trunk, and 10 to 12 feet above the ground. You can retrieve your food by hooking the loop you tied in the rope with your stick or walking staff, and pulling it down.

Other precautions campers should take in bear country include cooking at least 100 yards from any tent, and maintaining a camp free of food scraps and food odors.

ZERO IMPACT

One thing that stands out in the Wind River backcountry is ample evidence that most of us have accepted the personal responsibility to care for our wilderness lands. Rarely will you find trash, food scraps, discarded items, noodles in lakes, or soap suds floating in streams. Most of us desire and expect an unconfined experience in the wilderness, free of burdensome

Lower Jean Lake on the Highline Trail.

regulations. Since Wind River travelers, as a rule, have embraced a no-trace ethic, regulations are minimal, and in most cases they simply embody common sense.

In a healthy wilderness environment, natural processes interact and maintain a delicate balance. But some impact by human visitors is inevitable. Consider employing some of the following practices to reduce your impact on the land and other visitors.

ON THE TRAIL

Trails in the Wind Rivers are your only means of accessing unfamiliar terrain. Staying on the trail protects the trailbed and the surrounding terrain and vegetation.

Travel single file on the trail to avoid creating multiple paths. Shortcutting switchbacks leads to erosion problems that are difficult to correct, and can destroy a good trail. Shortcutting over rugged terrain often requires as much time and more energy than staying on the trail.

If you travel cross-country, travel in small groups, and spread out to avoid creating a worn path. Restrain the urge to build cairns along your route; let following visitors find their way as you did.

CAMPING

The intricate nature of the Wind River landscape affords a vast potential for "perfect" spots in which to camp. Only the most obvious trailside campsites are mentioned in this guidebook. Most backcountry visitors prefer private sites, far from sight and sound of others.

While searching for a campsite, invest the extra effort to go beyond the 200-foot set-back rule from lakes, streams, and trails. Screen your camp from the view of other visitors, and consider using earth-tone equipment (gray, green) that blends in with the surroundings.

Many travelers tend to concentrate their use around streams and lakeshores. If you camp well away from water sources, you allow animals and other visitors free access to that water. Remember that cold air sinks into low-lying areas after dark. Choose a durable site on higher ground where temperatures will be several degrees warmer.

In heavily used areas, choose an existing campsite to reduce the spread of impacted sites.

In many areas of the Wind Rivers, particularly near and above timberline, the only possible camping areas are in meadows. Look for a site in a dry meadow where the vegetative cover is minimal.

Large groups have heavy impacts on camping areas. Groups should try to avoid camping in sensitive alpine areas, and they should attempt to use established sites wherever they camp. Groups should be aware of their visual impacts on other visitors' feelings of solitude, and groups should keep noise to a minimum.

Be a good neighbor while in camp, and allow ample room between camp-sites. Loud noises, shouting, clanging cookware, shooting, and bonfires are out of place in a wilderness setting.

Not all visitors are seeking solitude during their wilderness visit, a fact attested to by the crowds that gather in places such as Island Lake, Titcomb Basin, and Big Sandy Lake. If you're searching for solitude, choose a lightly used area instead.

CAMPFIRES

Unless otherwise posted, campfires are allowed in the Wind Rivers below timberline. But some visitors may be uncertain where timberline is. Timberline is generally defined as the upper limit of continuous forest, which lies at about 10,400 feet in the Wind Rivers. Above that point there may still be trees, though they are stunted, gnarled, and isolated in groves. Even higher are krummholz trees—a ground-hugging mat of conifers.

For cooking, you should always carry a small, lightweight backpack stove. But to many visitors, the warmth and spirit of a campfire is an integral part of their outdoor experience. If you choose to build a campfire, do so only below timberline, where downed wood is in obvious surplus. Never strip branches from standing trees or use an ax or saw to hack away at downed trees; gather your wood from the ground instead. And use existing fire rings rather than building new ones.

If no fire ring is available, or if you are camping in a previously unused location, dig a shallow pit, well away from the roots of trees and shrubs, down to bare mineral soil. Build your fire in the pit, and try to keep it small.

A ring of rocks that will be blackened by the fire is unnecessary.

Before breaking camp, drown the fire with water, and make sure the ashes are cold. Remove any unburned refuse from the ashes and pack it out. Scatter the ashes and any unused firewood, cover the pit, and scatter forest litter over the site.

BACKCOUNTRY SANITATION

Even biodegradable soaps can have an adverse effect on fish and aquatic vegetation. If you use soap for washing, dispose of the waste water where it can percolate through the soil, at least 200 feet from your campsite, water sources, or draws and gullies that are potential watercourses. As an alternative to soap, sand and gravel are effective for cleaning dirty cookware and don't pollute water sources.

Human waste should be buried in a "cat hole" 4 to 6 inches deep, where the biologically active layer of bacteria and fungi will aid in decomposition. Be sure the cat hole is far from campsites, water sources, and potential watercourses.

We all know that we must pack out any refuse we bring into the backcountry, and you can reduce the amount of trash by repackaging foods. If you find trash along the trail or in campsites left behind by thoughtless travelers, pack it out as well. Paper can be burned, but plastics and aluminum create a difficult mess to clean up if placed in a fire.

STOCK USE IN THE BACKCOUNTRY

Horses, mules, burros, llamas, and even goats are used for packing and transportation in the Wind River backcountry. Since stock use has the potential of significantly impacting resources, stock users can reduce their impact by following the guidelines listed below.

- Bring only the minimum number of stock necessary to support your trip.
- Observe trail conditions and hold horses from skirting shallow puddles and minor obstacles so you don't create multiple paths.
- Avoid shortcutting switchbacks, which can quickly ruin the trailbed.
- Tie stock to mature trees well off the trail for short periods only. Hobble nervous horses to further protect trees and to prevent excessive trampling of vegetation.
- Select a durable campsite, and maintain the distance restrictions from lakes, streams, and trail that apply to the wilderness area you are visiting.
- Use highlines, picket pins, or temporary hitch rails well away from your campsite.
- Select a durable site between trees, preferably a site with rocky ground or minimal vegetation, for highlining your stock. Move your picket pins frequently to avoid overgrazing and excessive trampling of vegetation.

- Use insect repellent on your animals to protect them and to help them stand more quietly.

- Consider using electric fences, rope corrals, or a plastic snow fence to contain your animals near your camp.

- Use feed bags or mangers when feeding your stock. Check the regulations concerning the use of weed seed-free hay or pelletized feed for the area you intend to visit. Use of non-weed-seed-free feed promotes the spread of noxious weeds.

- Water your stock at gravel bars or rocky locations at a stream or lake to avoid impacting delicate vegetation.

- Before leaving camp, remove picket pins, dismantle hitch rails, and scatter manure into surrounding vegetation.

HISTORY

Ever since humans first ventured into west-central Wyoming, the Wind River Range has drawn people into its remote interior, but the range has remained a major barrier to travel. As early as 10,000 years ago, Paleo-Indians used the Wind Rivers and surrounding valleys while hunting big-game animals for food and clothing. Trails were forged through the range over time, and two of them are generally followed by today's Indian Pass and Washakie trails. Prehistoric vision quest sites, stone circles, and big-horn sheep traps and drive fences indicate the importance of the Wind Rivers to pre-European cultures, though travel in these rugged mountains was never easy.

The Crows bestowed the name Wind River to the valley east of the range, for the constant winds blowing off the mountains. Early fur trappers called the range Spanish River Mountains, after Spanish explorers named the Green River "Rio Verde."

Following the Louisiana Purchase of 1804, Lewis and Clark began their epic expedition in an attempt to establish possession and control over the new territory. The British, however, were also seeking to gain control of the Northwest, and their Hudson's Bay Company monopolized the fur trade in the region by the early nineteenth century.

In 1811, John Jacob Astor founded Fort Astoria at the mouth of the Columbia River, attempting to usurp the British trade monopoly, until the War of 1812 forced the abandonment of the fort. The Astorians returned to the United States, and en route, unknowingly became the first white men to cross the hills of South Pass at the southern end of the Wind Rivers, a pass undoubtedly used for centuries before by Indians.

In 1822, Andrew Henry and William Ashley established the Rocky Mountain Fur Company, and two years later a group of company trappers, including Jedediah Smith, William Sublette, James Clyman, and Thomas Fitzpatrick,

Squaretop Mountain.

traveled to the Wind River Valley. They attempted to cross the Wind Rivers at Union Pass, but were stopped by snow. They returned to the Wind River Valley where they met a group of Crows. The Crows told them of a much easier crossing of the mountains—South Pass—a crossing that was later to become a vital passage over the Rocky Mountains on the westward migration over the Oregon Trail.

By 1825, Ashley held the first of fourteen rendezvous at the height of the Rocky Mountain fur trade era. At rendezvous, company wagons loaded with supplies traveled from Saint Louis to a predetermined location, where trappers would exchange their beaver pelts and resupply for another season of trapping beaver in icy mountain streams. Several rendezvous were held west of present-day Pinedale, and during that era the upper Green River Basin became the center of commerce in the Rocky Mountains.

Thus was born the legendary mountain man, and many of the trappers have been immortalized in place names of today, including Jim Bridger, Thomas Fitzpatrick, David Jackson, and Captain Benjamin L. E. Bonneville, to name but a few.

In 1832 the U.S. Army granted Bonneville a two-year leave to explore the West. He soon became active in the fur trade, which he described as a "smoke screen" to gain possession and control of the western territories.

Trappers ventured into the Wind Rivers in search of beaver, but it is likely that few of them explored into the lofty interior of the range, high above where beaver would be expected to dwell. Bonneville crossed the range at South Pass on his trip west, taking the first wagons across that pass on the Continental Divide.

After wintering in Pierre's Hole, Idaho (today's Teton Basin), Bonneville and a party of trappers traveled east, once again crossing South Pass en route to beaver streams in the Bighorn River drainage. Once east of the Wind Rivers, however, Blackfeet made off with much of the trappers' supplies. Bonneville then decided to return to a cache of supplies near the Green River. Rather than returning via the roundabout route over South Pass, his party opted to attempt a direct route across the Wind Rivers, becoming the first white men to penetrate the interior of the range.

They ascended the forks of the Popo Agie River on horseback and entered the rugged alpine reaches of the range near the Continental Divide, but they found no apparent route over the mountains. Bonneville and his companions proceeded to climb to the highest summit in the area to survey a westward route through the range.

Although it is reasonable to assume that the mountain that now bears his name was not the peak Bonneville climbed, for the party was south of that peak and its technical difficulty surely would have turned them back, Bonneville's peak is still a matter of debate and conjecture. Many believe that the peak Bonneville climbed could be Mount Chauvenet, near the Bears Ears Trail, or possibly Wind River Peak. Whichever peak he climbed, the colorful prose in Washington Irving's book *The Adventures of Captain Bonneville* tells that the party was awestruck with the grand panoramas of majestic mountains, panoramas that have changed very little in the ensuing years.

By 1842, Lieutenant John C. Fremont, an Army topographer, was sent west by the U.S. Army Corps of Engineers to survey a wagon road as far as South Pass—a route that would soon become the Oregon Trail. Among Fremont's companions was Kit Carson, a former trapper with intimate knowledge of the Green River country.

The popular opinion among army officers and mountain men of the day was that the highest peak in the Rocky Mountains was located in the Wind Rivers. Fremont's zeal for discovery led him beyond South Pass and to the western slopes of the Wind Rivers. He was determined to scale this peak and establish its elevation with barometric measurements.

Fremont led his party, atop mules, into the interior of the range from the vicinity of Boulder Lake. Based on Fremont's report, it has been established that the party crossed a pass at the head of Monument Creek (west of Lester Pass), descended past Little Seneca Lake, and camped at Island Lake (so named by Fremont).

From there the party set out to ascend their peak—present-day Fremont Peak, which, due to its size and location, *appears* to be the highest summit from many vantage points in the region. Suffering from altitude sickness, Fremont was unable to complete the ascent on their first day of climbing, but Kit Carson did scale nearby Jackson Peak. The following day, Fremont and five companions made another assault on the peak, and this time all succeeded. Barometric measurements gave the peak an elevation of 13,570 feet, very close to the currently established elevation of 13,745 feet.

From 1843 to 1865 thousands of emigrants crossed South Pass on the Oregon Trail, en route to Utah, California, and the Pacific Northwest, but few remained behind in Wyoming. By 1857, the first government road in Wyoming was constructed under the supervision of Brigadier General F. W. Lander, a road leading from South Pass to Fort Hall, Idaho. This shortcut to the Oregon Trail became known as the Lander Cutoff, and county roads closely follow the route today. Travelers heading for the Sweetwater and Big Sandy trailheads from South Pass follow the Lander Cutoff Road.

Emigrants eventually began to settle in the high valleys surrounding the Wind Rivers by the 1870s. Poor soils and a cold, dry climate were unsuitable for farming, but vast grasslands were ideal for the raising of sheep and cattle. Over time, tensions between sheep and cattle ranchers reached the breaking point. Cattle ranchers, fearing that sheep were destroying the range, established boundary lines that sheep and their herders were prohibited from crossing, lest they experience "frontier justice."

In June of 1885, near Raid Lake on the South Fork Boulder Creek, cattlemen attacked a sheep camp, bound the herders, and clubbed the sheep to death. Raid Lake, Raid Peak, and Ambush Peak were named in memory of this event. Later, in 1902, 2,000 sheep and one herder were killed on the New Fork River by masked raiders working for local cattlemen.

One of the emigrants who left a lasting legacy in the Wind Rivers was

Finis Mitchell, who settled with his family near the western slope of the range in 1906. Mitchell began exploring the Wind Rivers on hunting trips with his father at an early age. By 1930, during the Great Depression, Mitchell was laid off from his railroad job in Rock Springs, so he and his wife headed for the Wind Rivers and established Mitchell's Fishing Camp in Big Sandy Opening.

Few lakes at that time contained fish, due to cascades and waterfalls that prevented fish migration, and those that did hosted native cutthroat trout. Thus Mitchell began a fish stocking program in the Wind River backcountry, hauling hatchery fingerlings in 5-gallon milk cans on the backs of mules. During the seven years the Mitchell's ran the fishing camp, they planted 2.5 million trout in 314 lakes. Anglers today owe a debt of gratitude to Mitchell, for the Wind Rivers now boast some of the finest backcountry fishing in the Rocky Mountains. Today the Wyoming Game and Fish Department is charged with fish stocking programs, and hundreds of lakes in the Wind Rivers now support several varieties of trout.

Mitchell was also responsible for naming many lakes and peaks in the range. He has scaled 244 peaks in the Wind Rivers, many of them first ascents. He has climbed his namesake, 12,482-foot Mitchell Peak, a dozen times.

Mitchell wasn't alone in the Wind Rivers during the Great Depression. Dozens of trappers and hunters plied their trades in the mountains then, and travelers today are likely to find some of the small cabins they left behind.

The Wind River backcountry has been protected by its remoteness, isolation, rugged landscape, and lack of significant extractable resources. People recognized the need to preserve the range in its natural condition early in the Twentieth century. The Bridger Wilderness was designated a primitive area in 1931, and was expanded to include the southern half of the range's west slope in 1937. The Popo Agie was designated a primitive area in 1932. The Wyoming Wilderness Act of 1984 expanded the Bridger Wilderness and Fitzpatrick Wilderness to their current acreage, and designated the Popo Agie Primitive Area as wilderness.

Today, tens of thousands of wilderness travelers flock to this relatively obscure mountain range each summer to fish, to climb mountains, to trek long distances, and to simply revel in the glorious panoramas of the "shining mountains."

WIND RIVER VEGETATION

Although the Wind River Range is dominated by ice-scoured bedrock, and soils are generally thin and low in nutrients, a wide variety of plant species thrive here. Most noticeable are the conifer forests that shade travelers and shelter campsites, and the fragrant wildflowers that splash their

colors across the meadows and tundra.

Many wildflowers and shrubs are widespread at various elevations, but conifers are more predictable in their distribution. Conifer forests are separated into belts on the mountain slopes, and their distribution is influenced by moisture, sunlight, and temperature.

The following is a brief discussion of vegetation zones in the Wind Rivers. Each trail described in this guidebook will offer more detailed information on what plants you'll see at specified locations. To better identify plants in the backcountry, refer to one of the books listed at the end of this chapter.

In the lowest elevations of the range, below 8,000 feet near trailheads such as Boulder Lake, Torrey Creek, and Green River Lakes, sagebrush dominates on the dry, rubbly moraines. Conifers here are widely scattered in competition for scant moisture and nutrients, and these include Rocky Mountain juniper and limber pine.

Groves of quaking aspen reside in sheltered recesses in this zone but are more prevalent on higher slopes, generally above 8,000 feet, where Douglas-fir becomes the dominant forest tree in a narrow belt on the range's west slopes. On the more gradual eastern slopes, Douglas-fir forms a broad band of forest up to about 8,500 feet.

Throughout much of the range, once you rise above 8,500 feet, you enter the lodgepole pine forest. This straight-boled tree, with light green needles in bundles of two, is the most widespread forest tree in the range. It often forms dense forests that can obscure views for miles on many wilderness trails. East of the divide, particularly in the Popo Agie Wilderness, lodgepole forests are more open, with little or no understory plants on the forest floor, and the boles of the trees are often gnarled and knotted with burls.

As you approach 10,000 feet, the landscape begins to open up, and expansive meadows filled with myriad wildflowers begin to appear. Lodgepole pines give way to forests of Engelmann spruce, whitebark pine, and occasionally subalpine fir. The Wind Rivers support one of the most extensive whitebark pine forests in the Rocky Mountains. This five-needled conifer produces large seeds that are an important food source to animals such as the red squirrel, Clark's nutcracker, and black bear.

Spruce and whitebark pine are the dominant timberline conifers in the Wind Rivers. As you rise above 10,000 feet, these trees become stunted; the whitebark usually attaining a rounded, spreading form with multiple heavy branches. The spruce maintains its conical, spire-shaped form.

In timberline meadows, the trees are confined to groves growing on rocky knolls that rise above minor basins. Trees here are often wind-flagged, shaped by the incessant high-elevation winds and blowing snow and ice.

Above timberline at about 10,400 to 10,500 feet, where rock, grass, and snow dominates the landscape, these tenacious trees can often be found growing in ground-hugging mats that resemble bonsai trees, again mostly on rocky knolls. These mats of weather-tortured trees are known as "krummholz"—meaning "crooked wood." These tree mats grow low enough to the ground to be buried in snow during the long winter season, and so they remain protected from the sandblasting effects of wind-blown snow and ice particles. Krummholz trees often grow on the leeward slopes up to about 10,800 feet, where drifting snow buries them during winter.

Above timberline, the tundra is decorated by numerous arctic and alpine wildflowers that are circumboreal in distribution—a flower you see at 11,000 feet in the Wind Rivers may also be common in the treeless tundra of Europe, Siberia, or northern Canada. Willows are also common in wet areas of the tundra, but they often grow only a few inches off the ground.

Canyons and north-facing and south-facing slopes in the Wind Rivers host microclimates that create a departure from the usual distribution of plants. In Pine Creek Canyon below Elkhart Park, for example, you'll find spruces in the canyon's shady confines at 7,500 feet, 2,500 feet below that tree's normal range. There, limited sunlight and ample moisture mimics the high-elevation environment where spruces grow. On the hot, dry south slopes of Whiskey Mountain above Torrey Creek, Douglas-firs and limber pines extend upward to nearly 9,000 feet, high above their normal range. On shady north-facing slopes throughout the Wind Rivers, you'll often find typical timberline trees growing, while the opposite south-facing slopes may host sagebrush, Douglas-fir, and aspen.

Perhaps the best reference for trees and wildflowers in the Wind Rivers is the book: *Alpine Wildflowers of the Rocky Mountains,* by Joseph F. Duft and Robert K. Moseley (Missoula, Montana: Mountain Press Publishing, 1989). Also refer to: Craighead, Craighead, and Davis, *A Field Guide to Rocky Mountain Wildflowers.* (Boston: Houghton Mifflin Company, 1963); and Shaw, Richard J., *Plants of Yellowstone and Grand Teton National Parks.* (Salt Lake City, Utah: Wheelwright Press, 1981).

WIND RIVER WILDLIFE

Nearly all wildlife species indigenous to the Rocky Mountains dwell in the Wind River Range. However, sightings of large mammals from backcountry trails are infrequent. A wide variety of birds, waterfowl on backcountry lakes, and rodents such as Uinta chipmunks, red squirrels, golden-mantled ground squirrels, and in higher elevations, yellow-bellied marmots and pikas, are likely to be your most common wild companions on backcountry trails. Other wildlife you may encounter include marten, coyote, beaver, badger, weasel, and bobcat.

Birds represent the greatest variety of wildlife in the Wind Rivers, and each life zone and habitat type hosts its own array of avian denizens. In the sagebrush-juniper-limber pine zone, common birds include the vesper sparrow, sage grouse, and Brewer's sparrow. Aspen groves support a greater variety of birds, such as ruffed grouse, mountain chickadee, robin, mountain bluebird, hermit thrush, Townsend's solitaire, and ruby-crowned kinglet.

Open forests of Douglas-fir often grow in proximity to aspen groves, and many of the same birds can be observed in this forest. In addition, northern flicker, yellow-bellied sapsucker, evening grosbeak, Cassin's finch, dark-eyed junco, chipping sparrow, and pine siskin use Douglas-fir forests.

Lodgepole pine forests host a wide variety of birds. Here you may observe Canada (or gray) jay, Steller's jay, brown creeper, pine grosbeak, Oregon junco, white-crowned sparrow, calliope hummingbird, and hairy woodpecker.

Timberline forests of spruce and whitebark pine provide habitat for blue grouse, red crossbill, Hammond's flycatcher, Williamson's sapsucker, raven, Clark's nutcracker, red-breasted nuthatch, and red crossbill.

Alpine tundra is limited in the variety of bird species it can support. Common birds in this cold, windswept life zone include rosy finch, water pipit, horned lark, and white-crowned sparrow.

Some birds use all life zones from the foothills to the alpine reaches of the range. Raptors are the most obvious birds that roam throughout the Wind Rivers, and these include golden eagle, red-tailed hawk, Cooper's hawk, American kestrel, and great gray owl. Ospreys are often seen near lakes and large streams, since they subsist on the abundant fish there.

Large mammals in and around the Wind Rivers include more than 5,000 elk and 20,000 mule deer. Mule deer are widespread throughout the range, and are likely to be observed almost anywhere in the backcountry. Elk spend

Moose are frequently observed in the Wind River backcountry.

the summer in alpine meadows near timberline, often staying close to conifer groves for shelter and protection from predators. The early- to mid-September rut is the best time to observe elk in the backcountry; even if you don't see them then, you're likely to hear the bugling of bull elk as they challenge other bulls for breeding dominance.

Whiskey Mountain (see hike 40), near Dubois, hosts the largest herd of Rocky Mountain bighorn sheep. Travelers on the Whiskey Mountain Trail, and on the alpine plateaus of Goat Flat, Ram Flat, and Shale Mountain, often observe flocks of bighorns that summer in the alpine reaches of the northeastern Wind Rivers.

Moose are probably the most frequently observed large mammal in the range, and they number about 5,000 in and around the Wind Rivers. Although moose prefer to feed on aquatic vegetation in shallow ponds, you're likely to observe them wherever you find thickets of willows, another of their favorite foods.

Black bears range throughout the Wind Rivers, and in recent years they have become frequent visitors to campsites around Big Sandy Lake, the Cirque of the Towers, and in the Dickinson Park area, including Smith Lakes. Grizzly bears are expanding their range throughout the Greater Yellowstone area, and they have been sighted with increasing frequency south of Togwotee Pass. In the Bridger Wilderness, grizzlies have been reported in the Roaring Fork area, north of Green River Lakes. There is a possibility that the great bears may continue to expand their range southward through the Wind Rivers.

WIND RIVER GEOLOGY

The Wind River Range owes its dramatic landscapes not only to intensive glaciation, but also to its parent rock—granite. Resistant to erosion and massive (with few fractures) in structure, granite is more than just igneous rock. Wherever you find granite, particularly in glacier-carved mountains, this rock defines the types of landforms you will see.

But Wind River rock is not all granite, though much of the range's backcountry is composed of resistant rocks. In the northern reaches of the range west of the Continental Divide, light and dark swirls of gneiss, composed of the same minerals as granite, is the dominant rock. Gneiss, unlike granite, is a metamorphic rock, having been derived from pre-existing rocks and shaped by heat and pressure deep within the Earth.

Granodiorite and granite are igneous rocks that cooled from a molten mass, called magma, far beneath the Earth's crust. Wind River granite is among the oldest in the Rocky Mountains, having formed 2.5 billion years ago. The magma that would become the Wind River Range flowed into even older existing rocks, and those rocks, found in the central Bridger Wilderness, are among the most ancient rocks on Earth, dated at 3.4 billion years.

Grave Lake and the peaks of the Continental Divide from the Bears Ears Trail.

Granite dominates the landscape in the Big Sandy and Cirque of the Towers area, in New Fork Canyon, and in the Fitzpatrick Wilderness east of the Continental Divide peaks. Granodiorite is more brittle than granite, but nevertheless forms some of the range's most prominent walls, such as those on the flanks of Mount Hooker. Much of the southern end of the range, where rubbly plateaus, and mountains that resemble huge boulder piles dominate the landscape, is composed of granodiorite.

To simplify descriptions in this guidebook, all but sedimentary rocks are collectively called granite or granitic rocks.

Following the intrusion of Wind River granite into the Earth's crust, geologists have found no evidence to suggest uplift of mountains where we now find the Wind River Range. But during this time the Wind River block was fractured along a series of faults that now roughly parallel the crest of the range.

The Wyoming landscape of 600 million years ago was first a coastal plain, then was submerged as a continental shelf beneath warm and shallow, tropical marine seas. For the following 350 million years, sediments accumulated that would later be compressed into dolomite, limestone, and sandstone that now rest along the eastern flanks of the range, and are exposed near Green River Lakes west of the Divide.

Beginning about 65 million years ago, compression of the Earth's crust in the Rocky Mountain region resulted in widespread faulting and began a mountain-building event called the Laramide Orogeny. At this time the ancestral Wind River Range was uplifted, exposing the ancient gneiss and granite core of the range to the forces of erosion, perhaps for the first time.

The mountains of the Rockies, including the Wind Rivers, were not suddenly thrust upward in a short-term catastrophic event; rather they inched upward over millions of years, and they continue to rise today.

As the Wind River block arose, it was tilted and thrust southwestward, burying much of the overlying sedimentary rocks on the west slope of the range. The eastern slopes of the range rise at a lower angle, preserving much of the veneer of sedimentary rocks. The rise of the Wind Rivers increased the gradients of streams, and the streams began to carry debris from the mountains and deposit the material in adjacent basins. Eventually the Wind River Range was buried in its own detritus, and the region once again became a level plain. But about 10 million years ago, renewed uplift and extensive erosion exhumed the Wind River block.

The flat erosion surface of the Wind Rivers rose with the renewed uplift, and this surface is preserved on the flat-topped summits of many peaks, and on alpine plateaus such as Goat Flat and Shale Mountain. Periods of recurring uplift were interrupted by periods of erosion, and another flat erosion surface unique to the Wind Rivers developed—the terracelike bench on the range's western slope. This bench and the minor fault zones that dissect it allow for the relative ease of travel in the Bridger Wilderness.

Until about 250,000 years ago, the Wind Rivers were gently sloping mountains, featuring stream-cut, V-shaped canyons. Then periodic cooling of the world's climate began. Vast ice sheets spread from the poles but did not reach Wyoming. Instead, high mountains such as the Beartooths, the Yellowstone Plateau, and the Wind Rivers hosted their own ice caps that flowed down the flanks of the mountains and into the valleys below.

Three major glacial events shaped the Wind Rivers into the mountains we see today. Much of the sedimentary rocks on the flanks of the range were removed, and the great sheets of ice, in places more than 1,000 feet thick, performed their artistry on the resistant granitic rocks, sculpting here, chiseling there; gouging, polishing, and rounding.

The ice flowed down existing valleys, widening and reshaping them into the U-shaped cross-sectional profile characteristic of a glacial valley. Large valley glaciers removed the lower reaches of tributary canyons, stranding the tributaries as hanging valleys, such as Porcupine Creek and Clark Creek in the Green River area. Glaciers scoured the benchland on the west slope, gouging out depressions that would later become lakes. East side canyons, without the bench to interrupt the glaciers' flow, were deeply carved from the flanks of the Continental Divide down to the floor of the Wind River Valley.

Steep-walled bowls, called cirques, were gouged by glaciers at the valley heads. Glacial ice plucked rocks from peaks, and sculpted them into pinnacles and spires, called horns. Knife-edged ridges, known as arêtes, were formed when cirques intersected from opposite sides of a ridge.

Some rocks buried beneath the ice were resistant and massive (without fractures) enough that glaciers were forced to flow over and around them, rather than removing them, polishing and rounding the rock into domes, or *roches moutonees* (sheep rocks). Look for these landforms on the benchland in the Bridger Wilderness, and in the canyon of Dinwoody Creek.

Rocks, boulders, sand, and silt were carried on the giant conveyor belts of ice, until the glaciers reached their terminal points on valley floors, where the melting and the advance of the glaciers reached a state of equilibrium. Here the glaciers deposited their loads of debris in a pile of unsorted material called a terminal moraine. Large lakes such as Green River Lakes, New Fork Lakes, Fremont Lake, Boulder Lake, and the Torrey lakes are impounded behind moraines at the foot of the range.

The last minor glacial advance began its retreat about 100 years ago, and today's glaciers are remnants of that episode. Fresh moraines lying below them attest to their recent retreat. Most of today's glaciers lie east of the Continental Divide, but all of them, both east and west of the Divide, nestle in sheltered, generally north-facing or northeast-facing cirques, and they extend down to elevations of about 11,000 feet. Shoshone National Forest officials state that there are forty-four active glaciers in the Fitzpatrick Wilderness, the largest of which covers 1,220 acres.

Erosion by streams and glaciers, sedimentation of lakes that will eventually become meadows, and minor uplift caused by occasional earthquakes continues today, but these processes are barely perceptible to backcountry travelers in the Wind Rivers.

GREEN RIVER LAKES TRAILHEAD

OVERVIEW

Green River Lakes, the third most popular trailhead to the Bridger Wilderness, lies in a broad U-shaped valley near the headwaters of the Green River, the principal tributary to the Colorado River. Lofty limestone peaks soar more than 3,000 feet above the trailhead, and bold granite crags and sheer canyon walls provide a provocative backdrop to the south, dominated by the Wind Rivers' most photographed landmark, Squaretop Mountain.

East of the long upper Green River valley, precipitous, trailless canyons plunge down the flanks of the valley, draining remote cirques and glaciers, and some of the range's highest peaks. Except to veteran mountaineers, most of those canyons are inaccessible.

To the west, south, and southwest of the trailhead, a high, lake-dotted tableland—the northwest extension of the vast, comparatively level bench that abuts the range's high peaks—dominates the landscape. This benchland is crisscrossed by many miles of good trails that offer access to dozens of high lakes, both above and below timberline, to prominent, glacier-carved canyons, and broad stretches of tundra, where the vistas are among the most dramatic in the range.

The Highline Trail, the principal artery in the trail network, reaches the high benchlands via the north-south-trending Green River canyon, one of many ancient fault zones that roughly parallel the crest of the Wind Rivers. So from its beginning, the Highline takes advantage of the fault zones that facilitate the easy passage of the trail throughout its 72.5-mile journey to Big Sandy.

Users of the Highline should expect to encounter many fellow travelers concentrated along the trail, at least as far as Trail Creek Park, beyond which various other trails tend to absorb and disperse travelers throughout the northern reaches of the Bridger Wilderness. The scenic Porcupine Trail is much less traveled than the Highline and offers an alternate route to the lake-filled tablelands above.

Travelers should bear in mind that the trailhead lies at about 8,000 feet, and considerable time and effort is required to reach the high country.

Finding the trailhead: From U.S. Highway 191, 5.2 miles west of Pinedale and 5 miles east of Daniel Junction (60 miles southeast of Jackson), turn north onto paved Wyoming Highway 352, signed for Green River Lakes Entrance, Bridger Wilderness.

This highway leads north up the broad Green River valley, passing the Cora post office after 4.2 miles and the signed, eastbound New Fork Road after 14.6 miles. The pavement ends after 25.4 miles at the boundary of the Bridger National Forest.

From the national forest boundary to the trailhead the road has a wide gravel bed, but it can be rough with washboards.

Ignore the left-branching Union Pass Road, 2.8 miles from the pavement's end, and continue the remaining 15.7 miles around the Big Bend of the river and up the increasingly narrow valley to a prominently signed junction.

Avoid the right-branching road to the campground and bear left; the sign points to the trailhead. After 0.2 mile, a spur forks left to the horse unloading area and trailhead. Hikers, however, bear right and reach their spacious trailhead after another 0.2 mile.

Toilets and water are available at the trailhead. Travelers arriving late in the day can stay overnight in the 35-site campground (a fee is charged), or use one of many undeveloped camping areas located at intervals all along the Green River Lakes Road within the Bridger National Forest.

THE TRAILS

- Highline Trail
- Porcupine Trail
- Clear Creek Trail
- Slide Lake Trail

SUGGESTED EXTENDED TRIPS

1) Highline-New Fork-Porcupine Loop; 32.6 miles, 4 to 5 days.

2) Follow the Highline to Summit Lake, take the Doubletop Mountain Trail to Palmer Lake (see hike 8), descend into New Fork canyon, and return to the trailhead via the Porcupine Trail; loop trip, 37 miles, 4 to 6 days.

3) Summit Lake area base camp; round trip, 32.6 miles, 4 to 7 days.

PLACES TO AVOID IF YOU'RE LOOKING FOR SOLITUDE

- Slide Lake
- Beaver Park
- Peak Lake

Green River and The Bottle from the Highline Trail.

1 HIGHLINE TRAIL—GREEN RIVER LAKES TO SUMMIT LAKE

General description:	An extended trip along the northernmost segment of the Highline Trail.
Distance:	16.3 miles, one way.
Difficulty:	Moderate.
Traffic:	Heavy.
Elevation gain:	2,400 feet.
Trailhead elevation:	8,050 feet.
Maximum elevation:	10,380 feet.
Topo maps:	USGS: Green River Lakes, Squaretop Mountain, Gannett Peak; Earthwalk: Northern Wind River Range.

Key Points:

- 0.0   Green River Lakes Trailhead.
- 1.9   Clear Creek Trail junction.
- 2.7   Green River bridge; junction with cutoff trail leading to Lakeside and Porcupine trails; stay left.
- 9.7   Bridge over Green River at Beaver Park.
- 11.0   Enter Three Forks Park.
- 13.4   Junction with New Fork Trail in Trail Creek Park; stay left.
- 14.2   Junction with unmaintained trail to Vista Pass; stay right.
- 16.3   Summit Lake; junctions with Doubletop Mountain and Pine Creek Canyon trails.

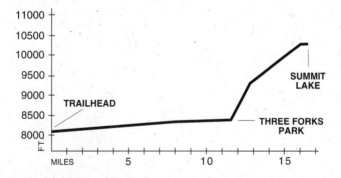

Best day hike destination: A short walk along the Highline Trail above lower Green River Lake offers outstanding vistas into the upper reaches of the Green River's 4,000-foot deep canyon, dominated by the towering granite stump of Squaretop Mountain.

A longer and more rewarding trip loops around the lower lake via the Highline and the Lakeside Trail (see hike 4), a day hike of 5.7 miles.

The hike: The northern segment of the Highline Trail—from Green River Lakes to Summit Lake—is one of the most popular trails in the range, for

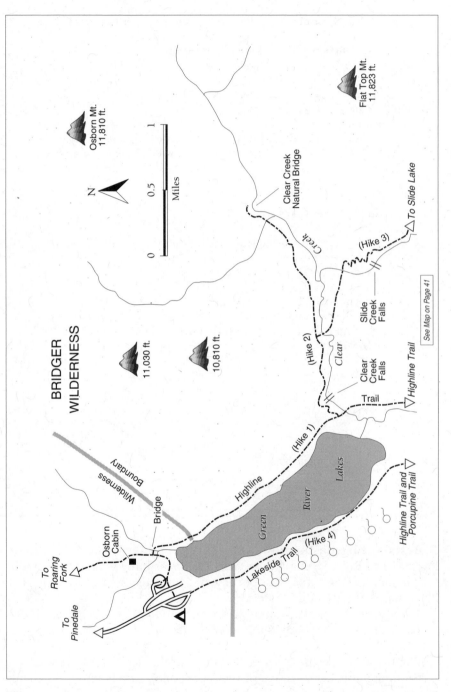

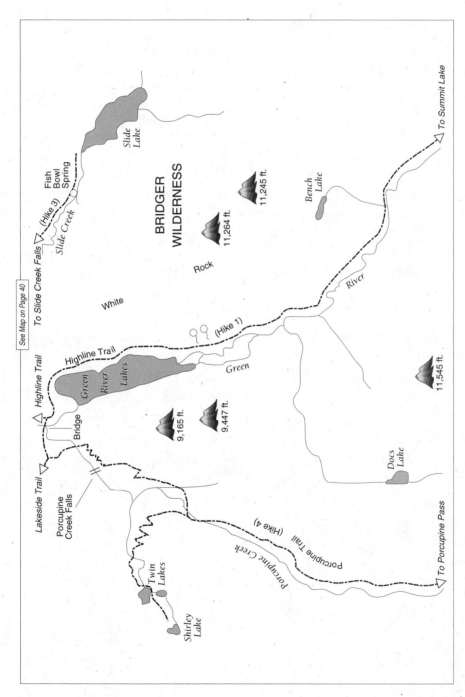

See Map on Page 40

BRIDGER
WILDERNESS

Slide Lake

Fish Bowl Spring

Slide Creek

(Hike 3)

To Slide Creek Falls

11,264 ft.

11,245 ft.

Rock

White

Bench Lake

River

(Hike 1)

Highline Trail

Green River Lakes

Green

11,545 ft.

Highline Trail

Bridge

Lakeside Trail

Porcupine Creek Falls

Docs Lake

To Summit Lake

Porcupine Creek

Porcupine Trail (Hike 4)

9,165 ft.

9,447 ft.

Twin Lakes

Shirley Lake

To Porcupine Pass

HIGHLINE—GREEN RIVER LAKES
TO SUMMIT LAKE

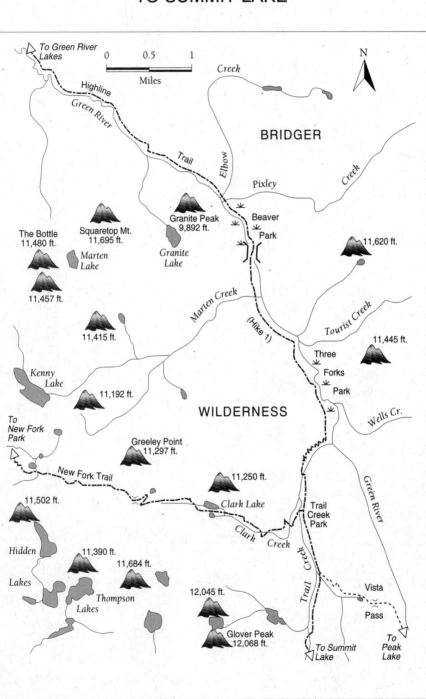

To Green River Lakes

Creek

0   0.5   1

Miles

N

Highline

Green River

BRIDGER

Trail

Elbow

Pixley

Creek

Beaver Park

11,620 ft.

The Bottle
11,480 ft.

Squaretop Mt.
11,695 ft.

Granite Peak
9,892 ft.

Marten Lake

Granite Lake

11,457 ft.

Marten Creek

(Hike 1)

Tourist Creek

11,445 ft.

11,415 ft.

Three

Forks

Park

Kenny Lake

11,192 ft.

WILDERNESS

Wells Cr.

To New Fork Park

Greeley Point
11,297 ft.

New Fork Trail

11,250 ft.

Green River

11,502 ft.

Clark Lake

Trail Creek Park

Clark Creek

Hidden

11,390 ft.

11,684 ft.

Lakes

Thompson Lakes

12,045 ft.

Trail Creek

Vista

Pass

Glover Peak
12,068 ft.

To Summit Lake

To Peak Lake

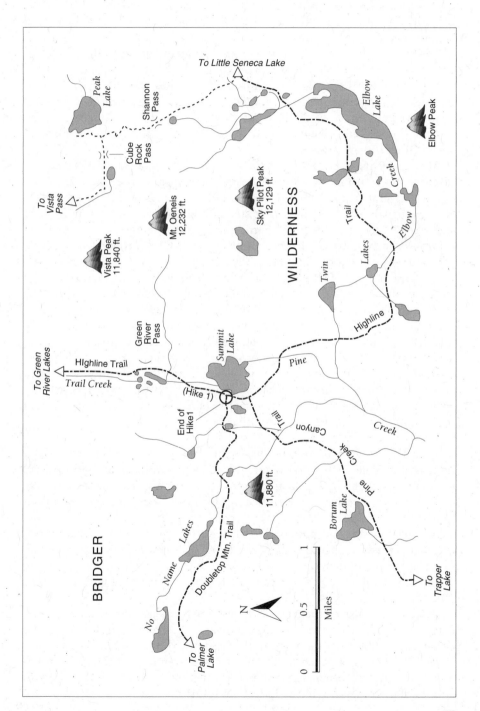

ample reasons. This memorable trail travels through the spectrum of western Wind River landscapes, from broad, rich meadows, open forests, and soaring canyon walls to spreading alpine meadows and ice-encrusted crags. And the trail boasts a smooth tread, a pleasant change from the Wind River's typically rocky, rough trails. Numerous trails that intersect this route offer a variety of possible loop trips.

The first 11.5 miles of the trail, winding along the banks of the beautiful, jade-tinted waters of the Green River to Three Forks Park, gain only 350 feet of elevation. From there to Summit Lake, however, the trail is more rigorous, gaining more than 2,000 feet in 4.8 miles. Fine camping areas are abundant along much of the trail, and water sources are frequent. Be sure to draw your drinking water from tributaries, not from the silt-laden waters of the Green River.

At the southwest corner of the hiker's parking lot, a trail sign on an old cabin points south into a minor forested draw, where the trail forks. The signed Highline Trail branches left here, descending the draw beneath an open canopy of lodgepole pine. The stock trail descends from the northwest and joins the foot trail after 250 yards, and together, hikers and equestrians continue gently downhill to the outlet of lower Green River Lake, where you find an information sign and trail register.

A lakeshore path forks right here, but bear left (north) and cross the sturdy bridge spanning the Green River. Just north of the crossing lies the Osborn Cabin, and the faint trail leading past it is a seldom used segment of the Highline, leading into the Roaring Fork drainage to the north.

Our trail curves east through level grasslands, then begins a long, undulating traverse above the lake's eastern shore. From these open, grassy slopes clothed in sagebrush and a scattering of aspen, narrowleaf cottonwood, and limber pine, travelers are rewarded with grand views that stretch across the lake's green waters and up the canyon to the cliff-edged monolith of Squaretop Mountain, a Green River landmark that remains in view for the following 9 miles.

An alpine ridge composed of limestone juts skyward to the east. That ridge, White Rock farther up the canyon, and a handful of neighboring peaks to the northwest and northeast, are remnants of the veneer of sedimentary rocks that covered the region prior to uplift of the Wind Rivers 65 million years ago.

Approaching the southern end of the lake, the signed trail to Clear Creek and Slide Lake branches left (see hikes 2 and 3), 1.9 miles from the trailhead. The Highline Trail then descends briefly into the willow thickets bordering the lakeshore and soon reaches the pole footbridge spanning wide and swift Clear Creek.

Beyond the crossing the trail skirts the brushy meadow and soon funnels between an open forest of lodgepole pine and the meandering waters of the Green River. About 2.7 miles from the trailhead, you reach the eastern abutment of a sturdy bridge across the river. A west-bound cutoff trail leads 0.3 mile from the bridge, across the meadow dividing the Green River Lakes, to join the Porcupine Trail in the lodgepole forest beyond.

Summit Lake on the Highline Trail.

The Highline Trail curves eastward beyond the bridge while gently climbing a pine-covered rise before descending to the meadow-fringed north shore of the upper lake. From here there are fine views across the lake to massive Squaretop Mountain and its satellite spire, The Bottle. The trail follows the lake's northeast shore, briefly climbing 100 feet above it midway around the lake, just beneath the overhanging dolomite and limestone cliffs of White Rock.

Descending back to the meadows fringing the lake, the trail alternates between Engelmann spruce forest and meadow openings rich with wildflowers that include shrub cinquefoil, lupine, blue flax, Everts thistle, blue harebell, groundsel, buckwheat, northern sweetvetch, larkspur, northern goldenrod, yellow Indian paintbrush, mountain bog gentian, and Richardson's geranium.

A variety of waterfowl may be seen on the lake feeding on aquatic vegetation and insects. Also watch for one of the world's most adept anglers— an osprey—diving into the lake to catch its unsuspecting prey. Although lake trout inhabit the waters of the upper lake, the glacial silt suspended in the river upstream is inhospitable to fish.

Near the upper end of the lake, several icy springs cascade across the trail, issuing from the porous limestones of White Rock, its ledges and cliff bands soaring 3,000 feet above and east of the trail.

From the upper lake, one of the most scenic segments of the trail follows. The trail winds among open, mostly lodgepole forest beyond the long grassy meadow above the lake as it follows the bends and curves of the swift, deep waters of the Green. The broken and fluted granite walls of Squaretop

Mountain, looming ever closer, allow travelers to gauge their progress up the canyon.

With the tree-fringed dome of Granite Peak and the east wall of Squaretop looming overhead, the trail soon reaches a pole footbridge over Elbow Creek about 8.8 miles in. Almost immediately thereafter it crosses the swift waters of Pixley Creek, also via a pole bridge.

Beyond the crossings the trail enters lovely Beaver Park, where parklike lodgepole forest, small meadows, the meandering river, and an abundance of fine camping areas combine to make Beaver Park a popular place for an overnight stay. Soaring cliffs and pinnacles jut skyward east of the park, hiding from view some of the loftiest peaks in the range.

Open forest and meadows continue as you proceed south through Beaver Park, soon reaching the sturdy bridge spanning the tumultuous waters of the Green, at 8,075 feet, 9.7 miles from the trailhead.

The trail ahead is sometimes rocky as it wanders through open stands of lodgepole pine and shady groves of Engelmann spruce. A bridge affords a dry crossing of Marten Creek at 10.1 miles, and beyond is a broad boulder field that forces the trail next to the brawling Green River.

Tourist Creek, both seen and heard tumbling down the aspen- and conifer-clad east wall of the canyon, marks the approach to Three Forks Park, where the main stem of the upper Green River, and its tributaries Wells and Trail creeks, all converge.

The trail skirts the western margins of the tall-grass meadows of the park. Here the Green meanders silently among scattered forest and meadow, and soaring, square-edged cliffs tower far above. There are a few fair campsites here, but the meadows remain mosquito-infested until late summer.

Beyond Three Forks Park, bid farewell to the Green River and begin the first major ascent thus far, climbing into the Trail Creek drainage. A series of gently graded switchbacks ascends southwest from the park through nearly viewless spruce and lodgepole forest, gaining 850 feet of elevation in 1.4 miles. Huckleberry and grouse whortleberry form a continuous green carpet in the understory of this shady forest.

Midway up this ascent, the forest breaks at an overlook high above tumbling Trail Creek. Here a grand view unfolds, reaching east into the trailless defile of Wells Creek and southeast into the upper canyon of the Green River to the lofty spires of Sulphur Peak.

Beyond the switchbacks, the trail traverses into a narrow canyon and crosses Trail Creek. There may be logs in place offering a dry crossing. It is also possible to boulder-hop the creek in low water. Otherwise you must wade the calf-deep, 15-foot-wide stream over slippery cobbles.

A gentle ascent through whitebark pine forest commences beyond the ford, leading 0.4 mile to a signed junction in the wildflower-speckled meadows of Trail Creek Park, at 9,300 feet. The right-branching New Fork Trail ascends westward into the rugged chasm of Clark Creek, and passes the Lozier Lakes chain en route to the New Fork Lakes Trailhead (see hike 5). Part of that trail can be used to loop back to Green River Lakes via Porcupine

Pass (see hike 4).

There are a few good campsites in Trail Creek Park among spruce and whitebark pine forest. The small meadows of the park are wildflower-rich, hosting the blooms of groundsel, dandelion, Indian paintbrush, one-flower daisy, dwarf goldenrod, and hairy arnica. Water is available from Trail Creek, a few yards west of the junction.

From that junction, the Highline climbs moderately for 0.8 mile through subalpine forest to the southeast-bound trail to Vista Pass. That unmaintained trail leads 3 miles to Peak Lake, lying among magnificent 12,000- and 13,000-foot crags in the headwaters cirque of the Green River. From Peak Lake, another trail runs 1.75 miles, via Shannon Pass, to rejoin the Highline in the Elbow Lake basin (see hike 11).

Continuing past that junction the trail soon hops across a small stream and ascends a moderate grade to a small, boulder-dotted meadow. The verdant alpine notch of Green River Pass now looms ahead on the southern skyline, flanked on the west by the broad, rocky slopes of 12,068-foot Glover Peak.

The trail steadily ascends toward the pass via upper Trail Creek canyon amid scattered spruces. The grade finally abates where it skirts the shores of several jewel-like tarns in alpine grassland well above timberline.

The summit of the pass is difficult to ascertain in this long, nearly level notch; when you pass above the shores of long Lake 10,362 you have crossed over into the Pine Creek drainage. Pause at the pass long enough to appreciate the view of the Trail Creek and Green River canyons. The canyon below is a classic example of a U-shaped, glacier-carved valley, bounded by soaring gray, cliff-edged alpine tablelands that rest 3,000 feet above the valley floor.

The raw beauty of the expansive alpine meadows and broad, lofty peaks that embrace the Green River Pass environs are ample rewards for your efforts. Stroll south down the gentle trail, hop across two minor streams, and soon you reach a signed junction above the west shore of large, round Summit Lake.

Although Summit Lake is an alpine gem, campsites around it are fully exposed to the view of other visitors, and also to the unpredictable mountain weather. The most sheltered sites can be found above the lake's east shore.

The junction is signed for Palmer Lake, and the west-bound trail (Doubletop Mountain Trail) is one of the most scenic alpine rambles in the Wind Rivers, passing No Name and Cutthroat lakes en route to Palmer Lake (see hike 8). Some travelers incorporate that trail into a loop that returns to Green River Lakes via New Fork Park and Porcupine Pass.

The Highline continues south from that junction for 150 yards to a junction with the southwest-bound Pine Creek Canyon Trail, signed for Trapper Lake (see hike 6).

To continue south on the Highline Trail, see hike 11.

2 GREEN RIVER LAKES TO CLEAR CREEK NATURAL BRIDGE

General description:	A rewarding, view-packed day hike.
Distance:	8.2 miles, round trip.
Difficulty:	Moderately easy.
Traffic:	Heavy.
Elevation gain and loss:	+400 feet, -100 feet.
Trailhead elevation:	8,050 feet.
Maximum elevation:	8,300 feet.
Topo maps:	USGS: Green River Lakes; Earthwalk: Northern Wind River Range.

See Map on Page 40

Key Points:

    0.0   Green River Lakes Trailhead.
    1.9   Junction with Clear Creek Trail; bear left.
    2.9   Junction with Slide Lake Trail; stay left.
    4.1   Clear Creek Natural Bridge.

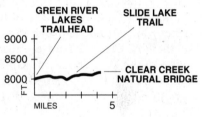

The hike: The core of the Wind Rivers is composed of granitic rocks that are highly resistant to erosion. But lying on the eastern flanks of the range, and in the Green River Lakes area in the northwest, are softer, more easily eroded layers of sedimentary rocks.

Natural bridges, formed by running water undercutting and subsequently penetrating a resistant, typically sedimentary wall of rock, are extremely rare in nature, but there are at least two natural bridges in the Wind Rivers.

One bridge can be found on lower Dinwoody Creek, east of the Continental Divide on the Wind River Indian Reservation, where access is restricted. But the Clear Creek Natural Bridge is easily accessible via the Clear Creek Trail from Green River Lakes.

This trip offers all the highlights of a Wind River trail—lakes, meadows, large streams, views of bold peaks—plus the chance to experience one of nature's rare erosional forms, a natural bridge carved through a narrow wall of limestone.

From the trailhead, follow the Highline Trail (see hike 1) for 1.9 miles above lower Green River Lake to the junction signed for Clear Creek Canyon, and turn left.

The Clear Creek Trail begins with a moderate northeast-bound ascent

Clear Creek Natural Bridge.

upon open slopes. Then it follows the rim of the canyon's lower gorge, passing above the thundering waterfall where Clear Creek plunges over a limestone precipice.

Beyond the falls is a pleasant, nearly level stretch of trail, leading at first through an open lodgepole pine forest, and later on opening up along the margins of an expansive meadow. Views also open up from the fringes of this spread, revealing the broken ramparts of 11,823-foot Flat Top Mountain, and an exciting array of bold crags soaring skyward farther up the canyon.

About 1 mile from the Highline Trail, the signed trail leading to Slide Lake (see hike 3) branches south. Instead, continue eastward; the sign points to Natural Bridge.

Our trail proceeds through open lodgepole forest, following the northern fringes of the meadow, where aptly named Clear Creek swings back and forth in wide, lazy meanders. Look up to the south wall of the canyon from this stretch of the trail to see the long white ribbon of Slide Creek Falls slicing through the forest there.

About 0.5 mile from the previous junction, the trail cuts across the northwest edge of the meadow, where the grasslands are enlivened by the blooms of blue harebell, subalpine daisy, yarrow, cinquefoil, and shrub cinquefoil. East of the meadow the trail enters a forest that was charred by a lightning-caused blaze in 1988, a burn where young lodgepoles are reclaiming the landscape.

The trail ahead closely follows the banks of large Clear Creek among blackened snags, soon reaching a log-crossing of a small tributary stream. Up ahead a prominent limestone rib drops off the northwestern flanks of Flat Top Mountain and blocks the canyon upstream.

Follow the streambanks north, presently on poor trail, and soon you will spy the small aperture in the rib through which Clear Creek flows. Follow the trail as it curves around the rib for the best view of Clear Creek Natural Bridge. There, Clear Creek flows north along the foot of this limestone spur, then turns abruptly west, flowing through the deep, arch-shaped cave the stream has carved. Echoes from the cave intensify the thunder of the cascading stream.

Where the creek enters the cave the opening is large, about 40 feet wide by 15 feet high. The exit opening is much smaller, 20 feet wide but only about 4 feet high.

The poor, unmaintained Clear Creek Trail continues up the canyon from the natural bridge for another 1.5 miles to Clear Lake.

3 GREEN RIVER LAKES TO SLIDE LAKE

General description:	A long round-trip day hike, or overnighter.
Distance:	11 miles, round trip.
Difficulty:	Moderately strenuous.
Traffic:	Heavy.
Elevation gain and loss:	+1,600 feet, -100 feet.
Trailhead elevation:	8,050 feet.
Maximum elevation:	9,490 feet.
Topo maps:	USGS: Green River Lakes; Earthwalk: Northern Green River Range.

See Maps on Pages 40 & 41

Key Points:

0.0   Green River Lakes Trailhead.
1.9   Junction with Clear Creek Trail; bear left.
2.9   Junction with Slide Lake Trail; bear right.
5.5   Slide Lake.

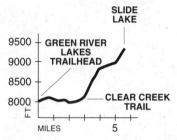

The hike: A large timberline lake embraced by towering walls and alpine summits is the destination of this rewarding trip. Although the trip can be completed in one long day, most people want to spend two or three days here absorbing the dramatic landscapes and fishing for the abundant brook trout that inhabit the lake.

From the Green River Lakes Trailhead, follow the Highline Trail (see hike 1) south for 1.9 miles above the east shore of lower Green River Lake, then turn left (east) onto the Clear Creek Trail (see hike 2). Follow that trail for 1 mile into Clear Creek canyon to the signed Slide Lake Trail and turn right (south).

This trail quickly leads to a footbridge spanning large Clear Creek. This precarious crossing consists of two sets of three logs, lashed together with cables, and meeting on a boulder in midstream. The logs are perched high above the creek's tumbling waters, and they flex and bounce as you cross. Exercise caution on this footbridge, particularly when the logs are wet. A good stock ford lies a few yards upstream from the bridge.

Beyond the crossing, head southeast across the meadow with its inspiring view up the canyon to Forlorn Pinnacle, the 11,640-foot spire to the northeast.

Slide Lake.

Footbridge spanning Clear Creek.

The trail carves a swath through the meadow, soon following its southern fringes beneath a shady canopy of Engelmann spruce and lodgepole pine. About 0.3 mile from the Clear Creek Trail junction, cross vigorous Slide Creek at a ford. Hikers may be able to avoid wet feet by searching for a log crossing several yards downstream.

Then the trail steadily ascends the shady, forested south wall of Clear Creek canyon via switchbacks. The grade ranges from moderate to steep, but the tread is fairly smooth. The dense canopy of spruce, lodgepole pine, and subalpine fir casts ample shade but hinders vistas.

Midway up the canyon wall, the trail edges close to dramatic Slide Creek Falls, a long, high-angle cascade that flows over the steeply dipping bedding plane of limestone. As you continue to gain elevation, the Tetons come into view in the northwest, nearly 60 miles distant.

After rising 800 feet in 1.5 miles, the grade slackens as the trail skirts a wet meadow, this one with a fine view of the fluted cliffs and spires on the southwest flanks of Flat Top Mountain, and of the bold towers of Lost Eagle Peak farther up the canyon.

Beyond the meadow the trail ducks into lodgepole forest and ascends gently to Fish Bowl Spring. Here a round, 6-foot-deep pool, set in limestone, is fed by springs issuing both from above ground and from within the pool. A large stream emerges from the pool, adding its waters to Slide Creek. True to its name, the pool is brimming with small trout.

Above the spring the trail ascends very steeply, at length becoming quite rocky for the final few hundred yards to Slide Lake. This beautiful lake lies in a deep cirque at 9,490 feet, with Flat Top Mountain to the north and Lost Eagle Peak to the southeast, each soaring more than 2,000 feet above its shores. Limestone cliffs rising south of the lake contrast with the dark gray gneiss that comprises the surrounding peaks.

Good campsites are scattered through the lodgepole-dominated forest near the outlet and above the north and northeast shores. A large log jam at the lake's outlet offers access to rocky points, where fishing for brookies is good, and to a few campsites along the southwest shores.

4 PORCUPINE TRAIL—GREEN RIVER LAKES TO NEW FORK TRAIL

General description:	An extended trip in the northern Bridger Wilderness, useful as part of a loop trip.
Distance:	12 miles, one way.
Difficulty:	Moderate.
Traffic:	Moderate.
Elevation gain and loss:	+2,740 feet, -1,180 feet.
Trailhead elevation:	8,050 feet.
Maximum elevation:	10,700 feet.
Topo maps:	USGS: Green River Lakes, Squaretop Mountain; Earthwalk: Northern Wind River Range.

Key Points:

0.0	Green River Lakes Trailhead.
0.3	Trail register in campground.
2.7	Junction with east-bound cutoff trail leading to the Highline Trail; stay right.
3.1	First ford of Porcupine Creek.
4.5	Junction with spur trail to Twin and Shirley lakes, just beyond second ford of Porcupine Creek.
4.9	Third ford of Porcupine Creek.
9.8	Porcupine Pass.
12.0	Junction with New Fork Trail.

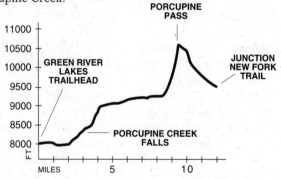

PORCUPINE

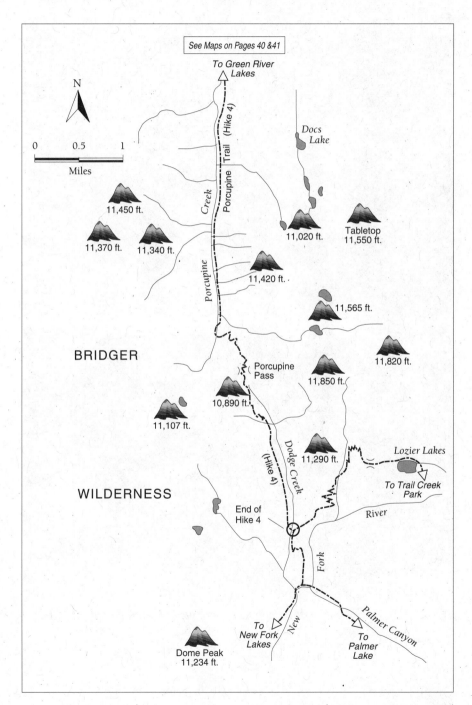

See Maps on Pages 40 &41

To Green River
Lakes

N

0   0.5   1
Miles

Docs
Lake

Creek

Porcupine Trail (Hike 4)

11,450 ft.

11,370 ft.   11,340 ft.

Porcupine

11,020 ft.

Tabletop
11,550 ft.

11,420 ft.

11,565 ft.

11,820 ft.

BRIDGER

Porcupine
Pass

11,850 ft.

11,107 ft.

10,890 ft.

11,290 ft.

Lozier Lakes

To Trail Creek
Park

(Hike 4)

Dodge Creek

WILDERNESS

End of
Hike 4

River

Fork

To
New Fork
Lakes

New

Palmer Canyon

To
Palmer
Lake

Dome Peak
11,234 ft.

The deep, U-shaped valley of Porcupine Creek, viewed from Porcupine Pass.

Best day hike destination: A 5.7-mile loop around lower Green River Lake (see hike 1) is an easy day hike for most hikers. Strong hikers might consider following the spur trail to Twin and Shirley lakes, accessed in the lower reaches of Porcupine Creek canyon, 4.5 miles from the trailhead. That trip involves a total of 2,100 feet of elevation gain and is 13.4 miles round trip.

The hike: Porcupine Creek, one of the upper Green River's major tributaries, drains a remote, U-shaped hanging valley of exceptional beauty. Groves of spire-topped spruce, meadows rich with tall grasses and colorful wildflowers; bold crags and avalanche-scarred canyon walls; and the overall verdant setting combine to make scenes in Porcupine Creek canyon more reminiscent of the Cascade Range than the Wind Rivers.

Despite Porcupine Creek's beauty, the canyon is seldom the destination of backcountry travelers, most of whom are usually en route to fish-filled lakes and high summits. Instead, this trail is usually used as a scenic leg of a loop trip originating at Green River Lakes, in combination with the Highline Trail and the New Fork or Doubletop Mountain trails.

From the southwest corner of the hiker's parking lot, a trail sign on an old cabin points to the trail, and from there it quickly descends into a minor forested draw to a signed junction. The Highline Trail forks left, so turn right (west), soon crossing a road below the parking lot and entering the campground. Turn left at the campground road and proceed to the trailhead proper; a trail register and mileage sign are located behind Campsites 10 and 11, where the trail begins.

The Lakeside Trail follows the west shore of lower Green River Lake, a pleasant, nearly level trail leading through a shady forest of lodgepole pine and Engelmann spruce. The understory features buffaloberry and common juniper, but wildflowers here are noticeably sparse; only groundsel and heartleaf arnica decorate the forest floor. One dozen small, spring-fed streams cascade across the trail as it traverses steep slopes west of the lower lake.

During the first mile the trail stays well above the lake. Then it drops to the rocky lakeshore, where anglers may be tempted to ply the lake's deep, green waters. Lake trout, arctic grayling, and mountain whitefish inhabit the lower lake.

On occasion the forest is thin enough to allow fine views across the lake and into the tower-rimmed canyon of Clear Creek. The gray granitic bedrock of the fluted walls and pinnacles that flank that canyon contrasts with the red, tan, and white cliff bands on the nearby west face of White Rock, a limestone outlier of the sedimentary veneer that buried the region more than 65 million years ago.

Beyond the shores of the lower lake the trail skirts the western edge of a broad, lodgepole-fringed meadow that separates the Green River Lakes. Continue along the meadow's edge to a signed junction. The sign pointing to Three Forks Park indicates a 0.3-mile cutoff trail that leads east through the meadow, brushy with shrub cinquefoil and willows, to a bridge spanning the Green River and a junction with the Highline Trail.

Bear right at that junction and continue on the level through the lodge-pole forest fringing the meadow, soon reaching the 15-foot wide main channel of Porcupine Creek. There may be logs in place just upstream to afford a dry crossing; if not, the cobble-bottomed stream is easily forded in low water (about 1-foot deep). Another channel beyond can be rock-hopped quite easily.

The trail ahead ascends 900 feet in 1.5 miles, rising via a series of moderately steep switchbacks through a forest of lodgepole and spruce. Once again, views are limited. After 0.5 mile of steady ascent a faint side path leads west to the brink of Porcupine Creek's gorge, with views of the thundering cascade of Porcupine Creek Falls.

When the grade on the main trail eventually eases, proceed through shady lodgepole forest and small meadows to the flower-rich banks of Porcupine Creek at 8,850 feet. Ford the creek again; here it is calf-deep and 12 to 15 feet wide. If the water level is low, it is possible to boulder-hop a few yards downstream. To avoid the ford some hikers have forged a path upstream on the east bank. It's about 100 yards to large logs spanning the creek.

Beyond the ford, briefly climb to a junction perched on a streamside bench. The spur trail to Twin and Shirley lakes departs northward from here, climbing 1,100 feet in 2.2 miles.

In the beautiful hanging valley of Porcupine Creek, 1,000 feet above the Green River's canyon, proceed southward along the tree-studded bench for 0.4 mile to a third crossing of the creek, 20 feet wide and shin-deep.

The following 1.5 miles are a scenic delight, passing alongside a lovely, narrow meadow, above which towers a host of splintered crags soaring 2,000 feet to the skyline. A diverse assemblage of wildflowers grows trailside, including Indian paintbrush, hairy and heartleaf arnica, mountain bluebells, cinquefoil, one-flower daisy, king's crown, short-styled onion, groundsel, mountain bog gentian, Colorado columbine, and shrub cinquefoil.

You may not see the canyon's namesake, porcupines, while traveling here, but their presence is certainly evident. On the scarred boles of lodgepole pines, porcupines have gnawed away the trees' bark to reach the inner bark, or cambium, their primary winter food. More likely seen here are moose, which frequent the canyon's willow thickets and, in the higher elevations, the elk that inhabit the alpine meadows in summer.

Fine camping areas are found throughout the canyon, and the best of them lie west of the creek. But, due to the confined nature of the canyon, it takes extra effort to establish camp beyond the 200-foot limit from the trail and creek. Try to make your camp as invisible to other travelers as possible.

Above the first long meadow, the trail, always close to increasingly small Porcupine Creek, alternates between groves of spruce and a series of smaller meadows. At length it leads into the boulder fields and subalpine meadows near the head of the canyon. At 8.5 miles is a fourth crossing, this one of a tributary of Porcupine Creek, which here is a much smaller stream and is easily boulder-hopped. Shortly thereafter, at 9,650 feet, pass the abandoned Jim Creek Trail. Not far past that junction is the fifth and final stream crossing en route to Porcupine Pass, also an easy rock-hop.

From here part of the trail ahead is visible as it switchbacks up the canyon's headwall to Porcupine Pass, the treeless alpine notch 1,000 feet above and to the southeast.

The following 1.1 miles to the pass ascend a series of well-designed switchbacks. The tread is smooth and the grade is moderate. Beginning in a grove of Christmas tree-sized spruces, the trail then enters an open timberline forest of whitebark pine and spruce. At length it breaks above timberline in a small, ice-gouged basin rimmed by minor moraines. Switchbacks then climb over the final, very steep alpine slopes to the windy 10,700-foot pass.

Pay heed here to some of the cushion plants adapted to the harsh alpine environment upon these north-facing slopes. Most noticeable are the blue blooms of sky pilot, sometimes called skunkflower for its pungent fragrance. Other flowers that are also restricted to the alpine zone include arctic sagewort and boreal sandwort.

The vistas that unfold atop the pass don't include any of the Wind Rivers' lofty Continental Divide summits, but they are befitting an alpine pass and grand enough to amply reward you for your efforts.

Porcupine Creek canyon, below to the north, is a fine example of a glacier-carved drainage, U-shaped and bounded by abruptly rising, fluted gray granitic cliffs. The canyon's walls frame a view of the volcanic plateaus of the Absaroka Range near Togwotee Pass some 40 miles to the north.

Southward, the view reaches into the canyon of New Fork River and beyond into Palmer Canyon, where precipitous talus fields and great ice-polished cliffs rise to a landscape of alpine tablelands.

From Porcupine Pass, the trail south into Dodge Creek is faint in places as it descends steadily across grassy alpine slopes and into a scenic, wildflower-rich bowl. Occasional cairns mark the way through this obscure stretch of trail.

Beyond the bowl the trail is more obvious, and the steady, moderate descent soon leads to a spruce-dominated timberline forest. Continue above the banks of Dodge Creek upon steep, east-facing slopes. The steep canyon of Dodge Creek offers little opportunity for camping.

Cross Dodge Creek 2.2 miles from the pass, which in low water is an easy rock-hop. The trail then curves around a minor ridge and joins the New Fork Trail in a grove of whitebark pine at 9,520 feet.

The nearest possible camping areas are located in New Fork Park, 1.5 miles and 600 feet below to the south, and at Lozier Lakes, 2.5 miles and 1,100 feet above to the east (see hike 5).

NEW FORK LAKES TRAILHEAD

OVERVIEW

The New Fork Lakes Trailhead, much like Green River Lakes, offers access to the high, lake-dotted benchlands in the northwest reaches of the Bridger Wilderness. New Fork Canyon, one of only five major west-side canyons, is much more open than the upper Green River canyon, with only scattered forests to shade travelers. Soaring canyon walls, among the largest expanses of unbroken granite in the range, dominate the canyon beyond the trailhead.

Not as heavily used as Green River Lakes, New Fork Lakes offers an attractive alternative starting point. The drive to the trailhead involves only 6.1 miles of rough dirt road, compared to the 17.5 miles of poor road to Green River Lakes. Moreover, trail miles are also shorter, but the trails involve a comparable ascent.

Finding the trailhead: Follow paved Wyoming Highway 352, the Green River Road, for 14.6 miles from U.S. Highway 191 (see Green River Lakes Trailhead) to the signed turnoff for New Fork Lakes.

Drivers approaching from the north via US 189/191 can reach the Green River Rd. by following signed Sublette County Road 23-149 east from that highway. Find the turnoff 46.3 miles southeast of Hoback Junction or 59.3 miles from Jackson. The gravel road leads 5 miles to the Green River Rd. then turn left (north) and drive another 6.3 miles to the New Fork Lakes Road.

The New Fork Lakes Rd. is a wide gravel road that tends to develop washboards. It winds eastward over rocky moraines for 2.7 miles to the boundary of the Bridger National Forest. About 0.75 mile beyond is a junction with the road to New Fork Lakes Campground.

Bear left (the sign points to the New Fork Trail), cross the dam at the outlet of lower New Fork Lake, and continue northeast above the lake's shoreline to the small trailhead parking area, opposite the entrance to Narrows Campground, 6.1 miles from WY 352.

There are a stock ramp and hitch rails at the trailhead.

In addition to the two campgrounds near the trailhead, travelers arriving late in the day can stay overnight in one of several undeveloped camping areas located between the national forest boundary and the dam at the lower lake.

THE TRAILS
- New Fork Trail
- Doubletop Mountain Trail
- Palmer Lake Trail

SUGGESTED EXTENDED TRIPS

1) A rigorous but rewarding long-distance trip follows the New Fork Trail to Trail Creek Park, thence the Highline Trail to Summit Lake, and returns via the Doubletop Mountain and Palmer Lake trails (the trip can also be taken in the opposite direction); semi-loop trip, 34.3 miles, 4 to 7 days.

2) New Fork Park base camp; round trip, 14 miles, 3 to 5 days.

3) Palmer Lake area base camp; round trip, 23 miles, 4 to 6 days.

4) Lozier Lakes base camp; round trip, 24 miles, 5 to 7 days.

5 NEW FORK TRAIL—NEW FORK LAKES TO TRAIL CREEK PARK

General description:	An extended trip in the northern Bridger Wilderness.
Distance:	16.5 miles, one way.
Difficulty:	Moderate.
Traffic:	Moderate.
Elevation gain and loss:	+3,480 feet; -2,080 feet.
Trailhead elevation:	7,895 feet.
Maximum elevation:	10,920 feet.
Topo maps:	USGS: New Fork Lakes, Kendall Mountain, Squaretop Mountain, Gannett Peak; Earthwalk: Northern Wind River Range.

Key points:

0.0	New Fork Lakes trailhead.
2.0	Junction with Boulder Basin (Lowline) Trail; continue straight ahead.
5.6	First ford of New Fork River.
6.3	Second ford of river.
6.7	Enter New Fork Park.
8.2	Junction with Palmer Canyon Trail; bear left.
9.3	Junction with Porcupine Trail; bear right.
11.6	10,680-foot pass west of Lozier Lakes.
14.1	10,920-foot pass east of Lozier Lakes.
15.0	Clark Lake.
16.5	Junction with Highline Trail in Trail Creek Park.

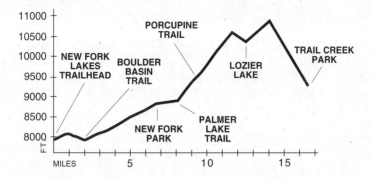

Best day hike destination: The sandy beach at the upper end of New Fork Lakes makes an attractive destination for a 3-mile round-trip day hike. Strong hikers can make the 14-mile round trip to New Fork Park in one long day.

The hike: The broad, open canyon of the New Fork River, bounded by some of the most impressive canyon walls in the range, offers a delightful and scenic way to reach the lake-dotted bench and high peaks region in the northern reaches of the Bridger Wilderness. The New Fork Trail is much less popular than trails beginning at the Green River Lakes and Elkhart Park entrances, but no less rewarding.

This trail surveys the spectrum of Bridger Wilderness landscapes, passing low-elevation glacial lakes, aspen groves, sagebrush-clad slopes, towering granite walls, timberline lakes, and alpine meadows, and offering grand vistas of the range's highest, glacier-draped peaks.

The New Fork Trail ascends the New Fork River's high-walled canyon to the lovely meadows of New Fork Park, then rises above timberline to the Lozier Lakes basin, and finally descends into the Green River drainage, past Clark Lake to Trail Creek Park. En route this trail passes junctions with the Lowline Trail (also known as the Boulder Basin Trail), the Palmer Lake Trail, and the Porcupine Trail.

The trail begins at the northeast corner of the parking lot and heads east above the north shore of upper New Fork Lake through an extensive grove of aspen. Pass an information sign and trail register and continue on a nearly level grade. The trail enters a minor draw, then curves briefly uphill around a low ridge—a small lateral moraine.

Beyond the moraine the trail begins a protracted traverse high above the lake on mostly open, sagebrush- and grass-covered slopes—a hot and dry stretch of trail. Views here stretch westward across New Fork Lakes to the Wyoming Range on the western horizon, 40 miles distant. Look eastward for a glimpse into the cliff-embraced lower reaches of New Fork Canyon.

The trail soon descends moderately to the upper end of the lake, where an inviting sandy beach appears in late summer. Pass several campsites set in aspen groves as you continue, soon skirting the northern margins of a

NEW FORK

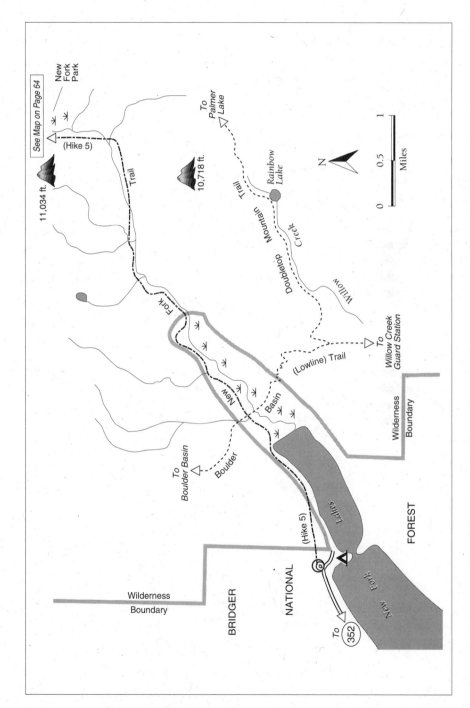

NEW FORK • DOUBLETOP MOUNTAIN & PALMER LAKE

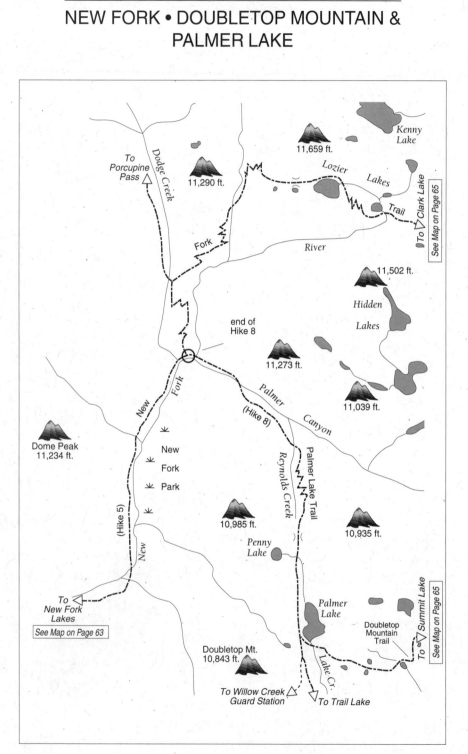

Kenny Lake

11,659 ft.

To Porcupine Pass

Dodge Creek

11,290 ft.

Lozier Lakes

Trail

To Clark Lake

See Map on Page 65

Fork

River

11,502 ft.

end of Hike 8

Hidden Lakes

11,273 ft.

New Fork

Palmer Canyon

11,039 ft.

(Hike 8)

Dome Peak
11,234 ft.

New Fork Park

Reynolds Creek

Palmer Lake Trail

(Hike 5)

10,985 ft.

10,935 ft.

New

Penny Lake

To New Fork Lakes

See Map on Page 63

Palmer Lake

To Summit Lake

See Map on Page 65

Doubletop Mountain Trail

Doubletop Mt.
10,843 ft.

Lake Cr.

To Willow Creek Guard Station

To Trail Lake

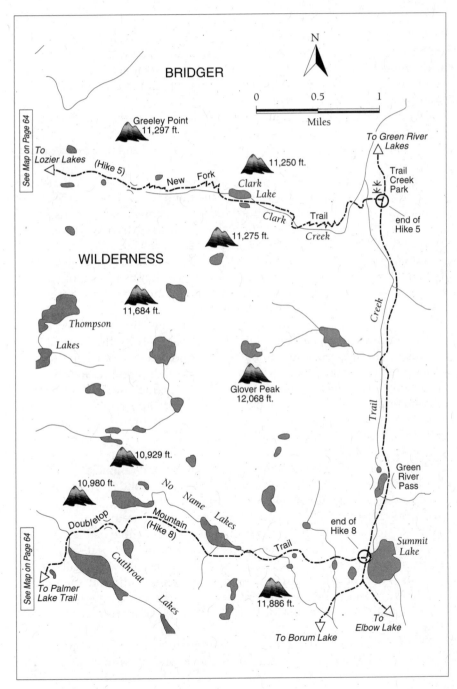

BRIDGER

N

0   0.5   1

Miles

Greeley Point
11,297 ft.

11,250 ft.

See Map on Page 64

To
Lozier Lakes

(Hike 5)

New   Fork

Clark
Lake

To Green River
Lakes

Trail
Creek
Park

Clark

Trail

end of
Hike 5

Creek

11,275 ft.

WILDERNESS

11,684 ft.

Thompson

Lakes

Creek

Glover Peak
12,068 ft.

Trail

10,929 ft.

10,980 ft.

No   Name   Lakes

Green
River
Pass

Doubletop

Mountain
(Hike 8)

end of
Hike 8

Summit
Lake

See Map on Page 64

To Palmer
Lake Trail

Cutthroat

Trail

Lakes

11,886 ft.

To
Elbow Lake

To Borum Lake

broad, willow-choked meadow.

Midway around the swampy expanse is a signed junction with the Lowline Trail, branching left (northwest) to Boulder Basin and right (south) to the Doubletop Mountain Trail. The latter requires a ford of the slow, meandering river and much bushwhacking through willow thickets to locate the tread south of the meadow.

Look northwest along the course of the Lowline Trail to a prominent outcrop of limestone high above the canyon. These sedimentary rocks, found on the range's west slope only between the New Fork and Green River's Big Bend, are more than 1.5 billion years younger than the granitic rocks that compose the core of the range.

About 1 mile beyond that junction the long meadow ends and scattered lodgepole pines begin to offer marginal shade. The trail contours above a chain of marshy ponds, where a variety of waterfowl, and possibly a moose, may be seen.

There are only four noticeable ascents en route to New Fork Park, and the first two are easily climbed beyond the ponds as the rocky canyon begins to twist and turn. Broken cliffs dotted with conifers and aspens rise to the north, and the canyon's south walls are scarred by many avalanche chutes plunging down from the tree-feathered ridge above.

Although the trail is seldom close to the river, either staying high above its many gorges or well away from its banks, a number of small streams cascade across the trail, allowing travelers to quench their thirst at convenient intervals (and after treating the water).

The canyon remains relatively open despite the cliffs that loom boldly above. There is a lack of substantial forest cover due to the bedrock that dominates the canyon floor, smoothed and polished by ancient glaciers. Lodgepole pine and aspen provide occasional shade, and the understory is decorated by a variety of shrubs and wildflowers, including Oregon grape, tobacco brush (Ceanothus spp.), buffaloberry, thimbleberry, red elderberry, gooseberry, pachystima, wild strawberry, cinquefoil, fireweed, Richardson's geranium, pearly everlasting, and blue harebell.

After ascending the third prominent grade the canyon becomes more confined, with sheer cliffs to the north and an array of pinnacles looming to the south. The trail closely follows the north bank of the river, soon reaching a ford of the New Fork where the river flows among large slabs and boulders, at 8,500 feet. If the water level is low, the crossing is not difficult; wade the slow-moving 12-foot-wide stream over its cobble bed. There may also be logs spanning the river just upstream. During high water, however, the river may be as much as 20 feet wide, and knee deep with a substantial current. Use good judgment and exercise extreme caution at such times. Some hikers elect to bypass the ford by continuing east on the north bank, but that route involves considerable effort to negotiate a steep, 0.5-mile boulder field.

The trail beyond the ford ascends moderately across open slopes dotted with erratic boulders and a scattering of lodgepole and whitebark pine and

Clark Lake and Continental Divide peaks, viewed from the pass east of Lozier Lakes.

subalpine fir. From here views open up to the north, following the northward bend of the canyon to the fluted granite walls embracing New Fork Park.

Soon the trail descends gently to the second ford of the New Fork, 0.7 mile from the first crossing, where the canyon makes a prominent bend to the north. Here the river is about 15 feet wide, shin deep, with a modest current. There may be a large spruce log across the river about 100 yards downstream.

A minor ascent ensues beyond the ford, quickly leading into beautiful, 1.5-mile-long New Fork Park, at 8,750 feet. The long meadows here are dotted with large erratic boulders and islands of forest composed of Engelmann spruce, lodgepole and whitebark pine, and subalpine fir. The meandering river bisects the park, isolating travelers from the best camping areas on the opposite side of the river. Several overused—and illegal—campsites lie alongside the trail; avoid using them.

No great peaks can be viewed from New Fork Park, but what the vistas lack in alpine grandeur is compensated for by the canyon's towering walls and jutting pinnacles that soar fully 2,000 feet above the canyon floor. On the west side of the park is a mile-long wall broken by chutes and buttresses, all part of the Dome Peak massif, one of the biggest walls in the Wind Rivers. Views also reach northeastward into the hanging valley of Dodge Creek (traversed by hike 4) and beyond to the rocky alpine highlands that rise above it.

New Fork Park is also notable for its profusion of wildflowers, which include bracted lousewort, cinquefoil, meadow rue, groundsel, yampah, fireweed, valerian, blue harebell, buckwheat, yarrow, green gentian, subalpine daisy, lupine, and cow parsnip.

The trail follows the park's western margin, passing beneath a scattering of conifers. Approaching the north end of New Fork Park, views open up to the northeast, exposing the unbroken granite walls bounding Palmer Canyon, a sheer face sweeping 1,500 feet skyward from the lower reaches of the canyon.

Soon you reach Dodge Creek, 1.8 miles from the last crossing of the New Fork River. The creek is about 12 feet wide but shallow. Rock-hop across the creek in late summer, or wade its shallow waters earlier in the season. There may be logs in place to afford a dry crossing.

Soon after crossing Dodge Creek watch for a junction with the Palmer Lake Trail (see hike 8), branching right (east). The New Fork Trail heads north; the sign points to Porcupine Pass. A moderate ascent ensues, gaining 675 feet in 1.1 miles through a subalpine forest of spruce and whitebark pine.

Upon reaching the signed junction with the north-bound Porcupine Trail at 9,500 feet, bear right and traverse northeast beneath an open canopy of whitebarks. Fine views stretch down the broad canyon of the New Fork to idyllic New Fork Park and the lofty fluted walls of Dome Peak.

The New Fork River rumbles through its canyon far below but is shielded

Peaks of the Continental Divide from Lozier Lakes basin.

from view by the slope's cloak of subalpine forest. Soon a series of switchbacks lead up and away from the canyon. In addition to the fine views, a variety of trailside wildflowers will also help to divert attention from the 500-foot, switchbacking ascent. These south-facing slopes host colorful blooms that include blue harebell, lupine, hairy arnica, yarrow, northern sweetvetch, green gentian, cinquefoil, groundsel, mountain dandelion, and arrowleaf balsamroot.

Soon the trail approaches a small tumbling stream; continue climbing switchbacks just west of the stream's banks. The grade eventually slackens as the trail enters a small, boulder-littered basin. It is easy to rock-hop the small stream.

Here, one-flower daisy, groundsel, Indian paintbrush, and mountain bluebells help to enliven the increasingly barren landscape. Timberline lies a short distance above, now, beneath an array of low crags.

The trail skirts the eastern edge of the basin and ascends steadily to another flower-rich meadow up-canyon. From there, follow more switchbacks eastward, climbing grassy slopes to timberline. Then the trail briefly levels off in a minor basin with another hop across a small stream.

The trail then continues at a gentler grade, leading across alpine slopes and past a small tarn to an unnamed pass at 10,680 feet. The pass hosts a fabulous array of colorful wildflowers, and the largest of the Lozier Lakes (10,590 feet) spreads out just below to the east. These details may escape your immediate attention, for an incredible tableau of peaks and glaciers unfolds before you.

From Gannett Peak to Stroud Peak, the sawtoothed crest of the Wind Rivers spreads out in a glorious panorama of unsurpassed alpine grandeur. The vistas from this pass, and from the next pass 2.5 miles ahead, are among the finest obtained from any trail in the range.

The trail descends gently eastward from the pass into the headwaters basin of the New Fork River, skirting the north shore of Lake 10,590. Good fishing for brook trout and good camping areas invite an overnight stay at this lovely timberline gem. Knobs of ice-polished granite rise north of the lake, and a broad wall of jointed bedrock marks the upper reaches of New Fork Canyon, to the south.

Rock-hop the lake's small outlet stream, then begin a moderately descending grade over wildflower-dotted slopes amid increasingly large groves of spruce and whitebark pine. The descent ends after 0.6 mile, at 10,400 feet at the south shore of round, meadow-fringed lower Lozier Lake, its shallow waters barren of fish. A plank bridge affords a dry crossing of the lake's outlet—the infant New Fork River.

To both the north and south of Lozier Lakes basin a trailless, lake-dotted alpine tableland extends for several miles. This rolling, ice-sculpted landscape of granite knolls and shallow basins beckons to adventurous travelers for days of satisfying exploration. Kenny Lake to the north and the Hidden Lakes chain to the south both harbor populations of brookies.

The trail once again inclines over grassy slopes beyond the lake, passes the last persistent stand of gnarled trees, then leads into a shallow, tarn-dotted basin. A viable cross-country route to the Hidden Lakes ascends the narrow gully from the southeast corner of the basin (consult the Squaretop Mountain quad).

After a final ascent of green tundra slopes, surmount a 10,920-foot pass and once again the towering northern peaks of the Wind Rivers burst upon the scene in a grand panorama. The yawning depths of the Green River canyon lie far below, with one dozen lofty crags rising nearly a mile above.

From south to north the peaks include the isolated spire of 12,198-foot Stroud Peak, above which rises the steep flanks of 13,020-foot Bow Mountain. To the left of Bow is the striking needle of 12,825-foot Sulphur Peak, and below it part of Stroud Glacier. Look past that glacier to gaze into the headwaters cirque of the Green River, to 12,775-foot Winifred Peak, through the gap of Knapsack Col and up to 13,185-foot Twin Peaks, snow-covered Mount Whitecap at 13,020 feet, and 12,957-foot Ladd Peak. Northeast of Ladd is the broad, snow-crowned summit of 13,804-foot Gannett Peak—Wyoming's highest. Below Gannett lies Minor Glacier, and to its north two more prominent Continental Divide peaks are visible beyond a prow-like knob above Clark Lake: craggy, red-streaked Mount Koven, 13,265 feet, and the broad plateau of 13,435-foot Rampart Peak.

Closer at hand, numerous alpine wildflowers enliven the treeless environs of the pass, including alpine bistort, one-flower daisy, cinquefoil, elephanthead, alpine goldenrod, Parry's townsendia, dwarf alpine arnica, arctic sagewort, and alpine dandelion.

The trail descends the open slopes below the pass, at first heading northeast toward a tarn, then beginning a series of switchbacks just north of Clark Creek's headwaters stream. Cross the runoff of an upslope spring, where mountain bluebells and monkey flowers grow in profusion, then descend across slopes masked with ground-hugging mats of spruce and an increasingly fine display of wildflowers.

At length you reach the floor of Clark Lake's basin, pass a grove of tall spruces, step across two small streams, and skirt a swampy meadow west of the lake. The trail then follows a low, boulder-covered moraine that separates Clark Lake from an unseen tarn to the south.

The Clark Lake environs offers good camping in a subalpine forest of spruce and whitebark pine. But because the small basin is confined, campers need to make an extra effort to camp at least 200 feet from the lake and trail (see *Bridger Wilderness Regulations*).

The lake harbors rainbow trout, and views from its shores are good. Bold granite cliffs soar 1,000 feet above to the north and south, and eastward views reach into the headwaters of the Green River, revealing a host of peaks, from Stroud in the southeast to Ladd in the northeast.

Cross the wide, shallow outlet of the lake via boulders, then descend a moderate grade down the narrow, boulder-choked canyon of Clark Creek. The spruce and pine forest steadily thickens while views become obscured as the rocky trail descends. About 0.7 mile below Clark Lake, rock-hop to the creek's south bank and then cross back to the north bank, following switchbacks down into Trail Creek canyon.

Approaching the end of the descent, cross Clark Creek one final time via a bridge, then negotiate a few more gently descending switchbacks to a ford of Trail Creek. When the water is low, boulder-hop your way across, but early in the season you must wade the 20-foot-wide, calf-deep stream, which has a moderate current.

Beyond the ford the trail enters Trail Creek Park, a string of flower-filled meadow openings amid groves of subalpine forest. Groundsel, dandelion, Indian paintbrush, one-flower daisy, dwarf goldenrod, and hairy arnica decorate the meadows, while bold cliffs and lofty alpine plateaus rise to the east.

The trail passes a number of good camping areas as it continues northeast from the ford, soon meeting the Highline Trail (see hike 1) at 9,300 feet.

SPRING CREEK PARK TRAILHEAD

OVERVIEW

Spring Creek Park, lying near the rim of a monumental moraine high above the northwest shore of Fremont Lake, is one of the least-used trailheads to the northern Bridger Wilderness. Trails lead from the trailhead into a landscape of granite domes, subalpine forests, and dozens of lakes on the southwestern reaches of the high benchland that stretches from Pine Creek canyon in the south to the west rim of the upper Green River in the north.

Fishing is a popular pastime in most of the lakes accessed from this trailhead. And the landscape here is "friendlier" than the alpine reaches of the bench farther north. An abundant forest cover of Engelmann spruce and whitebark and lodgepole pine surrounds the lakes south of Borum Lake, where there are sheltered campsites and ample firewood. The lower elevations here—right around 10,000 feet, translate to warmer nights than in the alpine heights.

A good gravel road leads from Pinedale to the trailhead turnoff, but the final 2.5 miles is a narrow, rough, one-lane forest road. A high-clearance vehicle is recommended, but cars can negotiate the road if driven with care.

Finding the trailhead: From U.S. Highway 191 near the west end of Pinedale, turn north where a large Wyoming Game and Fish Department sign points the way to the Soda Lake Wildlife Habitat Management Area.

Follow the pavement north through a residential area of Pinedale for 0.25 mile, then continue north on gravel Sublette County Road 23-119, a good wide road that can be occasionally rough with washboards.

After 5.1 miles bear left at the turnoff to the Wildlife Habitat Management Area, and bear left again after another 1.6 miles, where a road branches right to Soda Lake. The road to the trailhead, signed for Willow Lake, leads another 2.7 miles to the Bridger National Forest boundary.

About 50 yards beyond the forest boundary (9.4 miles from Pinedale), turn right onto Forest Road 10053, signed for Spring Creek Park. This one-lane dirt road leads 2.5 miles to the spacious trailhead parking area. Along the final 0.6 mile of the road there are very rough, rocky, and eroded stretches. Do not attempt to follow the extremely rough road beyond the parking area unless you're driving a high-clearance, four-wheel-drive vehicle.

THE TRAILS

- Glimpse Lake Trail
- Pine Creek Canyon Trail
- Trapper Creek Trail
- Palmer Lake Trail
- Doubletop Mountain Trail

SUGGESTED EXTENDED TRIPS

1) Trail Lake area base camp; round trip, 20 miles, 4 to 6 days.

2) Borum Lake base camp; round trip, 23 miles, 4 to 7 days.

3) Follow Glimpse Lake and Pine Creek Canyon trails to Summit Lake, thence the Doubletop Mountain Trail to Palmer Lake. Return to Trail Lake via the Palmer Lake Trail and take the Trapper Creek Trail to the trailhead; loop trip, 30.5 miles, 5 to 7 days.

PLACES TO AVOID IF YOU'RE LOOKING FOR SOLITUDE

- Trapper Lake

6 GLIMPSE LAKE & PINE CREEK CANYON TRAILS— SPRING CREEK PARK TO SUMMIT LAKE

General description:	An extended trip leading to the Highline Trail midway between Green River Lakes and Elkhart Park trailheads.
Distance:	13.5 miles, one way.
Difficulty:	Moderate.
Traffic:	Moderate.
Elevation gain and loss:	+2,940 feet; -840 feet.
Trailhead elevation:	8,230 feet.
Maximum elevation:	10,350 feet.
Topo maps:	USGS: Fremont Lake North, Squaretop Mountain, Gannett Peak; Earthwalk: Northern Wind River Range.

Key points:

0.0	Trailhead parking area.
0.9	Junction with Trapper Creek Trail; bear right toward Glimpse Lake.
6.0	Junction with Pine Creek Canyon Trail above Glimpse Lake; turn left (north).
8.8	Junction with Section Corner Lake Trail on west shore of Trapper Lake; stay right.
9.8	Junction with unmaintained trail to Trail Lake; stay right.
10.8	Junction with west-bound trail to Heart Lake at Gottfried Lake; bear right.
11.5	Borum Lake.
13.5	Junction with Highline Trail at Summit Lake.

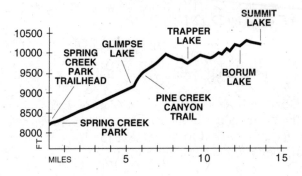

Best day hike destination: A short trip of 4 to 5 miles round trip leads to the ridge overlooking Fremont Lake, Pine Creek and Fremont Creek canyons, and the high peaks along the crest of the Wind Rivers. Strong hikers, or horseback riders, can make the 12-mile round trip to Glimpse Lake in one long day.

The trail: Following the shortest, least rigorous, and least frequently traveled trail to Summit Lake, this scenic trip tours the lake-filled landscape high above Pine Creek canyon. Varied scenery, distant views of high summits, abundant fishing opportunities, and comfortable forested camping areas combine to make this trail an attractive alternative to more popular trails leading to the Summit Lake region.

Since much of the route lies at relatively low elevations—by Wind Rivers standards—this trail opens up earlier in the season and is usually passable by late June in most years.

From the large trailhead parking lot follow the four-wheel-drive road eastward and uphill; a sign near the trail register points to Trapper Lake. The rough and rocky road leads generally northeast for 0.9 mile, passing through groves of aspen and stands of lodgepole pine, to a signed junction south of two marshy ponds in Spring Creek Park.

To reach the Trapper Creek Trail (see hike 7) bear left, staying on the road. The trail signed for Glimpse Lake forks right, briefly skirts the lily-covered pond, then ascends gently for 0.3 mile through aspen forest to a trail sign on the shoulder of a narrow ridge. Stay to the right here. A left-forking trail descends to the cow-cropped meadows of Spring Creek Park, visible below.

The next 4.8 miles to the junction above Glimpse Lake gain 1,250 feet of elevation over fairly smooth tread with an overall gentle grade. The trail generally follows a narrow ridge high above and west of Fremont Lake. Forest cover alternates from lodgepole stands to aspen groves with sunny openings of sagebrush.

Along much of this stretch of trail travelers can enjoy dramatic views of Soda Lake to the south. To the southeast and east is Fremont Lake and the precipitous gorges of Fremont and Pine creeks, including Long and Upper

74

GLIMPSE LAKE & PINE CREEK CANYON TRAILS
• TRAPPER CREEK

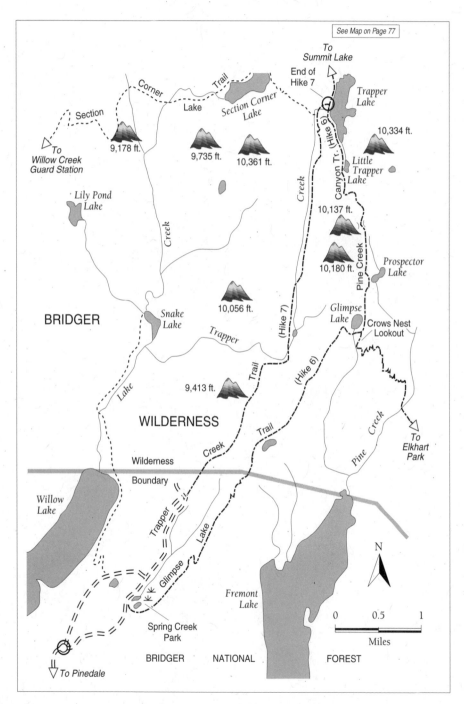

See Map on Page 77

To Summit Lake

End of Hike 7

Trapper Lake

Corner Trail

Section Corner Lake

10,334 ft.

Section

To Willow Creek Guard Station

9,178 ft.

9,735 ft.

10,361 ft.

Little Trapper Lake

Lily Pond Lake

Canyon Tr. (Hike 6)

Creek

10,137 ft.

Prospector Lake

Pine Creek

10,180 ft.

BRIDGER

Snake Lake

10,056 ft.

Trapper

(Hike 7)

Glimpse Lake

Crows Nest Lookout

Lake

Trail

(Hike 6)

9,413 ft.

WILDERNESS

Trail

Pine Creek

To Elkhart Park

Creek

Wilderness

Boundary

Willow Lake

Trapper

Glimpse Lake

Fremont Lake

N

Spring Creek Park

0   0.5   1

Miles

To Pinedale

BRIDGER   NATIONAL   FOREST

75

GLIMPSE LAKE & PINE CREEK CANYON TRAILS
• PALMER LAKE

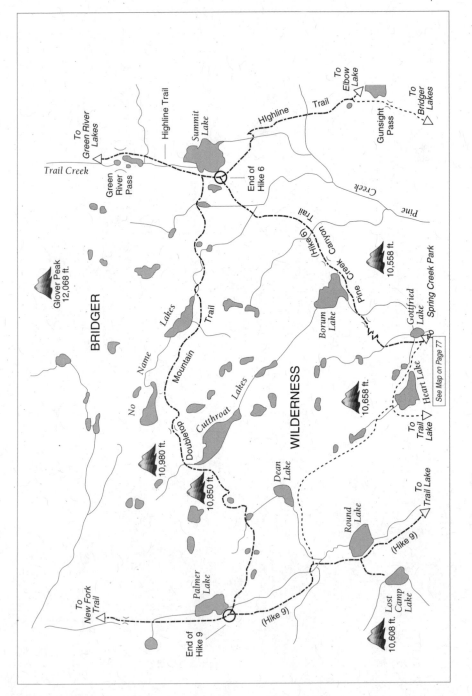

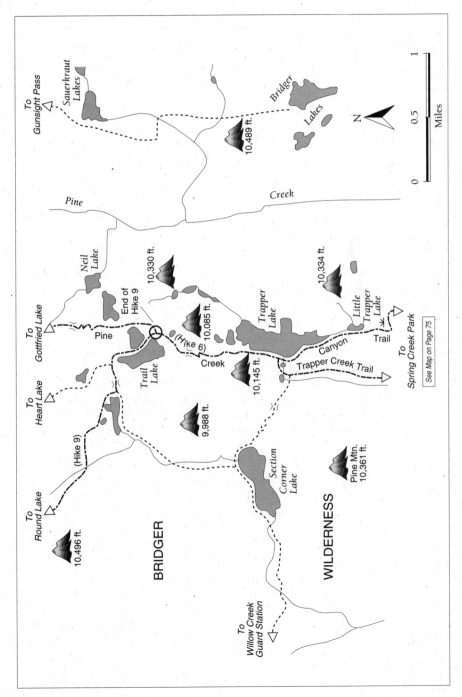

Long lakes. Above those canyons lies the rim of the knobby, tree-dotted, mid-elevation bench that spreads eastward to the foot of the Wind Rivers' high peaks. From north to south those summits are: 13,020-foot Bow Mountain, 12,972-foot Mount Arrowhead, 13,620-foot Mount Helen, 13,569-foot Mount Sacagawea, 13,745-foot Fremont Peak, 13,517-foot Jackson Peak, and 13,001-foot Knife Point Mountain.

Just beyond the signed Bridger Wilderness boundary the trail curves around the ridge 200 feet above a marshy pond. Soon whitebark pine and subalpine fir supplant lodgepole pines and dominate the forest ahead.

At length the blue oval of 9,373-foot Glimpse Lake comes into view, and the trail quickly descends 150 feet to its south shore. Rimmed by a forest of whitebarks, firs, and aspens, with a broad boulder field abutting the southwest shore, the lake lies in a picturesque, peaceful setting. Good camping areas are above the southeast shore, and the lake hosts a healthy population of brook trout.

After crossing the lake's outlet—usually an easy rock hop, curve around the east shore and briefly ascend a low ridge. Here the trail meets the Pine Creek Canyon Trail at 9,450 feet (see hike 13).

Vistas open up from this ridgetop junction, but to enjoy the best views follow the trail south along the ridge 300 yards to a high prominence called Crows Nest Lookout. The view here reaches far below into Pine Creek's rocky defile and into the lower reaches of the Fremont Creek canyon, embraced by ice-polished granite. Follow with your eyes that creek's whitewater torrent up to Long Lake, perched on a bench 300 feet above Pine Creek canyon. The road to Elkhart Park can be seen high on the opposite wall of the canyon, beyond which a broad, densely forested terrace extends eastward toward the high peaks.

From that junction a pleasant, nearly level stretch of trail leads past shallow, meadow-fringed Prospector Lake (home to brook trout). It then enters spruce and whitebark forest among small meadow openings that host the blooms of subalpine daisy, hairy arnica, valerian, lupine, and bracted lousewort.

The trail ahead ascends a moderate grade, including several switchbacks, and tops out on a viewless 9,920-foot divide. This is the first in a series of minor ridges crossed by this trail. Descending to the northwest, the trail passes through dense forest before opening up alongside an oval, marshy meadow. It then proceeds through lovely, tree-fringed meadows, traversing above the west shore of Little Trapper Lake (home to cutthroat trout). Continue down the narrow valley to the shores of large Trapper Lake, at 9,682 feet.

Views extend north across the lake to the tree-feathered granite knobs that foreground the distant pyramid of 12,068-foot Glover Peak, rising west of Summit Lake. The trail follows the curving west shore of the lake, passing several overused campsites that lie much too close to the shore and the trail.

Gottfried Lake on the Pine Creek Canyon Trail.

About 100 yards past the easy crossing of Trapper Lake's outlet is a signed junction. The west-bound trail leads to the Trapper Creek Trail (see hike 7), Section Corner Lake, and ultimately to the Willow Creek Guard Station. Instead, continue north around the long west shore of the lake.

Good camping areas can be found west and north of the lake, and fishing here for cutthroats can be productive. The lake is surrounded by a moderately dense forest of lodgepole and whitebark pine and Engelmann spruce. Grassy openings in the forest are enlivened by an abundance of wildflowers. East of the lake, bold granite knobs rise 600 feet from the lakeshore.

After following Trapper Lake's west shore, pass a pair of shallow tarns, then begin a moderate to steep, 200-foot ascent to another low ridge at 9,900 feet, 0.8 mile from the last junction. The subalpine forest and a number of snags obscures much of the view north.

The trail becomes quite rocky as it descends northeast from the ridge. Occasional tree-framed views reach down to Trail Lake and the unnamed lake just east of it. There is an unmaintained trail leading down to Trail Lake, but the junction is obscure and easy to miss. That trail turns north, leading downhill, 0.2 mile below (northeast of) the ridge, and 150 yards northeast of a small, trailside tarn (see hike 9 for more information on that trail).

Soon the trail leaves the forest, opening up in a beautiful basin between four easily accessible lakes: Trail Lake and an unnamed lake to the west, and another unnamed lake and Neil Lake to the east. Trail Lake harbors arctic grayling, while the other lakes are productive rainbow and cutthroat fisheries.

Good camping areas abound in the broad basin, nestled among glacier-polished bedrock, small meadows, and groves of stunted conifers. Good views extend eastward beyond the lakes to a broad alpine ridge crowned by the knob of 11,948-foot Elbow Peak.

From the Trail Lake basin, the trail leads north into the forest, then ascends 200 feet via switchbacks to the third minor ridge at 10,000 feet. From there traverse gently downhill through forest and meadow, into the confined bowl harboring Gottfried Lake (cutthroats and rainbows). Here the Heart Lake Trail branches left and ascends 100 feet in 0.3 mile to 10,014-foot Heart Lake (home to rainbows).

The main trail continues north above the west shore of Gottfried Lake, passing the remains of an old trapper's cabin along the fringe of an increasingly narrow meadow. It then ascends 300 feet to yet another ridge at an elevation of 10,200 feet. From there the trail winds its way down toward the outlet of Borum Lake. Along the way are inspiring views of several lofty peaks, including Fremont Peak (13,745 feet), Mount Sacagawea (13,569 feet), Henderson Peak (13,115 feet), Mount Helen (13,620 feet), Sky Pilot Peak (12,129 feet), and Mount Oeneis (12,232 feet).

Borum is a picturesque lake lying in a broad basin just below timberline. Granite knobs surround the lake and, combined with groves of stunted spruce and whitebark pine, the lakeside environs offer good camping areas with a modicum of shelter, particularly west of the lake. The scenic basin and good cutthroat fishing make the lake an attractive place for an overnight stay.

The lake's outlet is easily crossed by travelers on foot via boulders, beyond which the trail ascends grass- and rock-covered slopes amid scattered timberline trees to a broad, 10,280-foot saddle, the fifth and final ridge crossing.

From this ridge, an alpine landscape unfolds before you, and the remaining scenic 1.2 miles to Summit Lake lead through small basins, past several tarns, across minor creeks, and over alpine grasslands.

Upon reaching the Highline Trail above Summit Lake, numerous trails are available to extend your trip (see hikes 8, 9, and 11).

7 TRAPPER CREEK TRAIL—SPRING CREEK PARK TO TRAPPER LAKE

General description:	An alternative to the Glimpse Lake Trail (see hike 6), useful as one leg of a loop trip.
Distance:	7.4 miles, one way.
Difficulty:	Moderate.
Traffic:	Light.
Elevation gain and loss:	+1,850 feet, -350 feet.
Trailhead elevation:	8,230 feet.
Maximum elevation:	9,682 feet.
Topo maps:	USGS: Fremont Lake North; Earthwalk: Northern Wind River Range.

See Map on Page 75

Key points:
- 0.0   Trailhead parking lot.
- 0.9   Signed junction with trail to Glimpse Lake in Spring Creek Park; stay left and follow the road.
- 2.3   Trapper Creek Trail branches right from four-wheel-drive road.
- 3.7   Surmount ridge at 9,400 feet.
- 4.5   First crossing of Trapper Creek.
- 5.2   Second crossing of Trapper Creek.
- 7.2   Junction with Section Corner Lake Trail; bear right (east).
- 7.4   Junction with Pine Creek Canyon Trail at Trapper Lake.

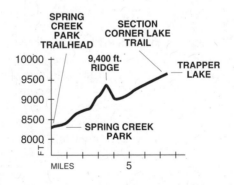

Best day hike destination: Strong hikers and those on horseback can make the 15-mile round trip to Trapper Lake in one long day.

The trail: The seldom-traveled Trapper Creek Trail offers an alternate route to Trapper Lake and the mid-elevation, lake-dotted bench between Pine Creek and Lake Creek. This trail offers a shorter route to Trapper Lake than the trail to Glimpse Lake (see hike 6).

The scenery en route, however, is not dramatic; rather, this is a peaceful trail passing through forests and long meadows. You aren't likely to encounter many other travelers. The trail is most useful as a quick means of access to Trapper Lake, and it can be used as one leg of a loop trip that tours the lake-rich country to the north.

From the trailhead parking area follow the first 0.9 mile of hike 6, along the four-wheel-drive road that leads northeast. Upon reaching Spring Creek Park and the junction with the trail to Glimpse Lake, stay left and continue following the rough road; the sign points to Trapper Creek.

The four-wheel-drive road skirts the shores of two marshy ponds and the meadows of Spring Creek Park. Cattle may block the way at times—a sizable herd congregates in the shady roadside forest during the heat of the day.

Groves of aspen and a forest of lodgepole pine and subalpine fir offer sporadic shade where their branches arch over the roadway. The meadows becomes increasingly narrow beyond a fenced-in cabin. Then the trail ascends a moderate grade into a minor draw.

At 1.4 miles, and 380 feet higher than the junction in Spring Creek Park, there is a *No Motor Vehicles* sign. Turn right onto the trail, avoiding the climbing, west-trending curve in the road.

The trail ahead, rocky in places, ascends a gentle to moderate grade through mostly viewless lodgepole pine forest, gaining 600 feet of elevation in 1.4 miles to a broad ridge at 9,400 feet. North of the ridge, the rocky trail descends steeply, losing 350 feet of elevation in 0.8 mile. The descent ends at an easy rock-hop crossing of small Trapper Creek.

The north-bound trail then leads 100 feet above the west bank of the creek, through lodgepole forest, for 0.7 mile before descending to another ford of Trapper Creek. If the water is high, you must wade across the sand-bottomed stream. In late summer the creek is often low enough to jump across.

Just beyond the ford is the old Bridger Wilderness boundary. The trail then skirts the eastern margins of a series of long and narrow, spruce-fringed meadows for 1.5 miles. Bold granite cliffs, plunging 1,000 feet from 10,361-foot Pine Mountain, form the west wall of this confined canyon.

The narrow meadows that occupy the canyon floor are decorated with the blooms of subalpine daisy, lupine, cinquefoil, northern goldenrod, bracted lousewort, hairy arnica, yarrow, and mountain bluebells.

At length you reach the head of the meadows and begin a steep 300-foot ascent over the rocky, badly eroded trail. At the top of this grind is a signed junction at 9,600 feet. The left-branching trail climbs 100 feet before descending 400 feet in 1 mile to large Section Corner Lake. This is a popular fishing destination for local outfitters who prize the lake's grayling and brook and brown trout.

Trapper Lake lies 0.2 mile to the east. To get there, turn right and climb briefly on the rocky trail through the forest to a rock-hop crossing of Trapper Creek just below a shallow tarn. Soon thereafter the climb ends at the signed junction with the Pine Creek Canyon Trail on the west shore of Trapper Lake.

8 DOUBLETOP MOUNTAIN & PALMER LAKE TRAILS—SUMMIT LAKE TO NEW FORK CANYON

General description:	A backcountry connecting trail useful as part of an extended trip.
Distance:	7.6 miles, one way.
Difficulty:	Moderate.
Traffic:	Moderate to Cutthroat Lakes, light from Cutthroat Lakes to New Fork Canyon.
Elevation gain and loss:	+780 feet, -2,270 feet.
Maximum elevation:	10,800 feet.
Topo maps:	USGS: Gannett Peak, Squaretop Mountain; Earthwalk: Northern Wind River Range.

See Maps on Pages 64 & 65

Key points:

0.0	Junction of Doubletop Mountain and Highline trails at Summit Lake.
1.1	Lower No Name Lake, 10,590.
2.3	10,800-foot divide between No Name and Cutthroat lakes.
2.6	Upper Cutthroat Lake, 10,595.
3.25	Marshy pond above Dean Lake.
4.3	Junction with Palmer Lake Trail at Palmer Lake; turn right (north).
7.6	Junction with New Fork Trail in New Fork canyon.

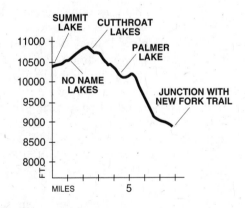

Finding the trail: The Doubletop Mountain Trail, signed for Palmer Lake, begins at a junction with the Highline Trail above the west shore of Summit Lake. This junction lies 150 yards north of the Highline's juncture with the Pine Creek Canyon Trail, which is signed for Trapper Lake. The terminus of this trail segment is located in New Fork Canyon, 0.5 mile north of New Fork Park and 1.1 miles south of the junction of the New Fork and Porcupine trails.

Glover Peak and the Continental Divide from the pass between No Name and Cutthroat lakes.

The trail: From Summit Lake to upper Cutthroat Lake the trail ascends gently over alpine grasslands featuring grand vistas. Then the trail drops below timberline to Palmer Lake and into the cliff-bound confines of Palmer and New Fork canyons. The steep, rocky section of the trail from Palmer to New Fork canyon is not recommended for stock parties.

From the junction with the Highline Trail at 10,350 feet, the Doubletop Mountain Trail ascends gently westward among scattered and stunted Engelmann spruce and whitebark pine, passing timberline meadows bounded by ice-polished bedrock and a number of small tarns.

After 0.5 mile the trail curves around a higher tarn, jogs southwest, and leads into the basin harboring the No Name Lakes. Hop across the small creek draining the lakes three times before reaching the narrow eastern bay of Lake 10,590, the easternmost No Name Lake. Both of the large lakes in this basin, and those in the Cutthroat chain ahead, are productive cutthroat trout fisheries.

This is true alpine terrain, with only a few persistent matlike conifers clinging to the rocky knolls on the north flanks of the narrow basin. Smooth, grassy slopes rise to a low ridge south of the lake, and the Glover Peak massif (12,063 feet) and its serrated crest rise sharply to the north. Travelers who choose to camp in this high basin are advised to seek a sheltered site among the rocky knolls that rise north of the lakes.

Beyond Lake 10,590, the gently inclined trail continues through alpine tundra to the slopes above the south shore of Lake 10,620. The trail then climbs to a low divide overlooking another attractive but much smaller lake

200 yards south of the trail. This lake, though higher than No Name Lakes, hosts a scattering of stunted trees around its shores, and thus offers camping areas with more shelter.

Next ascend a short but steep stretch of trail, topping out on a 10,800-foot saddle dividing the Cutthroat and No Name lake basins. From here a glorious panorama of lofty peaks unfolds, stretching from snow-crowned Gannett Peak in the northeast to Knife Point Mountain, near Indian Pass in the southeast. To the west, a sliver of the largest Cutthroat Lake is visible below, and on the far western horizon, across the upper Green River basin, lies the Wyoming Range, 40 miles distant.

The allure of these grand vistas never dims, but take heed, too, of the varied and colorful alpine wildflowers growing at your feet. Among them are the purple blooms of Parry's townsendia, one-flower daisy, and the unique and aptly named elephanthead; the yellow blooms of cinquefoil; and the white flowers of alpine bistort and marsh marigold.

West of the divide the trail is poor and the tread is very rocky, slowing the pace considerably. Reach the northwest end of upper Cutthroat Lake 0.3 mile and 200 feet below the divide. The basin harbors numerous tarns located in secluded recesses, where travelers will find suitable camping areas.

The trail briefly follows above the northwest shore of the lake, descends slightly to curve around a tarn, then drops steeply into a minor basin and passes above yet another tarn. Here stunted spruce and whitebark pine dot the landscape. Another slow-going, rocky descent ensues past that tarn, leading to the shores of a marshy pond on the floor of a narrow draw.

Dean Lake lies 0.3 mile southeast down that draw, via an easy, straightforward cross-country route alongside the stream. The Heart Lake Trail, connecting Round Lake to Gottfried Lake, runs along Dean Lake's south shore. Sheltered campsites among tall subalpine conifers and fishing for brook trout may offer enough incentive to some travelers to make a detour to Dean Lake.

The trail ahead briefly ascends grassy slopes to gain the broad ridge to the west. From the ridge it quickly descends to a pair of tarns, passing between them, then winds across a broad, grassy bench dotted with spruces and spreading, multi-boled whitebark pines.

That pleasant stretch soon ends at the rim of the Palmer Lake basin. Here the trail begins a steep and rocky, 200-foot descent. En route are fine views to the rock- and grass-covered twin domes of Doubletop Mountain and Dome Peak and its sheer, fluted cliffs rising above New Fork Park, both to the west; and north to the bold granite walls bounding lower Palmer Canyon.

An easy rock hop leads across Lake Creek just below the outlet of Palmer Lake. Ignore a steep, boot-worn path climbing west up the slope, and curve northwest on the trail to a junction along the lake's west shore. The southbound trail leads past Round Lake to Trail Lake and Section Corner Lake (see hike 9). But turn right instead, heading north along the west shore of Palmer Lake at 10,165 feet.

This pleasant, meadow-fringed lake may attract anglers with its population of brook trout, but nearby slopes are too steep for camping. Better camping areas can be found to the north near Penny Lake.

Beyond Palmer Lake, the trail ascends gentle grassy slopes to the narrow valley above. Jump across the outlet of Penny Lake 0.6 mile from the last junction; that lake lies 250 yards west of and above the trail in a shallow bowl. A brief climb ahead leads to a prominent grassy saddle at 10,320 feet, overlooking the granite-bound defile of Palmer Canyon 1,000 feet below.

A gradually descending traverse leads north from the saddle and into the head of precipitous Reynolds Creek canyon. A series of moderately graded switchbacks follows, shaded by spruce forest. Approaching Palmer Canyon, the trail crosses the steep chute carved by Reynolds Creek, which may be dry in late summer. In early summer the chute is a torrent of snowmelt.

Beyond the chute the trail curves northwest, still descending, among small spruces and avalanche debris. It soon reaches the floor of Palmer Canyon and meanders through flower-rich openings to a ford of Palmer Canyon's creek. The crossing is usually a boulder hop even if the water is fairly high. At the peak of snowmelt, however, wading may be necessary. At such times the creek may be about 12 feet wide and as much as knee-deep, with a moderate current.

The broad sweep of smooth granite cliffs, rising nearly 2,000 feet above the canyon in a lateral distance of only 0.3 mile, forms an exciting backdrop as the trail climbs briefly from the ford to the north side of the canyon. Soon it passes into a subalpine forest of spruce, whitebark pine, and subalpine fir and winds through fields of gigantic boulders and small meadow openings. Then the route descends deeper into the forest, losing another 200 feet of elevation, to a ford of New Fork River.

If the water is low, rock-hop across the river. During high water hikers must wade across the shin-deep waters, where the current is modest.

The trail ahead follows the grassy, tree-shaded riverbank 200 yards to the junction with the New Fork Trail, 0.25 mile above New Fork Park (see hike 5) and 1.1 miles below that trail's junction with the Porcupine Trail (see hike 4).

9 PALMER LAKE TRAIL—PALMER LAKE TO TRAIL LAKE

General description:	A backcountry connecting trail useful as part of an extended trip.
Distance:	4.3 miles, one way.
Difficulty:	Easy.
Traffic:	Light.
Elevation gain and loss:	+380 feet, -700 feet.
Maximum elevation:	10,250 feet.
Topo maps:	USGS: Squaretop Mountain, Fremont Lake North (part of the trail, from Lake Creek to Trail Lake, is not shown on the map); Earthwalk: Northern Wind River Range.

See Maps on Pages 76 & 77

Key points:

0.0 Junction with Palmer Lake and Doubletop Mountain trails at Palmer Lake.

1.1 Junction with east-bound Dean Lake Trail; bear left (south).

1.5 Junction with west-bound trail to Lost Camp Lake on west shore of Round Lake; continue straight ahead (south).

3.5 Junction with west-bound trail to Section Corner Lake at east end of Coyote Lake (Lake 9,678); bear left, heading east.

3.7 Junction with north-bound trail to Heart Lake; stay right, heading for Trail Lake.

4.3 Junction with Pine Creek Canyon Trail south of Trail Lake.

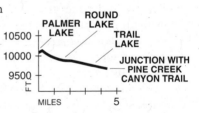

Finding the trail: This trail begins at the southwest corner of Palmer Lake and heads south at the unsigned junction with the east-bound segment of the Doubletop Mountain Trail, 4.3 miles west of Summit Lake. Palmer Lake can also be reached by following the Palmer Lake Trail 3.3 miles from the New Fork Trail above New Fork Park.

The trail: This backcountry trail is one of the least frequently used trails on the high, lake-dotted bench west of Pine Creek canyon. Local outfitters developed part of this trail and are the most frequent users of trails in this area; you may encounter some of their camps and packstrings along this route.

Although the route is far from the high country, it is a pleasant trip through subalpine forests and meadows, and it offers access to five fish-filled lakes en route. Running water along the route may be scarce in late summer, but nearby lakes offer a reliable supply for drinking (after treatment).

The following description follows the trail from north to south; in that direction the route is mostly downhill.

From 10,165-foot Palmer Lake, the south-bound segment of the Palmer Lake Trail briefly ascends a grassy slope, then levels off after 250 yards. It then passes an obscure, unsigned junction with the very faint Doubletop Mountain Trail, branching right (southwest).

The next 1 mile of trail is a pleasant, moderate descent across grassy slopes west of the narrow draw harboring Lake Creek. The descent ends at the northern margin of the broad, grassy valley north of presently visible Round Lake, where the trail splits. The left fork immediately crosses Lake Creek, which may be dry in late summer, then meets the signed east-bound trail to forested Dean Lake, less than 0.5 mile away and 250 feet above.

The left fork trail then bends south, soon recrossing Lake Creek. The right fork trail stays west of the creek, avoiding both crossings; both trails rejoin beyond the second crossing.

Proceed south through the broad meadow, soon reaching the shore of aptly-named Round Lake (9,952 feet). After skirting the shore for 175 yards, watch for a well-worn path heading west and climbing to the low gap on the skyline. That path leads 0.4 mile to 9,816-foot Lost Camp Lake, which features good fishing for brook trout.

Round Lake lies in a wide, open valley, surrounded by low, forest-covered ridges. There are good camping areas in the spruce and whitebark pine forest on the bench west of the lake and above the trail.

Beyond Round Lake, the trail ascends briefly upon grassy slopes, then enters subalpine forest and begins a steady, moderate descent. Views open up to include an array of rocky domes to the south that punctuate this high, lake-terrace region. On the eastern horizon rises the broad, rocky mass of 11,362-foot Guiterrez Peak.

At a point about 0.5 mile below Round Lake, both USGS and the Earthwalk Press maps show the trail continuing south another 2 miles to Section Corner Lake. That trail, however, is difficult to locate on the ground, and a more frequently used trail, one forged by outfitters, leads to that lake by a longer, but gentler route that also offers access to Trail Lake.

The well-worn outfitters' trail bends southeast into an attractive grassy basin, where the descent levels off. The trail then curves to a crossing of Lake Creek, which may be flowing here in late summer. Earlier in the season, when the water is flowing vigorously, the ford is still an easy rockhop. Several cold, reliable springs augment the creek's volume just downstream from the crossing.

The trail then heads generally southeast, nearly on the level, passing through a series of small, meadow-carpeted basins. It soon reaches the north shores of sprawling Coyote Lake (Lake 9,678), populated by grayling. Follow the rocky trail around to the eastern end of the lake to an unsigned junction,

1.9 miles from Round Lake. Bear left (east). (The right fork, also forged by outfitters, continues around Coyote Lake before descending to Section Corner Lake in 1.5 miles.)

The trail then ascends briefly into a forested draw, topping out after 0.2 mile at another unsigned junction above a grass-fringed pond. The left-branching trail ascending the slope to the north leads 0.9 mile to Heart Lake. But bear right and continue southeast above the shore of the pond, curving around its shores and heading toward the now-visible northern bay of Trail Lake. Pay no heed to the abandoned segment of the above-mentioned trail to Heart Lake on the left (north).

The trail stays above the eastern shore of 9,753-foot Trail Lake, and just west of a smaller, unnamed lake. Fine camping areas and good fishing in the four nearby lakes make the Trail Lake environs an attractive area for an overnight stay. Fine views with a foreground of lakes and granite knobs stretch eastward to a dramatic array of jagged summits rising from 12,000 to 13,000 feet.

Beyond Trail Lake, the trail bends south and ascends briefly through subalpine forest to the junction with the Pine Creek Canyon Trail, 0.6 mile from the previous junction. Summit Lake lies 3.9 miles to the northeast via that trail, and the Spring Creek Park Trailhead lies 9.6 miles to the southwest (see hike 6).

ELKHART PARK TRAILHEAD

OVERVIEW

A paved access road, a high-elevation starting point, and easy two-day trail access to some of the grandest alpine terrain in the Rocky Mountains—these qualities account for Elkhart Park's popularity. This is the most heavily used Bridger Wilderness trailhead, featuring two huge parking lots that remain filled to capacity throughout the summer season.

Perched high on the rim above Fremont Creek and Pine Creek canyons at the edge of the Wind Rivers' western bench, this trailhead offers access to high lake basins and a network of backcountry trails that involve minimal elevation gain. The exception is the rigorous Pine Creek Canyon Trail, a strenuous down-and-up route more reminiscent of a trail in the Cascades or Sierra Nevada than a typical gentle Wind River trail.

Users of trails beginning here should expect to encounter a continuous stream of fellow travelers en route to the Titcomb Basin environs. Titcomb Basin's popularity is due not only to its widespread recognition as *the* place to go in the Wind Rivers; it also happens to be one of the classic alpine cirques in the Rocky Mountains. Bold cliffs, small glaciers, and sawtoothed spires exceeding 13,000 feet in elevation surround the basin's large lakes and tundra.

Throughout the summer at Island Lake, and at Titcomb and Indian basins, the tundra is studded with the tents of climbers and backpackers. No problem if you don't mind company after a two-day, 15-mile trek into the backcountry. For more solitude, follow the Pole Creek Trail to Pole Creek and beyond toward Cook Lakes, Chain Lakes, or Bald Mountain Basin; or follow the Highline Trail toward the Elbow Lake area.

Finding the trailhead: From U.S. Highway 191 in Pinedale, 100 miles north of Rock Springs or 79 miles southeast of Jackson, turn northeast onto a paved road prominently signed for Half Moon and Fremont lakes. The turnoff is located where the highway (Pinedale's main street) describes the only pronounced curve in town.

The road is paved for the entire 14.5-mile distance to the trailhead, but cracked pavement along the first half of the road makes the drive rough. En route ignore signed spur roads leading to Fremont and Half Moon lakes. Beyond the latter the road begins to climb steadily and becomes narrow and winding.

At length the road curves past a dramatic viewpoint, then continues the remaining short distance into Elkhart Park. About 200 yards past an A-frame information station the road forks. The left fork leads to Trail's End Campground and the north parking lot for the Pine Creek Canyon Trail. The right fork quickly leads to the south parking lot, for users of the Pole Creek Trail. Here there are toilets and drinking water, and corrals and unloading facilities for packstock.

Travelers arriving late in the day may not find a campsite in the popular, 8-site Trail's End Campground (fee area), but they may find space in one of several undeveloped camping areas alongside the road to the trailhead.

THE TRAILS

- Pole Creek Trail
- Seneca Lake Trail
- Highline Trail (from Summit Lake to North Fork Lake)
- Indian and Titcomb Basin Trails
- Miller Lake and Sweeney Creek Trails
- Pine Creek Canyon Trail

SUGGESTED EXTENDED TRIPS

1) Follow the Pole Creek Trail to Pole Creek, then the Highline Trail over Lester Pass, and return to the trailhead via the Seneca Lake and Pole Creek trails; semi-loop trip, 25.2 miles, 3 to 5 days.

2) Titcomb or Indian Basin base camps; round trip, 30 miles, 5 to 7 days.

3) Fremont Creek-Pine Creek loop, via Seneca Lake and Highline trails to Summit Lake, return via Pine Creek Canyon Trail; loop trip, 35 miles, 4 to 7 days.

4) Long Lake base camp; round trip, 4.2 miles, 2-plus days.

5) Miller and Sweeney lakes, via Pole Creek, Miller Lake, and Sweeney Creek trails; round trip, 8.6 miles; semi-loop trip, 10.9 miles; 1 to 3 days.

6) Cook Lakes base camp, via Pole Creek or Seneca Lake-Highline trails; round trip, 27 to 32 miles, 4 to 6 days.

7) Pole Creek-Highline-Fremont trails loop, via Pole Creek, Barnes Lake, Timico Lake Trail, return via Fremont Trail to Pole Creek, and return to the trailhead via either Pole Creek Trail or Highline and Seneca Lake trails over Lester Pass; semi-loop trip, 32 to 35 miles, 4 to 7 days.

PLACES TO AVOID IF YOU'RE LOOKING FOR SOLITUDE

- Titcomb Basin
- Indian Basin
- Island Lake
- Seneca Lake
- Jean Lakes

10 POLE CREEK & SENECA LAKE TRAILS— ELKHART PARK TO LITTLE SENECA LAKE

General description:	An extended trip leading to the Highline Trail near Titcomb Basin.
Distance:	10.4 miles, one way.
Difficulty:	Moderate.
Traffic:	Heavy.
Elevation gain and loss:	+2,000 feet, -550 feet.
Trailhead elevation:	9,350 feet.
Maximum elevation:	10,400 feet.
Topo maps:	USGS: Fremont Lake North, Fayette Lake, Bridger Lakes; Earthwalk: Northern Wind River Range.

Key points:
- 0.0 Elkhart Park Trailhead.
- 3.3 Junction with trail to Miller Lake in Miller Park; bear left.
- 5.1 Junction with south-bound trail to Sweeney Lakes; stay left.
- 5.5 Junction with Pole Creek Trail; turn left (northwest).
- 5.8 Barbara Lake.
- 7.0 Hobbs Lake.
- 7.5 Ford Seneca Lake's outlet creek.
- 8.8 Surmount 10,400-foot ridge west of Seneca Lake.
- 9.5 Junction with unmaintained trail to Lost Lake at north end of Seneca Lake; bear right.
- 10.4 Junction with Highline Trail above Little Seneca Lake.

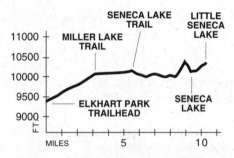

Best day hike destination: Miller Park, 3.3 miles from the trailhead, is a lovely, flower-filled subalpine meadow, featuring fine views of high summits from Glover Peak in the northwest to Jackson Peak in the northeast.

Another worthwhile destination lies above Photographers Point, 4.5 miles from the trailhead. From there, enjoy grand views of the above-mentioned peaks and the ice-chiseled defile of Fremont Creek canyon 2,000 feet below.

Also, Miller and Sweeney lakes, 3.7 and 4.5 miles from the trailhead respectively, lie in pleasant meadow and forest settings. They offer fishing for brook and golden trout (see hike 14).

The hike: Following one of the most popular trails in the Wind Rivers, this trip leads through extensive forests, past meadows rich with wildflowers, and beyond ice-polished domes to timberline lakes near the foot of the lofty crest of the range.

This trail offers the easiest and fastest means to access the alpine regions of the Bridger Wilderness, including incomparable Titcomb Basin, and so the route is heavily used by climbers, backpackers, and anglers who enjoy majestic alpine scenery at its finest. Travelers in search of solitude are advised to either avoid this trail or to use it after Labor Day when the throngs of backpackers have diminished.

The trail seems longer than its distance would suggest, with miles of viewless travel in heavy forest. Many ups and downs make this trip to the high country an arduous, one- to two-day journey.

The trail begins behind the information sign at the northeast corner of the parking lot. The initial 3.3 miles of the trail are uneventful, beginning beneath a shady canopy of lodgepole pine and heading north from the trailhead over smooth tread.

Soon the trail curves southeast into the headwaters draw of Faler Creek, where the tread becomes rocky and the forest is dominated by Engelmann spruce. Small meadows open up periodically in the draw, watered by Faler Creek.

Beyond the head of the draw, continue climbing at a gentle to moderate grade, curving north through a heavy, viewless forest of lodgepole and spruce. The trail crosses the signed Bridger Wilderness boundary after 2.8 miles, at 10,050 feet. From there the gently inclined trail bends northeast and traverses the upper reaches of Miller Park, a sloping subalpine meadow enlivened by the blooms of lupine and buttercup.

The forested fringes of this broad spread offer the first views of the bold, serrated northern peaks of the range, including the broad dome of 13,745-foot Fremont Peak, the Wind Rivers' second highest summit.

On the southeastern edge of Miller Park, ignore the signed, east-bound trail leading 0.3 mile to Miller Lake, a popular destination of day hikers and equestrians (see hike 14). The main trail curves northeast, climbing gently back into the forest for 0.5 mile to another, drier meadow. From this opening enjoy views southeast along the face of the range, including the broad 9,000- to 10,000-foot bench that abuts the alpine crest of the Wind Rivers, and such notable peaks as jagged Mount Bonneville and the bold pyramid of Temple Peak.

The trail ahead proceeds through a high landscape of bare, ice-polished granite, scattered subalpine forest, and small meadows. Numerous tarns line the way, the only source of water until Eklund Lake at 5.5 miles.

After 4.5 miles, round a prominent bend in the trail above Photographers Point, at 10,350 feet, where suddenly a grand panorama unfolds. The yawning, glacier-gouged canyon of Fremont Creek lies far below, and beyond it, the high terrace. This knobby landscape of bedrock scraped bare by ancient glaciers and dotted with stunted conifers, stretches north and east to the

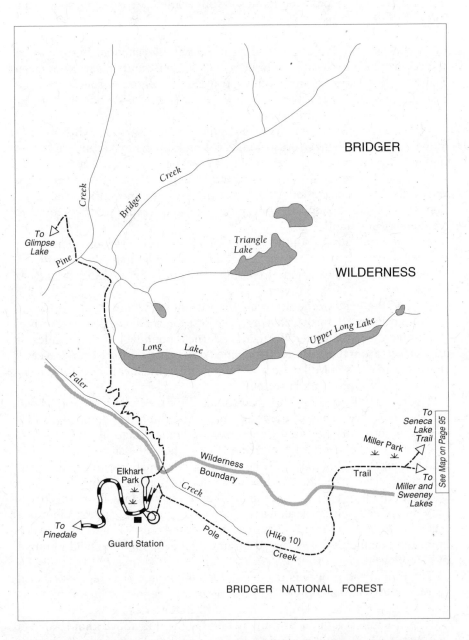

foot of the high peaks. From Glover Peak in the northwest to Mount Lester, near Seneca Lake, in the northeast, the horizon is filled with a dramatic array of ice-encrusted crags that thrust skyward in bold relief.

The trail ahead winds among the spruce and whitebark pine forest, soon

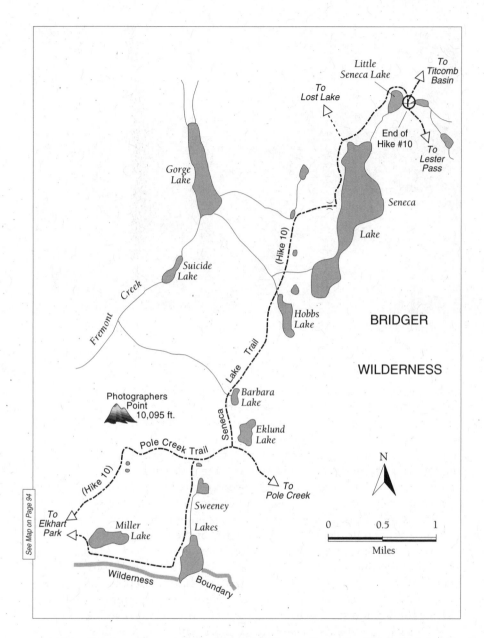

See Map on Page 94

reaching the signed, south-bound trail leading to Sweeney Lakes in 0.9 mile (see hike 14). From that junction, in a broad saddle next to a shallow tarn, quickly mount a forested rise and descend briefly to the junction with the Pole Creek Trail (see hike 15). The Pole Creek Trail heads southeast toward the shores of Eklund Lake, visible through the forest below.

Instead, bear left on the Seneca Lake Trail and head northwest along the forest's edge above 10,250-foot Eklund Lake. The trail descends steadily to small but inviting Barbara Lake, at 10,200 feet. Fair campsites can be found

The Continental Divide looms behind Seneca Lake. Fremont and Jackson peaks at left center.

above the east shore, and the lake hosts a population of rainbow trout.

Hop across Barbara Lake's small outlet and continue around the west shore before beginning a steady, 200-foot descent via switchbacks. En route the forest opens up enough at times to allow distant views of the broad upper Green River basin. With the deep gorge of Fremont Creek canyon in the foreground, the Wyoming Range rims the western horizon.

Emerging into a meadow-floored basin rimmed by granite knolls at the bottom of the descent, head past a grass-fringed tarn and then ascend 150 feet in 0.2 mile through a scattered spruce and whitebark pine forest. The trail opens up on grassy slopes near the top of the grade.

A minor descent ensues, leading to the shores of 10,070-foot Hobbs Lake, another timberline gem. Trailside cliffs funnel the trail nearly into the lake's waters midway around it. Travelers can gaze into its depths and perhaps spot some of the rainbow trout that lurk there. Good camping areas lie on benches and in the small basin lying east of the long, narrow lake.

Hobbs Lake's outlet is an easy rock hop. A gentle, forested descent of 0.3 mile beyond the lake leads to the banks of the tumultuous outlet creek of Seneca Lake, which lies less than 0.5 mile to the east.

There may be poles in place to afford a dry crossing. If not, wade the swift creek (which may be knee-deep before August) between tumbling cascades. The trail doesn't follow this stream, as might be expected, but instead takes a roundabout route to Seneca Lake.

Begin climbing again, gaining 150 feet in 0.3 mile, past a tarn to a narrow saddle. Then descend 200 feet north and past another tarn, after which the trail curves northeast just before reaching another granite-rimmed basin.

The rocky trail then begins a moderate to steep, 400-foot ascent over the following 0.6 mile. The trail heads for the smooth granite ridge rising on the eastern skyline, ascending a narrow draw amid thinning forest and bare granite. At length the trail reaches the narrow crest of the bedrock ridge at 10,400 feet, and sprawling, 1.4-mile-long Seneca Lake spreads out 100 feet below.

From the ridge descend steadily north down steep slopes to the lake's west shore. Just like the trail around Hobbs Lake, portions of this trail may be submerged when the lake's waters are high. Proceed on an undulating course around Seneca's west shore, reaching a signed, northwest-bound trail to Lost Lake above Seneca's north shore.

Despite Seneca Lake's great size, camping areas are scarce and most of the shoreline is inaccessible. Nevertheless, many travelers choose the lake for their first night's stay on the trail.

A short distance east and southeast of the junction with the Lost Lake Trail, at the lake's north end, is one of the few possible camping areas at the lake. Although the campsites are scenic, located among granite knobs, stunted trees, and meadows, too many people camp here and signs of overuse are apparent. Travelers seeking solitude will seldom find it here.

Those who are too exhausted to continue will enjoy good fishing for rainbows and the evening alpenglow on the hulking masses of Peak 11,550 and Mount Lester, looming skyward east of the lake.

Seneca Lake, at 10,250 feet, lies very near timberline, and nearby vegetation reflects the rigors of the high elevation, a short growing season, and a deep, long-lasting snowpack. Scattered stands of whitebark pine and spruce grow on drier sites in the basin, clumping in groves to conserve heat, or in ground-hugging mats (krummholz) where their foliage is protected in winter beneath an insulating blanket of snow. Low-growing willows form discontinuous thickets among erratic boulders and bedrock in the grassy, flower-speckled meadows.

These timberline meadows host the typical assemblage of wildflowers found in the Wind Rivers, including the yellow blooms of buttercup and cinquefoil, the white blooms of alpine bistort and marsh marigold, the blue shades of lupine and mountain bluebells, the flaming red flowers of Indian paintbrush and rose crown, and the delicate pink, bell-shaped flowers of mountain heather.

Beyond Seneca Lake, amble through rocky terrain, curve around a group of tarns, then follow the west and north shores of Little Seneca Lake on rocky tread. Little Seneca also supports a rainbow trout fishery, but the nearby steep, rocky slopes offer no opportunities for camping.

Just beyond and east of Little Seneca Lake the trail meets the Highline Trail, branching right and left. The nearest camping areas lie more than 0.5 mile away, either in the alpine lake basin beneath Lester Pass to the southeast (see hike 16), or near the junction of the Highline and Indian Pass trails to the north (see hike 11).

11 HIGHLINE TRAIL—LITTLE SENECA LAKE TO SUMMIT LAKE

General description:	A high-elevation segment of the Highline Trail, in the northern reaches of the Wind Rivers between Green River Lakes and Elkhart Park.
Distance:	11.2 miles, one way.
Difficulty:	Moderate.
Traffic:	Moderate.
Elevation gain and loss:	+1,300 feet, -1,350 feet.
Maximum elevation:	11,050 feet.
Topo Maps:	USGS: Bridger Lakes, Gannett Peak; Earthwalk: Northern Wind River Range.

Key points:

0.0	Junction of Highline and Seneca Lake trails above Little Seneca Lake; turn north onto Highline.
0.4	Junction with Indian Pass Trail leading to Titcomb Basin; bear left.
2.3	Bridge over Fremont Creek at Fremont Crossing.
2.4	Junction with northern terminus of Lost Lake Trail; turn right.
4.2	Ford of Fremont Creek at inlet of Lower Jean Lake.
5.1	Upper Jean Lake.
6.0	11,050-foot pass dividing the Jean Lakes and Elbow Lake basin.
6.3	Junction with Shannon Pass Trail; bear left toward Elbow Lake.
6.9	First ford of Elbow Creek above north end of Elbow Lake.
9.1	Second ford of Elbow Creek above Twin Lakes.
9.7	Junction with unmaintained trail to Pass Lake, Gunsight Pass, and Bridger Lakes; bear right.
10.5	Ford Pine Creek; ignore trail ascending east bank of creek.
11.2	Junction with Pine Creek Canyon Trail above west shore of Summit Lake.

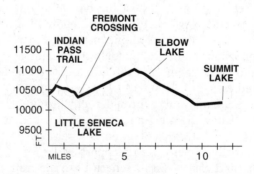

Finding the trail: This segment of the Highline Trail begins above the east shore of Little Seneca Lake, 0.9 mile northeast of Seneca Lake and the junction with the Lost Lake Trail, and 1.5 miles northwest of Lester Pass.

The trail: This segment of the Highline is arguably the most spectacular trail in the range. The route travels through grand alpine terrain in the shadow of towering crags, staying above 10,000 feet throughout its length. Stunted groves of timberline forest lie at either end of this segment; in between is a raw landscape of alpine lake basins seemingly just released from the grip of an ice age.

From the signed junction of the Highline and Seneca Lake trails, turn northeast onto the Highline Trail. It rises gently at first above an unnamed lake, then curves into a narrow, boulder-choked draw, following moderately ascending switchbacks. The trail gains 200 feet of elevation in 0.4 mile, passing among ice-scoured bedrock and a few persistent groves of krummholz spruce and whitebark pine.

Topping out amid boulders on a narrow, 10,600-foot saddle, an array of bold alpine summits suddenly comes into view. To the northeast, rising above the deep notch of Indian Pass, is snow-crowned Jackson Peak (13,517 feet), and beyond it is broad Fremont Peak (13,745 feet), and mounts Sacagawea (13,569 feet) and Helen (13,620 feet), all forming the east wall of Titcomb Basin. Bobs Towers and Mount Woodrow Wilson (13,502 feet) bound the north wall of the basin, and farther northwest rises Mount Arrowhead (12,972 feet) and Bow Mountain (13,020 feet).

Just below and northeast of the saddle is a junction, and travelers bound for Titcomb and Indian basins will turn right (see hike 12), but the Highline goes left, bound for Fremont Crossing. The trail runs north above a shallow basin among groves of stunted spruce and whitebark, descending moderately to an easy rock-hop crossing of the outlet of a large, unnamed tarn.

The trail ahead proceeds northwest for 1.9 miles, with minor undulations over rocky knobs and into small, tarn-dotted basins. Patches of stunted trees, combined with ample water and convoluted terrain, offer good camping opportunities along this stretch of trail to Fremont Crossing.

The sturdy bridge spanning Fremont Creek is a welcome sight; a ford of this deep, wide, and swift stream would be difficult even in late summer. Fremont Crossing lies in a lovely little basin surrounded by bare, ice-polished granite, with stunted conifers around its margins and verdant meadows spread across the basin floor. Lofty summits form a serrated skyline to the north and east, while broad alpine ridges rise to the western horizon.

The Highline curves northeast through meadows from the crossing, intersecting the unmaintained Lost Lake Trail after 0.1 mile. If time and energy allow, don't miss the 0.5-mile side trip to Big Water Slide, a thundering cascade where Fremont Creek plunges over a granite ledge. To get there, follow the Lost Lake Trail westward, through meadows and along the north shore of a large Fremont Creek pond, shown as a marshy area on the topo map. At the west end of that pond, leave the trail and follow a well-worn path southeast, through the forest and along the pond's southwest shore for another 0.1 mile to the brink of Big Water Slide. Good camping areas lie nearby, and fishing in the pond can be productive.

The Highline ascends steadily over a rocky tread from Fremont Crossing, angling northwest through small basins and across glacier-carved, corrugated

HIGHLINE

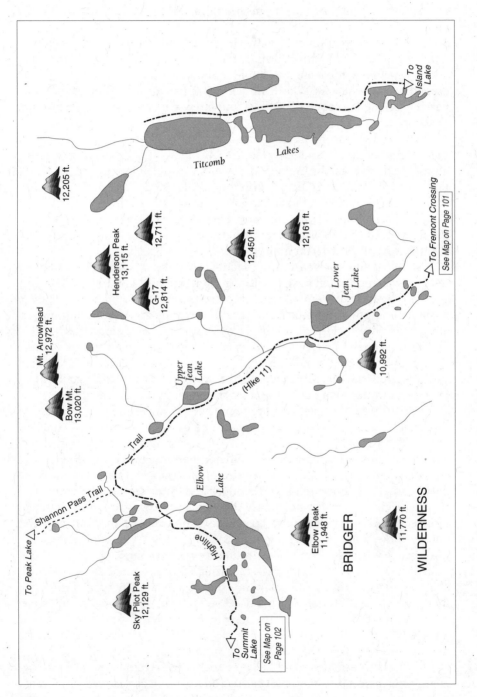

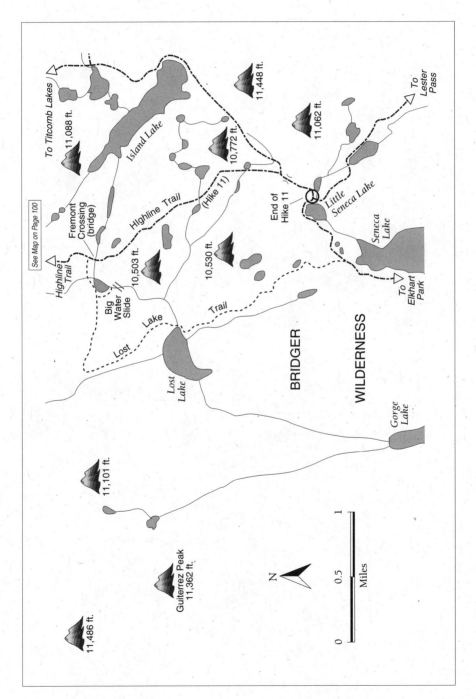

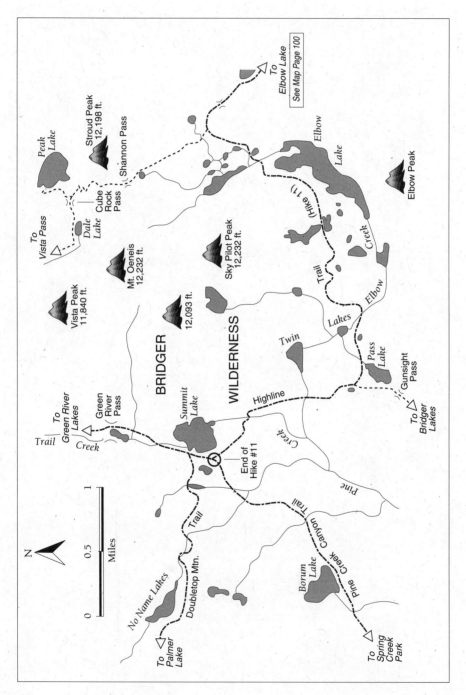

slopes. En route watch for a large cascading creek roaring down the north-east wall of the valley, draining remote Lake 11,052, lying far above. Perched on the rim of that wall are a jumble of massive boulders—glacial erratics—that appear as if they could topple at any time.

Topping out between a trio of timberline tarns, 400 feet above Fremont Crossing, the trail then begins a protracted traverse on steep alpine slopes 100 feet above mile-long Lower Jean Lake. The backdrop of peaks jutting skyward from the lake's shore is dramatic. There is little opportunity for camping around the lake; slopes of grass and bedrock rise abruptly from the shores.

Staying high above the lake, pass several tarns before finally descending steadily to its inlet and a ford. The crossing is deep and swift, but a boulder-hop facilitates a dry crossing in late summer. The trail re-crosses the creek 0.25 mile ahead, but some travelers stay on the creek's west bank to avoid the fords, following an easy course through a boulder field and meadows to rejoin the trail beyond the second ford.

The trail continues northwest at a gentle grade, ascending the confined alpine valley. About 1 mile above Lower Jean Lake the terrain opens up alongside Upper Jean, an alpine gem resting in a deep basin embraced by great crags that rise more than 2,000 feet above its shores. Eastward, the spires of Titcomb Needles form an exciting backdrop, and combined with the peaks rising overhead and enclosing the basin, Upper Jean Lake ranks as one of the most dramatic settings accessible by trail in the range.

To the northeast are the twin pyramids of 13,115-foot Henderson Peak and 12,814-foot G-17 (one of the USGS surveyor's classifications that remain on many unnamed peaks in the Wind Rivers). North of Henderson rises the slender, snow-streaked spire of 13,205-foot American Legion (or Bechtel) Peak. And piercing the sky north of the lake is the fluted south face of aptly named Mount Arrowhead.

The trail follows the southwest shore of 10,799-foot Upper Jean Lake. Then it rises moderately, gaining nearly 200 feet of elevation in 0.25 mile, to a short traverse above Lake 10,935. Beyond that lake the route winds briefly upward among erratic boulders and grassy alpine slopes, and soon mounts a broad saddle at 11,050 feet. Here the rubbly masses of 12,232-foot Mount Oeneis and 12,129-foot Sky Pilot Peak dominate the view.

The trail descends gently from the pass across boulder-dotted tundra and past a small tarn, reaching the northwest-bound trail to Shannon Pass (visible on the skyline above) and Peak Lake after 0.3 mile.

Stroud Peak, rising to 12,198 feet, (1,000 feet above and east of Shannon Pass), is one of the more frequently climbed peaks in the Wind Rivers. An easy, non-technical ascent (class 2) begins near this junction, climbing grassy, southwest-facing slopes to a prominent gap southeast of the peak. From there a steep ridge northwest leads to the summit. Stroud's position west of the crest of the range allows sweeping vistas that include many of the north-ern peaks of the Wind Rivers west of the Continental Divide and distant mountain ranges that include the Gros Ventres and the Tetons.

Bow Mountain and Mount Arrowhead from Lower Jean Lake.

Bearing left at the Shannon Pass Trail junction, continue a meandering descent into one of the classic alpine lake basins in the range. There are no trees visible here; everywhere you look there are wide stretches of alpine tundra, lakes and tarns, and ice-scoured bedrock. Erratic boulders rest atop rocky knolls, plucked from the basin's walls and left behind by a retreating glacier.

Upon reaching the basin floor, pass among tarns to a ford of 10-foot-wide, deep, and swift Elbow Creek, a difficult crossing in early summer. Hikers may jump across the creek where it narrows downstream from the ford. When the creek is low in late summer, boulders offer a convenient dry crossing.

Few hardy souls brave the austere surroundings to camp in the exposed reaches of the basin, but good, open camping areas abound here. Slightly more sheltered sites can be found above the northwest shore of Elbow Lake in a corrugated landscape of granite knobs, small meadows, and tarns.

Beyond the crossing, the trail heads west to climb the slopes above the basin, then it curves south, traversing 100 feet above massive Elbow Lake at 10,777 feet. Soon it follows a southwesterly course north of the infrequently visible lake. The rocky dome of 11,948-foot Elbow Peak overshadows the southern reaches of the basin, its stony flanks rising 1,200 feet from the lake's somber waters.

The trail ahead crests low granite knolls and dips into minor, tarn-dotted basins. After traveling 1.75 miles from the ford of Elbow Creek, begin a 400-foot descent, at first via a shallow, rocky draw, then upon slopes clothed in spruce and whitebark pine. The trail emerges from the subalpine forest to views of Elbow Creek thundering down a narrow gorge, its bed choked with boulders and its banks tangled with willow thickets.

Soon the trail reaches the creek at a ford, about 0.1 mile upstream from the crossing shown on the topo map, where the waters briefly widen and the current slackens. During late summer you can easily cross the creek via a rock hop, but earlier in the season you must wade across. The creek's waters are usually only shin-deep and 10 to 12 feet wide, with a modest current.

From the crossing, the newer segment of the Highline (not shown on the topo map) ascends briefly to a grassy, boulder-dotted bench with views down the canyon to meadow-fringed Twin Lakes (supporting a golden and rainbow trout fishery). Skirt the grass-bordered shores of two tarns and jump across the small, seasonal stream draining Pass Lake. Quickly thereafter, ignore a boot-worn path ascending southwest to Pass Lake, 100 yards up the draw. Pass Lake offers a few fair campsites above its west shore, and the lake hosts cutthroat trout.

Immediately beyond that junction, an old, closed segment of the Highline forks right. Instead, continue west and gain a low ridge among stunted conifers. Pause here to enjoy the grand view of towering summits behind you before they fade from view beyond the ridge.

A steep and rocky descent west of the ridge quickly leads past another informal trail to Pass Lake and Gunsight Pass. The descent continues to a junction, 0.2 mile below the ridge, with the formal but unmaintained trail to Pass Lake.

Beyond that junction the trail emerges onto the floor of a grassy basin,

Bridge spanning Fremont Creek at Fremont Crossing, on the Highline Trail.

contours around a tarn, and, amid increasingly large spruces and whitebarks, follows a few switchbacks down to a bridge spanning the boulder-filled cataract of Elbow Creek.

The trail then leads on a traverse high above Pine Creek canyon, heading northwest beneath a shady canopy of conifers. It gradually descends 120 feet in 0.3 mile and meets a north-bound trail leading up-canyon toward Summit Lake, following the east bank of the stream.

Bearing left, quickly descend to Pine Creek, where there may be logs in place to afford a dry crossing. If not, expect a shin-deep ford of the creek's swift waters.

A steady, moderate ascent ensues, gaining 200 feet in 0.7 mile. The trail leads south, then abruptly curves north along a broad ridge clothed in a thinning forest, where grouse whortleberry forms a green mat on the forest floor.

At length the scene opens up in rolling alpine meadows, and soon the broad waters of Summit Lake unfold to the north. Green River Pass, the low notch north of the lake, frames a fine view of the gray, imposing canyon walls of the Green River canyon.

Staying well above the lake, the nearly level trail curves above the southwest shore and meets Pine Creek Canyon Trail (see hike 6), signed for Trapper Lake, branching southwest. About 150 yards farther the Doubletop Mountain Trail (see hike 8), signed for Palmer Lake, branches west. The Highline Trail continues north, leading to the Green River Lakes Trailhead in 16.3 miles (see hike 1).

12 INDIAN PASS TRAIL TO TITCOMB BASIN

General description:	A popular backcountry spur trail useful as part of an extended trip.
Distance:	5.25 miles, one way.
Difficulty:	Moderate.
Traffic:	Heavy.
Elevation gain and loss:	550 feet.
Maximum elevation:	10,650 feet.
Topo maps:	USGS: Bridger Lakes, Gannett Peak, Fremont Peak South; Earthwalk: Northern Wind River Range.

Key points:

0.0	Junction with Highline and Indian Pass trails; bear right.
1.2	Island Lake.
2.2	Junction of Indian Pass and Titcomb Basin trails; turn right to reach Indian Basin, left to reach Titcomb Basin.
5.25	Reach north end of upper Titcomb Lake.

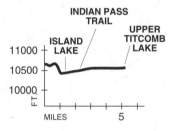

Finding the trail: This trail branches northeast from the Highline Trail, 0.4 mile north of the junction of the Highline and Seneca Lake trails above the east shore of Little Seneca Lake, and 1.9 miles southeast of Fremont Crossing.

The trail: Of the many spectacular alpine trails in the Wind Rivers, the trail to Titcomb and Indian basins outranks them all for the ease of access and for the grandeur of the scenery. More than one dozen alpine lakes; a dramatic backdrop of sweeping walls capped by slender spires and bold crags—including some of the highest peaks in the range; and ample, though austere, camping areas all combine to make the Titcomb/Indian Basin environs one of the most heavily visited areas in the Bridger Wilderness.

The basin is a mecca for climbing parties, a convenient base for ascents of the glaciers and the lofty northern peaks of the range, including Gannett Peak. But you don't need to be a rock climber or alpinist to enjoy the vast panoramas and the sense of accomplishment gained from scaling the surrounding summits. Fremont and Jackson peaks can both be attained via non-technical but strenuous routes beginning in Indian Basin. Routes to

INDIAN PASS TRAIL TO TITCOMB BASIN

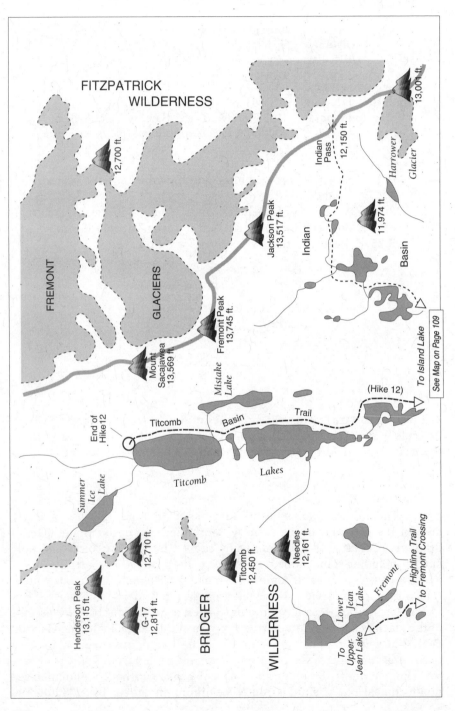

FITZPATRICK WILDERNESS

FREMONT

GLACIERS

12,700 ft.

Jackson Peak 13,517 ft.

Indian Pass 12,150 ft.

13,001 ft.

Harrower Glacier

Indian

11,974 ft.

Basin

Fremont Peak 13,745 ft.

Mount Sacajawea 13,569 ft.

Mistake Lake

See Map on Page 109

To Island Lake

(Hike 12)

End of Hike 12

Titcomb   Basin   Trail

Summer Ice Lake

Titcomb   Lakes

Titcomb

12,710 ft.

G-17 12,814 ft.

Henderson Peak 13,115 ft.

BRIDGER

Titcomb 12,450 ft.

Needles 12,161 ft.

WILDERNESS

Lower Jean Lake

To Upper Jean Lake

Fremont

Highline Trail to Fremont Crossing

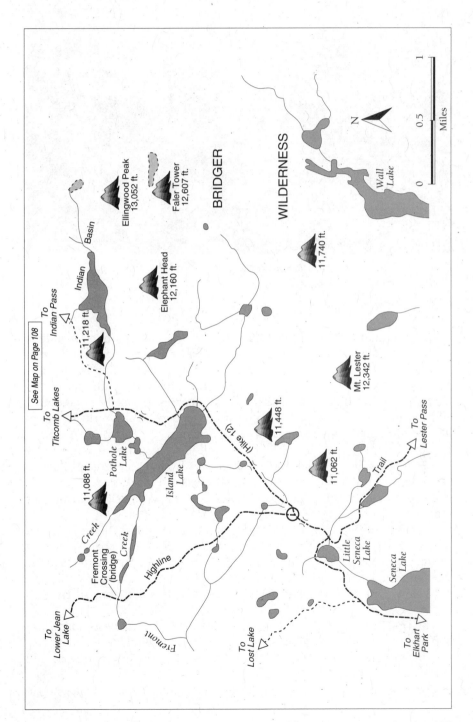

See Map on Page 108

To Indian Pass

To Titcomb Lakes

Indian Basin

11,218 ft.

Ellingwood Peak
13,052 ft.

Faler Tower
12,607 ft.

Elephant Head
12,160 ft.

BRIDGER

WILDERNESS

11,740 ft.

11,088 ft.

Pothole Lake

Creek

Fremont Crossing (bridge)

Creek

Highline

Fremont

To Lower Jean Lake

Island Lake

(Hike 12)

11,448 ft.

11,062 ft.

Mt. Lester
12,342 ft.

Trail

To Lester Pass

Little Seneca Lake

Seneca Lake

To Lost Lake

To Elkhart Park

Wall Lake

N

Miles

0   0.5   1

Fremont Peak, Jackson Peak, and Indian Pass, from the junction of the Highline and Indian Pass trails.

those summits require considerable effort; route-finding among boulders, ledges, and snow-covered slopes; and ample experience and good judgment.

Camping areas are widely available along this trail, but only Island Lake offers a modicum of shelter among stunted conifers. Titcomb and Indian basins lie above timberline, and though the basins are likely to be dotted with backpacker's tents, the terrain is variable enough to allow private camping spots among the bedrock knolls and meadows.

From its junction with the Highline Trail just below and northeast of a 10,600-foot saddle, the well-worn Indian Pass Trail descends gently northeast onto the floor of a shallow basin. It crosses a small stream, then inclines—gradually at first, moderately later on—as it ascends toward another saddle.

The grade levels off in another 10,600-foot saddle, passes to the right of a tarn, then proceeds past a scattering of krummholz whitebark pine and spruce into another saddle just beyond, flanked by ice-scoured knobs to the west and a tall, broken cliff to the east. From that notch Island Lake sprawls out below, with views of the majestic ice-clad spires that enclose Titcomb Basin.

The trail is rocky northeast of the saddle as it steadily descends nearly 300 feet in 0.4 mile. The grade levels off around the boulder-dotted, grassy southeast shore of 10,346-foot Island Lake, home to rainbow, cutthroat, and golden trout.

Curve around the east shore of the lake, then ascend 200 feet via a north- ·

110

east-trending draw to surmount another broad saddle. A gently descending traverse leads another 0.2 mile to a junction above the inlet of Pothole Lake (Lake 10,467). Here the Indian Pass Trail branches right and the Titcomb Basin Trail continues straight ahead to the north.

Travelers bound for Titcomb Basin quickly reach a ford of Indian Basin's creek. You may need to search upstream for a dry crossing via boulders. The trail ahead skirts the east shore of a tarn, mounts yet another 10,600-foot notch, then leads past the east shores of Lake 10,548 before briefly ascending to one final saddle next to a shallow tarn.

The trail then descends gently via alpine slopes to the east shore of Lower Titcomb Lake (Lake 10,575), the largest in the Titcomb chain. Follow the east shore amid alpine meadows and ice-polished bedrock to the upper lake at 10,598 feet. That lake occupies the entire basin floor, with smooth rock walls rising above. The trail continues around the east shore and into the alpine meadows beyond, where the tread becomes obscure.

Good camping areas can be found between Pothole Lake and lower Titcomb Lake, and the diligent traveler will find many other possible camping areas. Pothole, the two large Titcomb lakes, and Mistake Lake all support golden trout fisheries.

13 PINE CREEK CANYON TRAIL—ELKHART PARK TO LONG & GLIMPSE LAKES

General description:	A day hike or overnighter, useful as part of an extended loop trip.
Distance:	6 miles.
Difficulty:	Strenuous.
Traffic:	Moderate to Long Lake; light to Glimpse Lake.
Elevation loss and gain:	-1,800 feet, +1,950 feet.
Trailhead elevation:	9,350 feet.
Maximum elevation:	9,500 feet.
Topo maps:	USGS: Fremont Lake North, Bridger Lakes; Earthwalk: Northern Wind River Range.

Key points:

0.0   Elkhart Park Trailhead.
2.1   Long Lake.
2.7   Pine Creek bridge.
6.0   Junction with Glimpse Lake Trail.

PINE CREEK CANYON

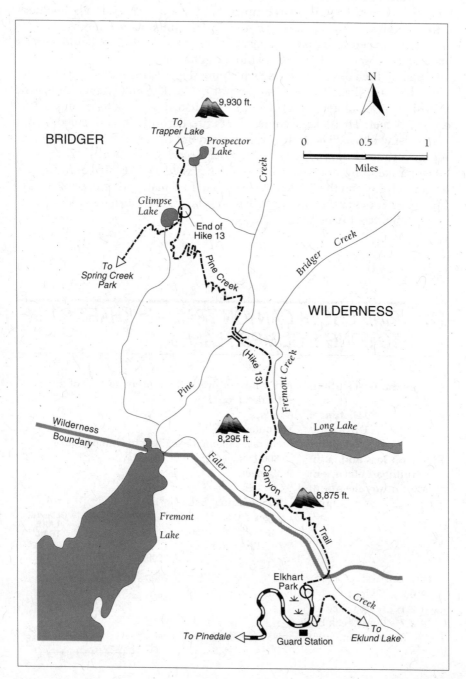

The trail: This trail, the most demanding route in the Bridger Wilderness, is most often dismissed by backcountry travelers beginning a trip from Elkhart Park. After all, the trail loses nearly 2,000 feet of elevation as it plunges into the depths of Pine Creek canyon, then *regains* all that lost elevation, and then some, to reach the canyon rim above Glimpse Lake.

The trail is steep, rocky, and crosses sun-drenched slopes where the sparse forest cover offers little shade. In fact, the trail is so rocky, steep, and rough, it is one of only nine trails in the Bridger Wilderness that are not recommended for stock parties.

The trail does have its attractions, however. First, it is seldom used. Second, it visits Pine and Fremont Creek canyons, among the deepest and most scenic gorges in the Bridger. Both are confined by ice-scoured canyon walls that soar 2,000 feet skyward. Long Lake, set deep in Fremont Creek canyon, is a worthwhile destination of a day hike, and it offers several fine campsites—the only suitable camps in the canyons.

This segment of the Pine Creek Canyon Trail is most useful as the return leg of a 35-mile backpack, via the Pole Creek, Seneca Lake, and Highline trails to Summit Lake (see hikes 10 and 11), and thence south to Pine Creek canyon (see hike 6). The down-and-up trek across the canyon is much easier with a lighter pack at the end of a trip.

The trail begins from the north parking lot in Elkhart Park, adjacent to Trails End Campground. From the north edge of the parking lot, fringed by whitebark and lodgepole pines, there are fine views stretching across the rocky trenches of Pine Creek and Fremont Creek canyons, to an array of lofty summits.

The trail quickly descends into a grassy draw draining Elkhart Park's trickling stream, then curves east to an easy crossing of larger Faler Creek, where Engelmann spruce make a brief appearance. Immediately beyond the crossing the trail enters the Bridger Wilderness.

The trail bends north and away from the creek while maintaining a gentle downhill grade, but the tread is invariably rough and rocky. Soon, though, the trail begins a steady plunge via steep, rocky switchbacks, descending rock-bound slopes dotted with lodgepole, spruce, and aspen. At length the knee-jarring descent follows above cascading Faler Creek, where Douglas-fir joins the scattered forest, heralding the warmer, drier environment here.

Soon the trail curves north and crests a minor saddle, then drops steeply into a sloping, conifer-clad draw. A brief ascent up the draw leads to the west shore of Long Lake, at 7,875 feet.

Stretching up the canyon for 1.5 miles, this aptly named lake lies deep in the rock-bound confines of Fremont Creek canyon, flooding the entire canyon floor. Fishing for brook, brown, and cutthroat trout can be productive in this deep lake, but large boulders and cliffs are major obstacles to access around the shoreline. Several good campsites lie west of the trail, set in a parklike forest of Douglas-fir and lodgepole pine.

The trail beyond Long Lake descends at a gentler grade down the narrow canyon of Fremont Creek, shaded by a canopy of Douglas-fir, subalpine fir,

Bridge spanning Pine Creek on the Pine Creek Canyon Trail.

Long Lake on the Pine Creek Canyon Trail.

and lodgepole pine. Broad Fremont Creek, the most vigorous stream in the canyons, thunders over its boulder-strewn bed below the trail.

About 0.6 mile from Long Lake, the trail reaches a signed junction with a trail leading 1.5 miles southwest to Fremont Lake. Bear right and cross the long, sturdy bridge spanning Pine Creek just downstream from its confluence with Fremont Creek.

Here at the trail's low point—7,550 feet—the canyon is rocky and confined, offering no opportunity to pitch a tent. Tall spruces shade the trail next to the bridge, but the trail quickly ascends to rocky slopes supporting scattered aspen groves, Douglas-fir and lodgepole pine. Switchbacks climb steadily above the canyon's confines, but the grade here is not as steep as it is on the opposite canyon wall.

Two miles above the bridge the trail switchbacks alongside Miller Creek (Glimpse Lake's outlet stream), then climbs the canyon rim at Crows Nest Lookout, where an outstanding view of the canyons, and the route, unfolds. About 300 yards farther is the junction with the Glimpse Lake Trail at 9,500 feet, 6 miles from Elkhart Park.

Good campsites can be found in the subalpine forest above the lake's southeast shore. To continue north on the Pine Creek Canyon Trail, see hike 6.

General description:	A day hike or overnighter.
Distance:	8.6 miles, round trip; or 10.6 miles, loop trip.
Difficulty:	Moderate.
Traffic:	Moderate.
Elevation gain and loss:	+700 feet, -200 feet, round trip; or +1,150 feet, loop trip.
Trailhead elevation:	9,350 feet.
Maximum elevation:	10,080 feet on round trip; 10,300 feet on loop trip.
Topo maps:	USGS: Fremont Lake North, Fayette Lake, Bridger Lakes; Earthwalk: Northern Wind River Range.

Key points:

0.0   Elkhart Park Trailhead.

3.3   Junction with Miller Lake Trail in Miller Park; turn right.

4.0   Miller Lake.

4.3   Middle Sweeney Lake.

5.3   Upper Sweeney Lake.

5.8   Junction with Pole Creek Trail; turn left to return to trailhead.

10.9   Elkhart Park Trailhead.

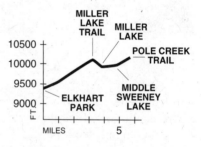

The trail: Most travelers on the Pole Creek Trail from Elkhart Park hurry past the trails to Miller and Sweeney lakes while en route to the fabulous high country of Titcomb Basin, Jean Lakes, or Cook Lakes. But day hikers, equestrians, and families with children are attracted to these peaceful sub-alpine lakes due to the ease of access and good fishing for brookies (Miller) and goldens (Middle Sweeney).

Long-distance trekkers en route to or from Elkhart Park will find the Miller Lake/Sweeney Creek trails to be a scenic diversion from the tedious Pole Creek Trail, adding only 0.7 mile distance to their trip.

From Elkhart Park, follow the Pole Creek Trail (see hike 10) for 3.3 miles to the signed junction in Miller Park, and bear right (southeast); the sign points to Miller Lake. A gentle uphill grade follows, leading 200 yards to a grassy, lupine-decorated saddle.

From there outstanding views stretch southeast along the front of the range, revealing such notable summits as Mount Baldy (11,857 feet), Angel Peak (12,402 feet), and Mount Victor (12,254 feet). Vistas to the northwest reach beyond the Wind Rivers to the distant peaks of the Gros Ventre Range.

The section of the trail from the saddle down to Miller Lake has been reconstructed since the Bridger Lakes quad was published. Now the trail

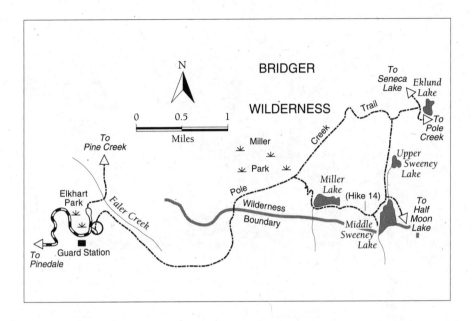

descends moderately, rather than the very steep old trail, via five switchbacks through whitebark pine forest to the grassy west shore of 9,850-foot Miller Lake.

As you follow the shoreline south, avoid numerous right-branching paths leading to campsites—unless you're looking for a place to spend the night. After crossing the lake's sluggish outlet stream, the trail bends east, following the south shores, where the tread becomes quite rough and rocky. There are more good camping areas south of the trail, above the lake.

This pretty lake lies in an open bowl that hosts stunted timberline conifers and wildflower-rich meadows. Rocky bluffs rise to the north, and forested slopes bound the bowl to the south.

The trail reaches the east end of Miller Lake 1 mile from the Pole Creek Trail. It then winds its way through a shady forest of Engelmann spruce and whitebark and lodgepole pine, skirting the fringes of a long, soggy meadow. The trail leads to the head of a narrow valley, passing a boggy spread shown as a tarn on the topo map. At the bog's southeast corner, a sign points down a faint, southeast-trending path leading 200 yards to Middle Sweeney Lake and campsites near its west shore.

For a rewarding round trip, follow that trail down to Middle Sweeney Lake, then return the way you came. For a longer trip that loops back to the trailhead, continue east on the main trail.

Bearing left at that junction, begin a gentle, forested ascent past a small trapper's cabin in ruins, and then above the northwest shore of Middle

Miller Lake.

Sweeney Lake. Campsites can be seen below, on benches between the trail and the lake. Most of the sites are close to the lakeshore and should be avoided.

The traverse above the lake ends next to trickling Sweeney Creek, 1.6 miles from the Pole Creek Trail. The unsigned Sweeney Creek Trail branches east and crosses the creek here, but bear left, staying on the well-worn trail that ascends the draw west of Sweeney Creek. Whitebark pines dominate the forest here, but the trees open up at times to reveal sloping meadows adorned with the colorful blooms of lupine, one-flower daisy, and yarrow.

The moderate ascent ends above the west shore of much smaller Upper Sweeney Lake, perhaps the most beautiful of the triad of lakes passed along this trail. The lake lies in a bowl beneath a skyline of rocky, tree-fringed knobs. There are many fine camping areas in the spruce, whitebark pine, and lodgepole pine forest above the shoreline.

The trail continues north beyond that lake, ascending a steady grade that first leads through spruce forest, and farther on ascends a sloping meadow. Upon approaching a broad, grassy saddle, the trail joins an abandoned segment of the Pole Creek Trail, beyond which our trail becomes obscure.

Continue north, skirting the west shore of a lovely tarn resting atop the saddle. Several yards north of the tarn is a junction with the Pole Creek Trail signed for the Sweeney Creek Trail.

Elkhart Park lies 5.1 miles west of this junction, and Eklund Lake lies 0.4 mile east. To continue on the Seneca or Pole Creek trails, see hikes 10 and 15.

15 POLE CREEK TRAIL—ELKHART PARK TO POLE CREEK

General description: An extended trip useful as one leg of a loop trip.

Distance: 9.3 miles, one way.

Difficulty: Moderate.

Traffic: Moderate to heavy.

Elevation gain and loss: +1,150 feet. -750 feet.

Trailhead elevation: 9,350 feet.

Maximum elevation: 10,450 feet.

Topo maps: USGS: Fremont Lake North, Bridger Lakes, Fayette Lake, Fremont Peak South; Earthwalk: Northern Wind River Range.

Key points:

0.0 Elkhart Park Trailhead.
3.3 Junction with Miller Lake Trail; bear left.
5.1 Junction with Sweeney Creek Trail; bear left.
5.5 Junction with Seneca Lake Trail; turn right.
6.3 Marys Lake.
9.3 Junction with Highline Trail at Pole Creek.

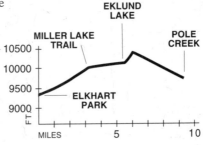

Finding the trail: The Pole Creek Trail officially begins at Elkhart Park. Find the southeast-bound segment of the trail above Eklund Lake, 5.5 miles from the Elkhart Park Trailhead.

The trail: After passing through largely uninspiring timberline terrain to Eklund Lake, the Pole Creek Trail then traverses a corrugated, glacier-carved landscape as it descends into the valley of Pole Creek, a major drainage in the central Wind Rivers.

There are numerous destinations in the Pole Creek environs that make convenient base camps, including Cook Lakes, Wall Lake, Bald Mountain Basin, and Chain Lakes. All these waters, including Pole Creek, offer good fishing for a variety of trout species, as well as an abundance of fine camping areas. In this area you will find much to keep you busy, including a variety of cross-country excursions to high passes, remote lake basins, and class 2 scrambles to the surrounding lofty peaks.

EKLUND LAKE TO POLE CREEK

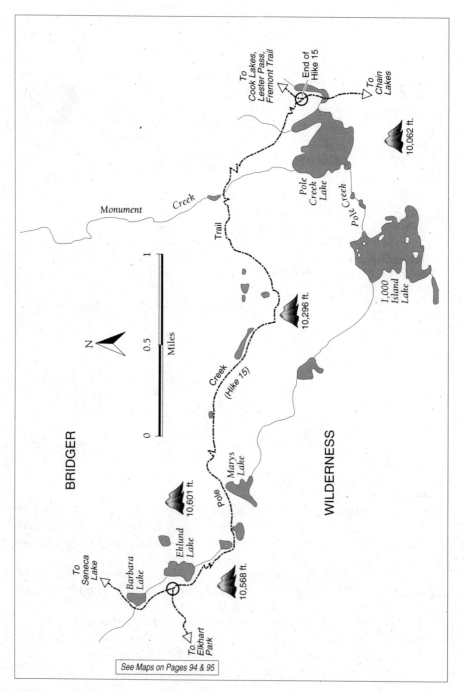

To Cook Lakes, Lester Pass, Fremont Trail

End of Hike 15

To Chain Lakes

10,062 ft.

Monument Creek

Trail

Pole Creek Lake

Pole Creek

1,000 Island Lake

10,296 ft.

N

1

0.5

0

Miles

Creek (Hike 15)

BRIDGER

Marys Lake

10,601 ft.

Pole

WILDERNESS

Eklund Lake

10,568 ft.

To Seneca Lake

Barbara Lake

To Elkhart Park

See Maps on Pages 94 & 95

Eklund Lake and the Continental Divide from the Pole Creek Trail.

From the Elkhart Park Trailhead follow the Pole Creek Trail (see hike 10) east 5.5 miles to a signed junction above Eklund Lake, at 10,300 feet. Bear right, staying on the Pole Creek Trail.

The trail skirts the rocky, meadow-fringed southwest shores of the lake, then begins a 150-foot ascent via switchbacks on slopes cloaked in a shady forest of Engelmann spruce and whitebark pine. As you gain elevation, breaks in the forest afford fine views of the bold peaks and spires encircling upper Fremont Creek and Titcomb Basin.

The grade abates at a tarn-filled notch, and the trail then skirts the shore-line of this and another tarn in quick succession. Meadows rich with wild-flowers, a light forest cover of timberline trees, and low granite knobs, with massive Baldy Mountain rising in the background, characterize the follow-ing 3 miles of the trail.

The trail ahead is a pleasant, mostly downhill stretch. It passes above inviting Marys Lake beyond the pair of tarns, then proceeds through the corrugated landscape of rocky knobs and minor draws that harbor mead-ows, willow thickets, and tarns.

Brilliant displays of wildflowers help to pass the time en route. Look for the blooms of one-flower daisy, Indian paintbrush, hairy arnica, and moun-tain bluebells. The forest of spruce and whitebark pine remains open and stunted along much of the distance to Pole Creek.

Occasional minor ascents interrupt the downhill trend of the trail, which invariably has a rocky tread. Views open up at times to reveal Mount Baldy and a host of other 12,000-foot mountains that bound the Pole Creek valley.

About 3.1 miles from Eklund Lake, rock-hop small Monument Creek, then descend more steadily, with the help of occasional switchbacks, to the signed junction with the Highline Trail, alongside a long, narrow pond in Pole Creek.

The sign points left (east) to Cook Lakes, and right (straight ahead) to Chain Lakes (see hike 16). Suitable campsites are found at Pole Creek Lakes, 200 yards west of Lower Pole Creek Crossing and 0.1 mile south.

16 HIGHLINE TRAIL—LITTLE SENECA LAKE TO NORTH FORK LAKE

General description:	A backcountry segment of the Highline Trail, all or part of which is useful as part of an extended trip beginning at either the Elkhart Park or Boulder Lake trailheads.
Distance:	18.9 miles.
Difficulty:	Moderate.
Traffic:	Light to moderate.
Elevation gain and loss:	+1,800 feet, -2,650 feet.
Maximum elevation:	11,100 feet.
Topo maps:	USGS: Bridger Lakes, Fremont Peak South, Horseshoe Lake; Earthwalk: Northern and Southern Wind River Range.

Key points:

0.0	Junction of Highline and Seneca Lake trails; turn southeast.
1.5	Lester Pass.
4.1	Junction with north segment of Cook Lakes Trail; bear right.
4.4	Upper Pole Creek Crossing.
4.5	Junction with south-bound Fremont Trail and east-bound south segment of Cook Lakes Trail; turn right (west).
5.4	Middle Pole Creek Crossing.
5.5	Junction with Pole Creek Trail; bear left.
5.6	Lower Pole Creek Crossing.
7.7	Junction with Bell Lakes Trail at Chain Lakes; bear right.
8.2	Junction with west-bound spur trail to Spruce Lake; stay left.
9.3	Junction with Timico Lake Trail at Barnes Lake; bear left.
9.8	Junction with east-bound segment of Timico Lake Trail (via Fall Creek); bear right.
12.8	Junction with south-bound Horseshoe Lake Trail; bear left.
14.2	Junction with North Fork Trail above Lake George; bear left.
17.1	Junction with Lake Ethel Trail above Macs Lake; stay left.
18.4	Junction with northeast-bound trail leading to Fremont Trail; turn right (south).
18.8	North Fork Lake.
18.9	Ford outlet of North Fork Lake.

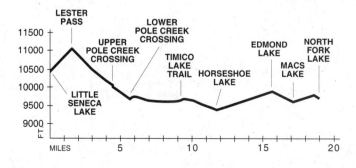

HIGHLINE • FREMONT

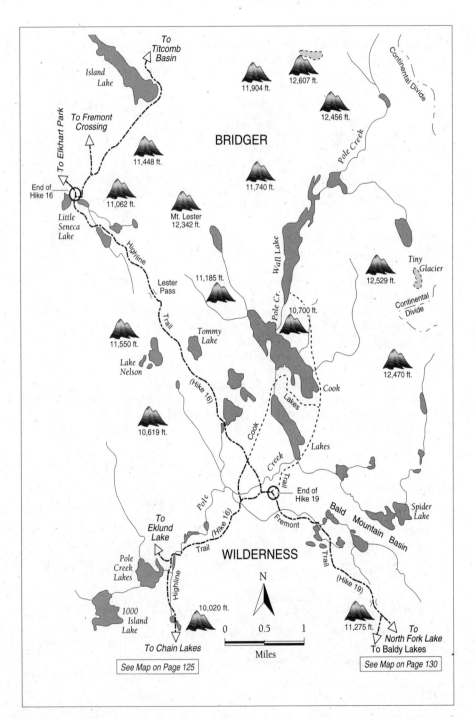

To Titcomb Basin

Island Lake

To Fremont Crossing

To Elkhart Park

11,448 ft.

BRIDGER

11,904 ft.

12,607 ft.

12,456 ft.

Pole Creek

Continental Divide

End of Hike 16

Little Seneca Lake

11,062 ft.

Highline

Mt. Lester 12,342 ft.

11,740 ft.

Wall Lake

Lester Pass

11,185 ft.

Trail

Pole Cr.

10,700 ft.

12,529 ft.

Tiny Glacier

Continental Divide

Tommy Lake

(Hike 16)

11,550 ft.

Lake Nelson

Cook

Lakes

12,470 ft.

10,619 ft.

Cook

Creek

Cook

Lakes

End of Hike 19

Trail

Spider Lake

To Eklund Lake

Pole

(Hike 16)

Fremont

Bald Mountain Basin

Pole Creek Lakes

Trail

WILDERNESS

Trail

(Hike 19)

Highline

1000 Island Lake

10,020 ft.

N

0   0.5   1

Miles

11,275 ft.

To North Fork Lake
To Baldy Lakes

To Chain Lakes

See Map on Page 125

See Map on Page 130

HIGHLINE

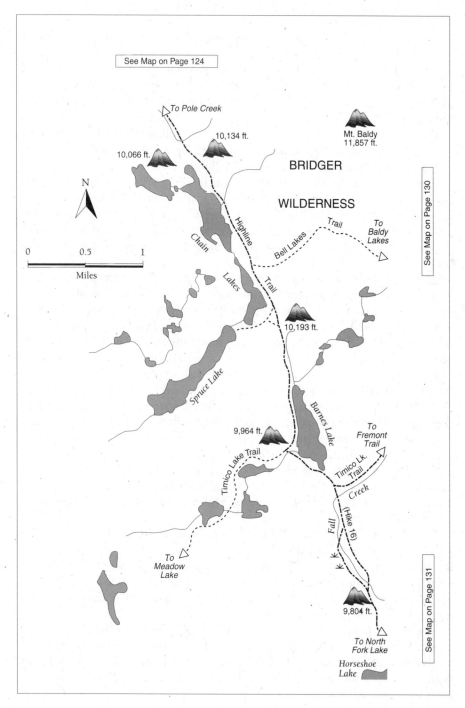

See Map on Page 124

To Pole Creek

10,134 ft.

Mt. Baldy
11,857 ft.

10,066 ft.

BRIDGER

N

WILDERNESS

Bell Lakes
Trail

To
Baldy
Lakes

Chain

Highline

0   0.5   1

Lakes

Miles

Trail

10,193 ft.

Spruce Lake

Barnes Lake

9,964 ft.

To
Fremont
Trail

Timico Lake Trail

Timico Lk.
Trail

Creek

Fall

(Hike 16)

To
Meadow
Lake

9,804 ft.

To North
Fork Lake

Horseshoe
Lake

See Map on Page 130

See Map on Page 131

Finding the trail: The northern terminus of this segment begins at the junction with the Seneca Lake Trail east of Little Seneca Lake, 10.4 miles from Elkhart Park Trailhead. The southern terminus is located at the ford of the outlet of North Fork Lake, 11 miles from Boulder Lake Trailhead.

The hike: This long-distance segment of the Highline Trail leads from the alpine heights of the northern Bridger Wilderness to the lake-dotted bench in the central part of the range. En route travelers cross 11,100-foot Lester Pass—the highest elevation attained on the Highline—then descend to three wide, swift crossings of large Pole Creek, fords that may be difficult during early summer high water.

From Pole Creek to North Fork Lake the trail follows a gentle, undulating route, staying below 10,000 feet while visiting a half dozen large lakes, wildflower-speckled meadows, and subalpine forests.

From Barnes Lake (9.8 miles from Little Seneca Lake) south to North Fork Lake, the trail passes through miles of forest charred in the 38,507-acre Fayette Fire of 1988. The blaze began from a lightning strike on the shores of Fayette Lake, in the western foothills of the range. The fire burned through the narrow belt of forest on the western slopes, finally burning itself out at timberline.

The high-elevation landscape here is dominated by bedrock, with thin, nutrient-poor soils; plant regeneration has been slow. A blanket of fireweed spreads a greenish cast across the slopes, contrasting with the blackened snags and sparkling bedrock. But lodgepole pine saplings, a common sight in places like Yellowstone National Park following the 1988 fires, are noticeably absent along much of this segment of the Highline.

Backcountry rangers can't keep up with falling snags in this area, so expect to find fallen trees blocking the trail in places between Barnes and North Fork lakes. Exercise extreme caution when traveling here during windy periods; snags can topple unexpectedly. With a jumble of fallen trees and a thick carpet of fireweed, camping areas are difficult to find in the burn. If you do camp here, choose a site away from fire-killed snags.

Travelers on foot or horseback can avoid the burned segment of the Highline by following the Timico Lake Trail from Barnes Lake to the Fremont Trail via Fall Creek. Then ascend over Hat Pass to reach North Fork Lake (see below).

From the junction east of Little Seneca Lake at 10,400 feet, follow the Highline Trail southeast, down to a rock-hop crossing of the small creek draining the lower lake in the Lester Pass basin. A 150-foot ascent follows, rising among boulders and a stunted band of Engelmann spruce and whitebark pine. Shortly after the grade abates, hop across the outlet of a larger lake and skirt around its northeast shore.

The broad, grassy saddle of Lester Pass looms ahead on the skyline, and the trail ascends toward the pass, past a few tenacious groves of krummholz and across tundra slopes dotted with ice-polished bedrock. Views expand with every step on the trail, until a memorable alpine vista unfolds at the crest of Lester Pass.

Enjoy the last views of the spires and crags encircling Titcomb Basin and upper Fremont Creek to the north, and then gaze southward, surveying the route ahead. The broad, rocky massifs and the expansive cirque of Bald Mountain Basin dominate the view.

A steady descent over rocky tundra ensues, leading to more gentle terrain in the basin below. The trail passes below Nelson Lake (home to golden trout), and soon traverses above the alpine shores of Tommy Lake (also harboring goldens). From Tommy Lake, the rocky trail leads down below timberline, dropping 400 feet to the meadow-fringed west shore of Lake 10,175, a productive brook and lake trout fishery.

After crossing this lake's outlet, a brief climb leads to another downhill grade to the junction with the north segment of the Cook Lakes Trail.

COOK LAKES TRAIL

The large Cook Lakes are well worth a visit, if time and energy allow. The northeast-bound Cook Lakes Trail reaches the lower lake, resting at 10,143 feet, after 0.6 mile. About 0.4 mile farther the trail follows the south shores of the upper lake, Lake 10,170. Both lakes harbor brook trout and offer many good camping areas among rocky knobs and stunted timberline forest. Wall Lake, a long, rock-bound alpine gem filled with golden trout, can be reached via an easy-to-follow trail leading north from Lake 10,170.

Travelers can rejoin the Highline and Fremont trails south of the Upper Crossing of Pole Creek by following the southern segment of the 2.8-mile Cook Lakes Trail.

From the Cook Lakes Trail junction, two trails diverge to the south, both leading down to Pole Creek. The trail to the right offers a shortcut, via a grassy draw, down to a knee-deep ford of Pole Creek and a junction with the west-bound Highline after 0.4 mile, saving 0.3 mile.

The official Highline, however, heads southeast for 0.4 mile, quickly ascends to a tree-crested notch between trailside domes, then leads down to the Upper Crossing of Pole Creek. During periods of normal stream flow, stock parties will find a good but long and deep ford in a pond of the creek. Backpackers can boulder-hop the creek above or below the ford.

Shortly after fording Pole Creek is the junction with the south-bound Fremont Trail (see hike 19), at 10,050 feet. The Highline turns west at the junction, following Pole Creek downstream through streamside meadows and past low domes and ice-polished slabs. Tall spruces and whitebarks form a discontinuous forest that fringes the rocky meadows.

Good views from this undulating stretch of trail reach up to the sawtoothed peaks at the canyon's head. There are many fine camping areas in the 2 miles between the upper and lower crossings.

About 0.4 mile from the Fremont Trail junction, pass the unsigned shortcut trail leading northeast back to the Highline/Cook Lakes trail junction. Soon the trail meets the small but wide stream draining Bald Mountain Basin, which you may have to wade until late summer.

The trail winds its way among more rocky domes, ducking in and out of the subalpine forest, past several tarns, and eventually cresting a 10,000-foot notch. The trail becomes very rocky as it steeply descends the other side, losing 200 feet of elevation beneath a shady spruce canopy.

After the trail levels off alongside the creek, lodgepole pine joins the ranks of forest. The trail meanders past alternating rapids and ponds in the large creek, until reaching the Middle Crossing of Pole Creek. Here the creek is about 50 feet wide, knee deep even in late summer, flowing with a moderate current over a bed of slippery rocks—exercise caution.

Beyond the ford the trail hugs the foot of a prominent dome for 0.1 mile to the terminus of the Pole Creek Trail (see hike 15), 9.8 miles from Elkhart Park Trailhead. Turn left (south) here; the sign points to Chain Lakes.

The Highline follows the shore of a linear pond in Pole Creek for 0.1 mile to the Lower Crossing at 9,750 feet, located just upstream from Pole Creek Lakes (with brook and cutthroat trout), where there are places to camp.

The ford here is about 40 feet wide and usually no more than knee deep in low water, with a modest current. An overused, pine-shaded campsite lies on a bench south of the ford, but it is much too close to the creek and the trail, and should be avoided.

The trail ahead follows the Wind Rivers' lake-studded western bench through a subdued landscape for the remaining distance to North Fork Lake. Beyond the ford a gradual ascent leads up a narrow, fault-controlled valley, passing forest-fringed meadows while following alongside a small, willow-bordered stream. Rock-hop the stream and mount a low, grassy saddle, then descend easily to the large, picturesque Chain Lakes, spreading out in a broad, shallow basin.

Midway around the first lake in the chain climb up and over a rocky knob that juts into the lake's waters, then follow the rocky, winding trail along the northeast shore among meadows, bedrock slabs, and glacial erratics. The massive, rubbly flanks of 11,857-foot Mount Baldy loom overhead to the east. Fishing for rainbows and cutthroats is often productive in this lake and in the following, smaller Chain Lake.

At 9,850 feet, 2 miles from Pole Creek, the trail meets the signed junction with the Bell Lakes Trail, its tread invisible in the meadows at the junction. That route offers quick access to the scenic Baldy Lakes basin, gaining 500 feet in 1.5 miles as it ascends through a narrow band of timberline forest.

From that junction, the Highline leads along the northeast shore of the second and smaller Chain Lake. After 0.5 mile an unsigned trail branches right (west), leading 0.4 mile to 9,797-foot Spruce Lake (good fishing for rainbows and cutthroats).

The trail then ascends gently toward a low gap on the southern skyline. Be sure to take the trail that stays in the forest west of the gap; another trail ascends directly to the gap but fades in a boggy meadow on the south side.

From the gap, the Highline descends gradually through a light forest of whitebark pine and spruce toward Barnes Lake. It passes through a finger of burned forest, a hint of what lies ahead. Once at the lake, traverse steep,

Fording Pole Creek at Lower Pole Creek Crossing.

pine-forested slopes above the west shore, soon curving southwest away from the lake. Steep terrain around the 9,747-foot lake offers few opportunities for camping, but a population of cutthroats may entice anglers to ply the lake's waters.

Several yards north of Barnes Lake's outlet is the west-bound Timico Lake Trail, a seldom-used route coming up from the obscure Meadow Lake Trailhead. Together, the Timico Lake and Highline trails lead southeast among slabs to the rock-hop crossing of the lake's sluggish outlet. A forested ascent follows, staying well above the lakeshore.

Opening up in a grassy saddle, views stretch northwest to distant alpine summits, with 0.75-mile-long Barnes Lake in the foreground. Views south from the saddle reveal the charred remains of the subalpine forest consumed in the 1988 fire.

A short distance down the trail from the saddle lies another junction; take time here to consider your options. Much of the Highline from here to North Fork Lake passes through a ghost forest of black and gray snags, with few camping opportunities, for the following 9.1 miles—a day-long journey for most backpackers.

The northeast-bound Timico Lake Trail, ascending the valley of Fall Creek to the Fremont Trail at timberline, avoids much of the burn. By following that trail, in combination with the Fremont, the distance to North Fork Lake is shortened to 7.1 miles, but the route involves a moderate ascent over 10,848-foot Hat Pass.

HIGHLINE • FREMONT

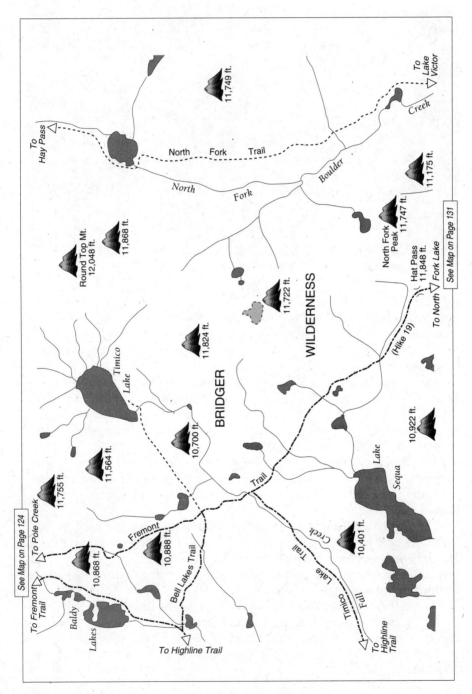

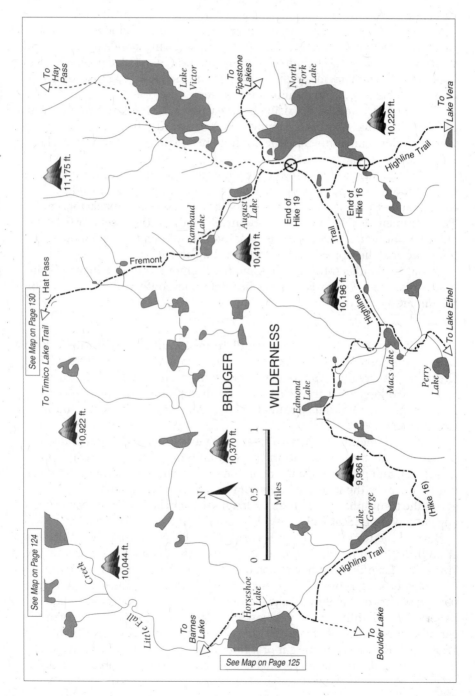

See Map on Page 130

To Timico Lake Trail

Hat Pass

To Hay Pass

11,175 ft.

Lake Victor

To Pipestone Lakes

North Fork Lake

10,222 ft.

To Lake Vera

Highline Trail

Rambaud Lake

August Lake

End of Hike 19

End of Hike 16

Highline Trail

10,410 ft.

Fremont

10,196 ft.

10,922 ft.

To Lake Ethel

BRIDGER

Edmond Lake

Macs Lake

Perry Lake

WILDERNESS

10,370 ft.

N

9,936 ft.

See Map on Page 124

10,044 ft.

Creek

Little Fall

To Barnes Lake

Horseshoe Lake

Lake George

0   0.5   1

Miles

Highline Trail

(Hike 16)

To Boulder Lake

See Map on Page 125

131

TIMICO LAKE TRAIL

From the junction south of Barnes Lake, at 9,770 feet, follow the Timico Lake Trail eastward, descending slightly into an expansive meadow. A good campsite lies south of the trail, in a grove of pines above Fall Creek.

The seldom-used trail, with occasional moderate uphill grades, stays above the northwest banks of the creek, alternately entering stands of spruce and whitebark and lodgepole pine or opening up into willow-clad meadows. Fall Creek ranges from a wide, placid stream in the meadows to a cascading roar of waters charging through miniature gorges.

The once-forested slopes rising southeast of Fall Creek were charred in the 1988 fire, but the blaze stopped its northward advance at the creek. Here travelers can appreciate the contrast between green forest and blackened snags.

Upon reaching a large, soggy meadow, the trail becomes obscure as it curves around the meadow's northeast margin. Beyond the meadow, ford the stream—an easy, shallow wade for backpackers and packstock alike. The trail then closely follows the southeast banks of the creek for 0.4 mile, entering another broad meadow. Massive 11,000- and 12,000-foot mountains encircle the upper reaches of the valley ahead.

About 2.25 miles from the Highline the Fremont Trail (see hike 19) joins in at 10,220 feet. North Fork Lake lies 4.8 miles southeast of this junction via the Fremont Trail.

The Highline Trail continues south from its junction with the Timico Lake Trail, descending 50 feet in 200 yards to a trouble-free ford of Fall Creek. Soon thereafter is a fork in the trail in the northern lobe of an expansive meadow. Follow either trail; they both require another ford of 15-foot-wide Fall Creek. The two trails rejoin after 0.75 mile, at the meadow's southern margin.

From the juncture of the two forks, a steady 200-foot descent leads past meadows and snags to the north shore of crescent-shaped Horseshoe Lake (brookies), and proceeds west. Soon the trail curves around the west shore but then leaves the lakeside and ascends among rocky knobs, staying well above the trout-inhabited waters. At length the trail leads back to the water's edge at a wide ford of Fall Creek, in a pond below the lake's outlet.

Beyond the ford the trail curves around the lake's south shore. Within a stretch of 0.3 mile, take care to avoid two right-branching spurs of the Horseshoe Lake Trail, both of which lead south to the Boulder Lake Trailhead.

A steady ascent of 200 feet ensues, following a confined draw to the narrow waters of 9,679-foot Lake George, which also supports a brook trout fishery. The Highline closely follows the lakeshore for 0.4 mile, then ascends southward, away from the shore, to a junction with the North Fork Trail along the western margin of a linear meadow. That trail also leads to the Boulder Lake Trailhead, through a landscape of rocky knobs and charred

Bearing left at that junction, follow the Highline as it winds past meadows, granite knolls, and minor draws south of Lake George. Soon the trail bends northeast and begins a gradual 200-foot ascent. Trailside snags frame views of a landscape dominated by ice-polished granite knobs and domes.

Crest a low ridge above barren Edmond Lake, then begin a 1.3-mile, 350-foot descent. The trail first skirts Edmond Lake, then a pair of tarns. Finally, it threads among knobs and snags to the junction with the Lake Ethel Trail (see hike 18), 200 yards east of Macs Lake at 9,658 feet.

The Highline turns northeast here, gently ascending a narrow valley harboring wet meadows and a trio of tarns, flanked to the north and south by prominent granite knobs. From the third tarn much of the burned forest is behind, and green spruces and lodgepoles begin to appear.

The trail crests a 9,850-foot saddle at the valley's head, then curves around the northern margins of a boggy spread to a signed junction. Here the Highline turns south, and it is signed for North Fork Lake. The northeast-bound trail, signed for Lake Victor, leads to the Fremont Trail in 0.3 mile.

The south-bound Highline crosses the soggy meadow where, in early season, hikers are likely to get their feet wet. A brief ascent among trailside knobs follows, and soon the trail joins a north-bound spur to the Fremont Trail along the west shore of North Fork Lake. A wide, usually knee-deep ford of the lake's outlet lies another 250 yards down the trail, marking the end of this segment of the Highline. To continue south, see hike 22.

Although the better camping areas at North Fork Lake lie above its east shores, there are fair sites near the ford. This large timberline lake, one of the gems of the central Wind Rivers, harbors a cutthroat trout population that promises to keep anglers busy.

BOULDER LAKE TRAILHEAD

OVERVIEW

Boulder Lake, the southernmost moraine-dammed lake in the western foothills of the Wind Rivers, is the lowest elevation trailhead covered in this book. Boulder Creek is a large stream that drains the bulk of the central Wind Rivers. Its canyon does not match the scale and depth of canyons farther north, but rather it is shallow and confined.

The Boulder Canyon Trail is a rocky, tedious route that gains minimal elevation to the forks of the canyon. Above the confluence of the Middle and North forks of Boulder Creek, trails diverge and climb steadily to the lake-dotted benchlands above. Much of the forest between the forks and North Fork Lake and Lake Vera was charred in a large forest fire in 1988.

But the Boulder Canyon Trail does offer direct access into the central reaches of the Bridger Wilderness. There, a network of trails, including the Fremont and Highline trails, can be used to devise a wide variety of rewarding loop trips that visit grand timberline landscapes.

This trail is popular with large groups and stock parties. Although the trail receives only moderate use, the area it traverses—as far as North Fork Lake and Lake Vera—is more confined than many areas in the Bridger Wilderness. Use is therefore concentrated in the few available camping areas.

The roads leading to the trailhead include good, graveled county roads and 3.3 miles of a rough, rocky, and potholed forest road that is passable to low-clearance vehicles.

Finding the trailhead: Follow U.S. Highway 191 to the small town of Boulder (store, gas, pub, and motel), 11.5 miles south of Pinedale or 88 miles north of Rock Springs. Prominently signed Wyoming Highway 353 branches east here. Follow its two-lane pavement east for 2.4 miles to the junction with Sublette County Road 23-125. Large signs pointing to Boulder Canyon Ranch and to various BLM destinations mark the turnoff.

Follow this good, wide, gravel county road north, bearing right at two signed junctions en route. After 6.8 miles, enter the Bridger National Forest, where the road deteriorates into a rough and rocky, one-lane dirt road. Proceed above the south shores of Boulder Lake, reaching the entrance to Boulder Lake Ranch after another 3.1 miles.

Bear left at this junction and follow the road as it quickly climbs to the crest of a moraine after another 0.1 mile. Here a spur road forks right to the stock users trailhead, signed for Horse Corrals and Packstring Assembly Area.

Hikers continue down the road for another 0.2 mile to their trailhead, signed for Backpack Assembly Area, located in an aspen grove north of the road alongside Boulder Creek, 10.2 miles from the pavement's end.

Travelers arriving late in the day can stay overnight in the 28-site Boulder

Lake Campground (fee area), at the road's end beyond the trailheads. Or choose one of several undeveloped sites located above the shores of Boulder Lake.

THE TRAILS
- Boulder Canyon Trail
- Lake Ethel Trail
- Fremont Trail (North Fork Lake to Pole Creek)

SUGGESTED EXTENDED TRIPS

1) Lake Vera base camp; round trip, 19 miles, 3 to 5 days.

2) Boulder Canyon Trail to Lake Vera, Highline Trail to North Fork Lake, return via Lake Ethel Trail; semi-loop trip, 17.3 miles, 3 to 4 days.

3) Boulder Canyon Trail to Lake Vera, Highline Trail to Junction Lake, Middle Fork Trail to Middle Fork Lake; round trip, 36.6 miles, 5 to 7 days.

4) Boulder Canyon Trail to Lake Vera, Highline Trail To Junction Lake, Middle Fork and Fremont trails to North Fork Lake, return via Lake Ethel Trail; semi-loop trip, 26.8 miles, 4 to 6 days.

PLACES TO AVOID IF YOU'RE LOOKING FOR SOLITUDE
- Lake Ethel
- Lake Vera

17 BOULDER CANYON TRAIL—BOULDER LAKE TO LAKE VERA

General description:	An extended trip in the central Bridger Wilderness.
Distance:	19 miles, round trip.
Difficulty:	Moderately strenuous.
Traffic:	Moderate.
Elevation gain and loss:	+2,400 feet, -100 feet.
Trailhead elevation:	7,300 feet.
Maximum elevation:	9,700 feet.
Topo maps:	USGS: Scab Creek, Horseshoe Lake, Halls Mountain; Earthwalk: Southern Wind River Range.

Key points:

    0.0   Boulder Lake Trailhead.
    0.4   Junction with Blueberry Lake Trail; stay right.
    1.1   Bridge spanning Boulder Creek.
    6.1   Junction with Lake Ethel Trail; turn right.
    9.5   Junction with Highline Trail at Lake Vera.

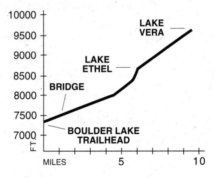

Best day hike destination: The old beaver ponds at 2.5 miles make a fine destination for a leisurely day hike. Or simply follow Boulder Creek as far as time and energy allow.

The trail: The Boulder Canyon Trail is the most direct route into the backcountry if destinations such as Fire Hole Lakes, North Fork Lake, Halls Creek, or Europe Canyon are your goals. The trail gains only 500 feet in the first 4.5 miles up Boulder Canyon, but it rises an additional 2,000 feet for the remaining distance to Lake Vera, making it one of the more rigorous trails in the Bridger Wilderness.

The final 5 miles of trail pass through forests consumed in the 1988 Fayette Fire. Campsites are scarce here and fallen snags are likely to occasionally block the trail.

Beyond Lake Vera, an expansive landscape of mostly unburned forest, flower-rich meadows, and large lakes compensate travelers for their efforts

Boulder Creek along the Boulder Canyon Trail.

on the Boulder Canyon Trail (see hikes 21 and 22).

Stock parties begin this trip from their hilltop trailhead above Boulder Lake. Backpackers begin next to the lakeshore, following the dirt road east from their trailhead 250 yards to a Boulder Canyon Trail sign, 50 yards short of a bridge over Boulder Creek. This trail leads into an aspen grove, soon reaching a maze of fallen logs spanning a sluggish stream. Beyond here the foot and stock trails merge.

Together, hikers and equestrians proceed into the broad mouth of Boulder Canyon, following a fenceline and passing outlying Boulder Lake Ranch

BOULDER CANYON

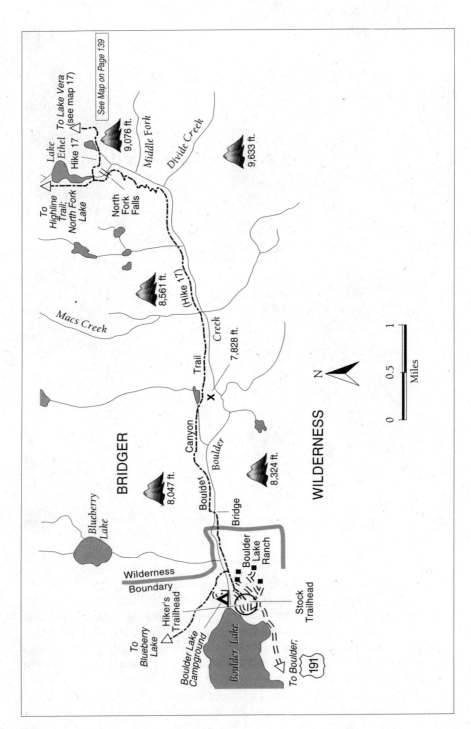

See Map on Page 139

To Lake Vera (see map 17)

Lake Ethel

Hike 17

Middle Fork

Divide Creek

9,076 ft.

9,633 ft.

To Highline Trail; North Fork Lake

North Fork Falls

(Hike 17)

8,561 ft.

Macs Creek

7,828 ft.

Creek

Trail

Canyon

Boulder

8,047 ft.

8,324 ft.

BRIDGER

WILDERNESS

Blueberry Lake

N

1

0.5

Miles

0

Bridge

Boulder Lake Ranch

Wilderness Boundary

Hiker's Trailhead

Stock Trailhead

To Blueberry Lake

Boulder Lake Campground

Boulder Lake

To Boulder; 191

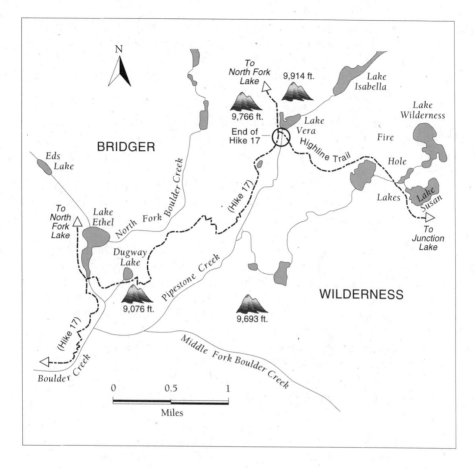

cabins. After 0.4 mile, next to a trail register, the Blueberry Lake Trail branches left (north) toward a bridge over Boulder Creek. Instead, bear right and continue up the canyon, soon joining an old, sandy roadbed and following it through open, sagebrush-studded flats scattered with lodgepole pines and aspens.

Shortly after entering the Bridger Wilderness the trail spans tumultuous Boulder Creek on a sturdy bridge, then continues up the canyon above the creek's north banks. The canyon is shallow, with granite walls and knobs rising north and partly forested slopes rising south, their rims lying only 1,000 feet above. At times the trail follows the creek closely through the depths of the canyon and shady groves of Engelmann spruce, subalpine fir, lodgepole pine, and Douglas-fir. But more often the rocky trail stays well above the creek upon sun-drenched slopes hosting a scattering of limber pine, Rocky Mountain juniper, and aspen.

Understory plants in the canyon are equally as diverse as the forest canopy. Shrubs here include common juniper, Oregon grape, thimbleberry, wild rose, buffaloberry, Rocky Mountain maple, snowberry, and bitterbrush. Wildflowers common to trailside slopes include a profusion of shortstyle onion, plus dogbane, arrowleaf balsamroot, wild strawberry, heartleaf arnica, sego lily, blue harebell, buckwheat, both red and white clover, and yellow mule's ears.

Views are restricted both up and down the canyon, and the first 4.5 miles of the trail are uneventful, save for the old beaver ponds passed at 2.5 miles. The larger of the pair is a shallow, 20-acre lake covered with pond lilies. Occasional Boulder Creek waterfalls come into view, offering an audio-visual diversion.

After 4.5 miles, at 7,800 feet, the rocky trail begins ascending in earnest, entering charred forest. Switchbacks climb beyond the confluence of the Middle and North forks of Boulder Creek and past the cascades of North Fork Falls.

The topo map shows the Boulder Canyon Trail crossing the North Fork below the falls, but on the ground it continues along the west banks of the creek to the outlet of 8,770-foot Lake Ethel, where the trail forks. The left branching trail, signed for Lake Ethel, continues generally northward toward the Highline Trail (see hikes 16 and 18). Lake Ethel, surrounded by blackened snags, offers a few poor campsites.

The Boulder Canyon Trail, signed for Lake Vera, crosses the North Fork via a footbridge, then winds eastward among low domes and charred lodgepole forest. Soon it skirts the shores of triangular Dugway Lake (no potential for camping), then negotiates moderate to steep grades leading away from the lake.

The grade briefly abates on approaching the wide, tumbling waters of the North Fork. Views through the charred forest reveal a landscape of low relief dominated by ice-scoured domes, once hidden from view by a thick mantle of pine forest. You quickly climb away from the North Fork, following switchbacks to a 9,400-foot saddle overlooking the canyon of Pipestone Creek. An ascending traverse of rocky slopes ensues, and green lodgepoles begin to appear.

About 0.7 mile from the saddle, the trail curves around a tarn and ascends slightly into the welcome shade of a spruce- and lodgepole-clad draw. It then traverses above Pipestone Creek to the outlet of Lake Vera, where it meets the Highline Trail, north-bound for North Fork Lake, and south-bound for Fire Hole Lakes (see hike 22).

Lake Vera is a pretty, V-shaped lake, surrounded by a mostly green forest of lodgepole and spruce. Benches above the lake offer fine campsites, and the lake's waters support an abundance of cutthroat trout. Granite domes encircle the 9,700-foot lake, and rocky points jutting from the shoreline offer deep-water fishing access.

18 LAKE ETHEL TRAIL—LAKE ETHEL TO MACS LAKE & THE HIGHLINE TRAIL

General description:	A backcountry connecting trail useful as part of an extended trip.
Distance:	4.4 miles.
Difficulty:	Moderate.
Traffic:	Moderate.
Elevation gain and loss:	+1,100 feet, -100 feet.
Maximum elevation:	9,680 feet.
Topo maps:	USGS: Horseshoe Lake; Earthwalk: Southern Wind River Range.

Key points:

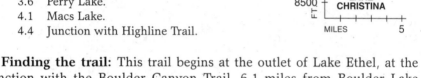

0.0   Junction with Boulder Canyon Trail; turn left (north).

1.2   Eds Lake.

2.4   Cross Macs Creek at outlet of Christina Lake.

3.6   Perry Lake.

4.1   Macs Lake.

4.4   Junction with Highline Trail.

Finding the trail: This trail begins at the outlet of Lake Ethel, at the junction with the Boulder Canyon Trail, 6.1 miles from Boulder Lake Trailhead.

The trail: This trail is perhaps the least attractive trail in the Bridger Wilderness, thanks to the 38,507-acre Fayette Fire of 1988. The entire route passes through a landscape of granite domes and a matchstick forest of charred lodgepole pine and spruce snags.

The steadily ascending trail passes five lakes en route to the Highline Trail, but campsites in the burned forest are scarce. Good fishing in the lakes along this trail is the primary attraction. This trail is most useful as the return leg of a loop trip that begins on the Boulder Canyon Trail, and uses either the Highline or Fremont trails to reach North Fork Lake (see hikes 21 and 22).

From the junction with the Boulder Canyon Trail at Lake Ethel's outlet, this trail heads north, following Lake Ethel's west shore at 8,770 feet. Fireweed blankets trailside slopes in the burned forest, its lavender summer blooms and greenery enlivening the bleak landscape.

Three campsites are found on the west shore, lying within a few feet of both the trail and the lakeshore—please avoid using them. Anglers may wish to pause long enough to sample the fishing for cutthroats. Just north of the lake you skirt the western margin of a meadow, where better campsites lie east of the trail. The trail then steadily ascends a desolate draw, gaining

LAKE ETHEL

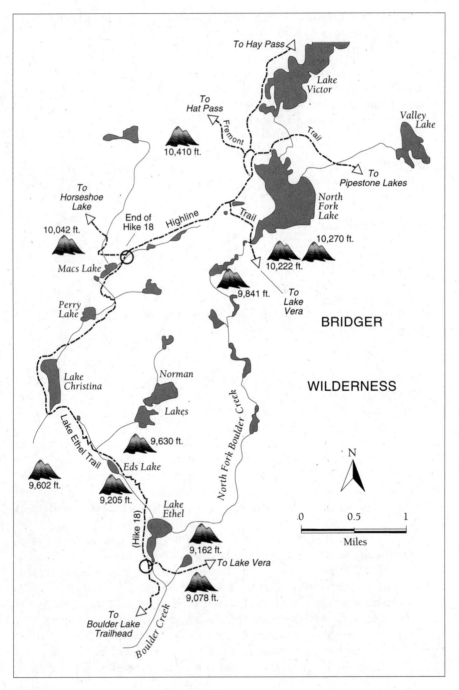

To Hay Pass

Lake Victor

To Hat Pass

Fremont

Trail

Valley Lake

10,410 ft.

To Pipestone Lakes

To Horseshoe Lake

North Fork Lake

10,042 ft.

End of Hike 18

Highline

Trail

10,270 ft.

Macs Lake

10,222 ft.

9,841 ft.

To Lake Vera

Perry Lake

BRIDGER

Lake Christina

Norman

WILDERNESS

North Fork Boulder Creek

Lakes

N

9,630 ft.

Lake Ethel Trail

9,602 ft.

Eds Lake

.0   0.5   1

9,205 ft.

Lake Ethel

Miles

(Hike 18)

9,162 ft.

To Lake Vera

9,078 ft.

To Boulder Lake Trailhead

Boulder Creek

350 feet to meadow-fringed Eds Lake, little more than a shallow pond rumored to harbor golden trout. Another ascent via switchbacks climbs the draw northwest from Eds Lake, crests a notch at 9,300 feet, then descends slightly to a traverse above the south shores of large Lake Christina at 9,255 feet.

Much the same as Lake Ethel, fishing in Lake Christina (for brookies) can be productive, and the few campsites here lie much too close to the lakeshore and should be avoided.

The trail dips down to a rock-hop of Lake Christina's outlet—Macs Creek—then climbs well above the west shore. Return to the lakeshore where the trail begins to curve around to skirt the north shore. Here are several inviting campsites shaded by green spruces and lodgepoles. These camps are wedged a few feet between the trail and lakeshore; please restrain the urge to use them.

The trail ahead leads to another rock-hop crossing of small Macs Creek above Lake Christina, then begins a steady uphill grade toward Perry Lake. The trail has been rerouted here since the publication of the Horseshoe Lake quad and now stays southeast of Macs Creek and Perry Lake. A few green trees hug the rocky and grassy shores of 9,382-foot Perry Lake, as they do the broken cliffs rising northwest of the lake.

Above Perry Lake, rock-hop Macs Creek once again, then begin a 275-foot ascent into another charred draw. Approaching the head of the draw, hop across Macs Creek for the fourth time, then begin a semi-circuit of the shallow Macs Lake basin, staying above the barren, island-studded lake.

About 200 yards east of 9,658-foot Macs Lake, after a fifth and final crossing of Macs Creek, you reach the end of the Lake Ethel Trail at the junction with the Highline Trail. To continue in either direction on the Highline, see hike 16.

19 FREMONT TRAIL—NORTH FORK LAKE TO POLE CREEK

General description:	A high-elevation segment of the Fremont Trail, useful as part of an extended trip.
Distance:	9.5 miles.
Difficulty:	Moderately strenuous.
Traffic:	Moderate.
Elevation gain and loss:	+2,050 feet, -1,600 feet.
Maximum elevation:	10,850 feet.
Topo maps:	USGS: Horseshoe Lake, Fremont Peak South; Earthwalk: Southern and Northern Wind River Range.

See Maps on Pages 124, 130 & 131

Key points:

- 0.0   Junction of Fremont Trail and southwest-bound spur to the Highline Trail above North Fork Lake.
- 0.2   Junction with Hay Pass Trail; bear left.
- 0.4   August Lake.
- 0.9   Rambaud Lake.
- 2.4   Hat Pass.
- 4.8   Ford Fall Creek at junction with west-bound Timico Lake Trail.
- 5.1   Junction with northeast-bound Timico Lake Trail; stay left.
- 5.2   Junction with Bell Lakes Trail; turn left.
- 6.1   Junction with Baldy Lakes Trail; turn right.
- 7.5   Junction with Fremont Trail; turn left (north) onto the Fremont.
- 7.9   10,850-foot pass above Bald Mountain Basin.
- 9.5   North end of Fremont Trail at Highline Trail junction, Pole Creek.

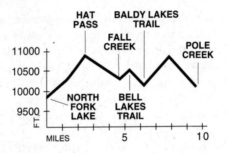

Finding the trail: The southern terminus of this segment is found northwest of North Fork Lake, 12.1 miles from Boulder Lake Trailhead. The northern terminus of the Fremont Trail lies south of the Upper Crossing of Pole Creek, 11.25 miles from Elkhart Park Trailhead.

The trail: This northernmost segment of the Fremont Trail is arguably its most scenic segment. The trail leads through the heart of the central Bridger Wilderness high country, staying at or above timberline for much of its length. Far-ranging vistas and rewarding side-trip opportunities—to Timico Lake, the lakes of Bald Mountain Basin, and Cook and Wall lakes—further add to this trail's appeal.

Long-distance travelers beginning at either Boulder Lake or Elkhart Park trailheads can use part or all of this segment, in combination with the Highline Trail, for a rewarding loop trip.

The segment begins above the northwest shore of North Fork Lake and leads north over a low rise and down to the fringes of a grassy expanse. Here the Hay Pass Trail branches right. Bear left instead, ascending the meadow northwest to August Lake, then following its west shore. Beyond the lake the trail ascends grassy slopes into a forested draw, leveling off around the shores of Rambaud Lake. The trail soon ascends another draw above this lake, flanked by rocky domes and timberline forest.

Beyond the draw begins a steady uphill assault of the alpine ridge ahead. Up and up the rocky trail winds, rising above timberline and onto the rocky

Bald Mountain Basin and peaks of the Continental Divide.

tundra, until it finally breaches the ridge at 10,848-foot Hat Pass. Here expansive vistas unfold to the northwest, stretching along the western flanks of the range, where massive peaks rise from the timberline forests of the range's western bench. Views to the south include such notable summits as Mount Bonneville and Temple Peak.

A moderate descent over slabs and tundra leads into the timberline basin below, where the trail crosses a small stream and then descends into the realm of stunted conifers. Several tarns dot the rocky landscape, and trees gain in number and stature as you descend.

At 10,200 feet, the trail crosses the infant Little Fall Creek 0.5 mile above Lake Sequa. This large lake and a pair of neighboring lakes to the west host brook trout and offer solitude in campsites sheltered by rocky knobs and timberline forest.

Beyond the creek crossing the trail angles uphill, levels off in the meadows of Fall Creek valley, and then fords Fall Creek just beyond the junction with the west-bound segment of the Timico Lake Trail (see hike 16). Here the Fremont and Timico Lake trails coalesce, and travelers then ford the broad, shin-deep waters of Fall Creek. The trail cuts north across the meadows of the wide valley floor, with fine views of the imposing mountains and tree-fringed domes that embrace this remote valley.

The trail quickly ascends a moderate grade from the valley floor, climbing through light forest for 0.3 mile to the signed Timico Lake Trail, which branches right (northeast), at 10,450 feet. Bear left here, and soon the grade abates atop a grassy bench. Follow the now-faint trail over the open flats to a four-way junction. Take time here to appreciate the fine vistas, and to consider your choices of trails to take.

Another trail leading 1 mile to 10,512-foot Timico Lake, unseen in the tundra, follows an open, straightforward course east from this junction. Timico Lake, lying in a broad, rock-bound bowl, offers good opportunities for solitude and brook trout fishing beneath the flanks of massive 12,000-foot mountains.

From the junction the Fremont Trail continues north 1.6 miles into the upper Baldy Lakes basin, where it is joined by the Baldy Lakes Trail. The Fremont Trail follows the most direct route north, staying above timberline much of the way. But it's a rigorous stretch. It climbs 350 feet to a 10,800-foot saddle, then descends 300 feet into a minor basin, and climbs 300 feet once again to another 10,800-foot saddle before finally dropping 300 feet to meet the Baldy Lakes Trail.

Many Fremont travelers opt to avoid that up-and-down route by following the Bell Lakes and Baldy Lakes trails. This detour involves less climbing, visits the scenic Baldy Lakes basin, but is 0.7 mile longer than the Fremont Trail. Travelers who choose this route should head west from the junction. The Bell Lakes Trail is faint for about 100 yards, but then becomes apparent where it enters the timberline forest and begins a steady descent. The forest cover quickly increases as the rocky trail loses elevation.

Midway down the grade the trail makes a brief climb to the wide shoulder of a ridge, then resumes the descent, soon reaching more level terrain along the shores of an inviting tarn rimmed by polished granite slabs. Just beyond the tarn is an easy rock-hop crossing of Baldy Creek. Then the trail curves northwest to meet the Baldy Lakes Trail.

The Bell Lakes Trail continues westward for 1.5 miles, descending to the Highline Trail at the Chain Lakes (see hike 16). Turning right onto Baldy Lakes Trail, immediately cross Baldy Creek, then follow a steady uphill grade through rocky terrain for 0.5 mile to 10,350-foot Baldy Lake. This lovely lake is tucked away in a secluded basin, with the broken cliffs of 11,857-foot Mount Baldy rising boldly to the north. A host of domes and alpine ridges bound the eastern reaches of the basin. A few good campsites and opportunities to land cutthroat trout may invite some travelers to stay the night here.

The often rocky, undulating trail continues past Baldy Lake and two higher tarns and then skirts a soggy meadow. It crosses Baldy Creek below a striking waterfall, where two channels of the creek plunge over a low precipice.

The trail then angles steeply uphill to the upper tier of the basin in a small meadow, where it joins the Fremont Trail at 10,480 feet. Turn left (northwest) and labor up the steep, eroded trail, passing a few tenacious clumps of krummholz spruce and whitebark pine clinging to trailside knobs. At length the trail hauls up at a rocky notch at 10,850 feet, where a grand panorama unfolds to the north. Better views can be obtained by dropping to the north for several yards across the tundra.

The lakes and rocky tundra of the broad cirque of Bald Mountain Basin spreads out below. Beyond lies the dome-studded upper valley of Pole Creek. A majestic array of lofty peaks rises north of that valley, including the stony pyramid of Mount Lester, the steel-gray spire of Mount Woodrow Wilson, snow-crowned Gannett Peak, the square-topped tower of Elephant Head, Fremont Peak, Harrower (or Ellingwood) Peak, and the sawtoothed crest of Knife Point Mountain—the southernmost 13,000-foot peak in the range, excepting Wind River Peak, lying 40 miles south.

From here you can visualize the arbitrary division between the "northern" and "central" Wind Rivers. South of Pole Creek, the peaks crowning the Continental Divide are lower and more massive than the lofty crags to the north. The most notable peak south of Pole Creek is pyramidal Angel Peak, straddling the Divide east of this vantage. This peak is prominent on the skyline from U.S. Highway 191 in downtown Pinedale. Angel Pass, the deep notch south of Angel Peak, offers class 2 access via talus and bedrock into the Alpine Lakes region east of the Divide.

The Fremont Trail, deeply eroded in places, descends steadily over the tundra into Bald Mountain Basin. Rock hop a minor stream west of an alpine tarn, then follow a winding course through the scenic basin, passing rocky knobs fringed with stunted trees and crossing expanses of meadow and ice-polished slabs.

The basin is well suited to off-trail exploration, and with a little effort travelers can have a lake or tarn to themselves. Only three lakes in the basin—Lake 10,450, Lake 10,442, and Spider Lake—host sizable populations of brook, golden, and cutthroat trout.

About 1.2 miles from the pass, cross another small stream via a rock hop at the inlet of a tarn, and quickly thereafter hop across its outlet. A descent ensues, following above the southwest banks of the stream, where the tree cover begins to increase below timberline. The trail then enters a pretty little valley, crossing slabs and meadows alongside the willow-bordered stream. Cross this stream at a wide and shallow ford. Upstream rocks offer a dry crossing for backpackers.

Continue to descend steeply into another tree-rimmed meadow, turning north across its soggy expanse. Then rise slightly to a low ridge, where trailside trees frame a fine view of 12,342-foot Mount Lester.

A short but steep and rough 150-foot descent toward audible Pole Creek ensues, down to the slab-dotted meadows along the floor of Pole Creek valley at 10,080 feet. Here the Cook Lakes Trail branches right (east), following the grassy streambanks for 0.5 mile to lower Cook Lake. Bear left here for 150 yards to the northern terminus of the Fremont Trail at the junction with the Highline Trail (see hike 16).

SCAB CREEK TRAILHEAD

OVERVIEW

The Scab Creek Trailhead, located on BLM-administered lands, lies just beneath the range's lake-filled benchlands, east of the town of Boulder. This is the second most lightly used trailhead in the southern half of the Bridger Wilderness, and the Scab Creek Trail offers the most direct access to the vast meadows of South Fork Boulder Creek, Middle Fork Lake, and Bonneville Basin. The trail is of interest not only for its scenic attributes, but because it offers a fine introduction to the flora and geography of the range's west slopes. Beginning in the western foothills, the trail ascends to the broad western bench, then follows that bench to its eastern margins, where it merges with the slopes of lofty alpine peaks. En route, travelers pass through most of the life zones on the Wind Rivers' west slope, from sagebrush, aspen groves, and stands of Douglas-fir, through the lodgepole pine belt, and into the timberline forest of Engelmann spruce and whitebark pine. Travelers who continue beyond Dream Lake to places such as Middle Fork Lake or Bonneville Basin will reach the alpine zone above timberline.

A good but obscure gravel road offers access to the trailhead, and is easily passable to any vehicle.

Finding the trailhead: Drive to the town of Boulder on U.S. Highway 191, 11.5 miles south of Pinedale or 88 miles north of Rock Springs. There Wyoming Highway 353 branches east, indicated by signs for Boulder Lake Ranch and Boulder Lake and Big Sandy wilderness entrances.

Follow the paved highway east, ignoring the turnoff to Boulder Lake after 2.4 miles. After driving 6.3 miles from Boulder, pass a cluster of tan buildings on the left, the U.S. Air Force Pinedale Seismic Research Facility.

About 200 yards east of the buildings, a gravel road branches left (north), and the turnoff is indicated only by a small, blue, Sublette County Road 23-122 sign. Follow this good gravel road as it leads east then north up the broad Spring Creek valley. Ignore a right-branching road after 0.8 mile, and bear left onto the signed Scab Creek Road about 1.4 miles from the pavement.

After 5.2 miles the road passes the Mountain Springs Ranch and begins climbing, winding over aspen-dotted moraines. About 8.5 miles from the pavement the road arrives at the small trailhead parking area, where a BLM sign indicates the Scab Creek Recreation Site. The trail begins on the north side of the parking area, behind a large destination and mileage sign.

The road continues ahead for about 300 yards, passes a stock unloading area, and ends at the small Scab Creek Campground, a pleasant site set among lodgepole pines and aspens. Here are tables, fire pits, and toilets. No water is available, so no fee is charged. There are also a few undeveloped camping areas back down the road on BLM-administered lands between Mountain Springs Ranch and the trailhead.

THE TRAILS

- Scab Creek Trail
- Rainbow Lake Trail
- Middle Fork Trail
- Fremont Trail (Dream Lake to North Fork Lake)
- Highline Trail (Dream Lake to North Fork Lake)

SUGGESTED EXTENDED TRIPS

1) Dream Lake or Raid Lake base camp; round trip, 22.6 to 27.4 miles, 4 to 7 days.

2) Rainbow Lake-Middle Fork Lake loop; semi-loop trip, 34.3 miles, 4 to 7 days.

3) Follow the Scab Creek Trail to Dream Lake, then take the Highline Trail to Junction Lake. From there follow the Middle Fork Trail to the Fremont Trail and return to the Scab Creek Trail via either the Fremont Trail or the unmaintained Crescent Lake Cutoff Trail; semi-loop trip, 26.5 miles, 3 to 5 days.

General description:	An extended trip leading to the Fremont Trail, midway between the Big Sandy and Boulder Lake trailheads.
Distance:	11.3 miles, one way.
Difficulty:	Moderate.
Traffic:	Moderate.
Elevation gain and loss:	+2450 feet, -450 feet.
Trailhead elevation:	8,200 feet.
Maximum elevation:	9,900 feet.
Topo maps:	USGS: Scab Creek, Raid Lake; Earthwalk: Southern Wind River Range.

Key points:

0.0	Scab Creek Trailhead.
2.1	Boundary Lake.
6.2	Junction with south-bound Lowline Trail at Little Divide Lake; stay left.
7.2	Lightning Lakes.
9.1	Junction of Scab Creek and Dream Lake trails; bear left.
9.4	Ford South Fork Boulder Creek.
9.6	Junction with unsigned, north-bound trail to Crescent, Bobs, and Sandpoint lakes; bear right.
10.5	Junction with Highline Trail at the outlet of Dream Lake; proceed straight ahead along west shore of Dream Lake.
11.3	Junction with Fremont Trail.

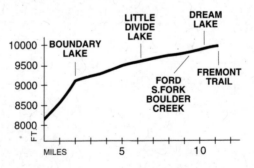

Best day hike destination: Strong hikers and anglers will find the 12.4-mile round trip to Little Divide Lake to be a rewarding day-long journey.

The trail: The South Fork Boulder Creek is born on the broken flanks of 12,585-foot Mount Bonneville. It gathers its waters in the alpine lakes of Bonneville Basin, then briefly tumbles through a narrow band of timberline forest before spreading out into the broad lakes dotting an incomparable 5 square miles of high meadows.

The Scab Creek Trail offers the quickest and easiest means to access the vast meadows and lakes of the South Fork Boulder Creek and the Mount Bonneville environs. A network of trails offers opportunities for extended trips, and adventurous backpackers will enjoy the numerous high cirque basins, cross-country routes, and non-technical routes to many of the high peaks near the South Fork's headwaters. Also, more than a dozen productive fishing lakes lie within a 2-mile radius of Dream Lake, and most are accessible via trail.

The only drawback to the meadows of the South Fork is the possibility of encountering bands of domestic sheep in summer. Before leaving for the trailhead, inquire at the Forest Service office in Pinedale to determine if sheep will be in your area of travel.

From the trailhead, only the western ramparts of the Wind Rivers' broad, mid-elevation bench are visible, forming an undulating rim clad in lodgepole pine, aspen groves, and sagebrush. From the foot of the range, slopes rise abruptly to the relatively gentle terrain of the bench. The trail follows suit, climbing steeply from the trail register and mileage sign at the trailhead. Shortly it meets a stock trail coming up from the horse unloading area. Together, hikers and equestrians follow switchbacks across an open slope of sagebrush and bitterbrush. Soon the grade slackens and contours north through an open forest of Douglas-fir, limber pine, and aspen.

Openings between the trees afford fine views west across the broad upper Green River basin to the distant Wyoming Range. The trail switchbacks again and then enters a narrow draw where it levels off in lodgepole pine forest. Pass the remains of an old cabin and then a sign proclaiming passage into the BLM's Scab Creek Primitive Area.

Beyond the sign the trail begins a steady ascent via switchbacks, leading toward the head of a steep draw. Trailside slopes are littered with granite slabs and boulders, and a scattered forest of lodgepole, aspen, and subalpine fir offers occasional shade. The 1,050-foot ascent from the trailhead ends next to the diminutive, beaver-dammed pond of Boundary Lake near the western rim of the bench. A short ascent above and east of the lake leads past the signed boundary of the Bridger Wilderness.

The following 3.3 miles of trail pass through a typical mid-elevation Bridger Wilderness landscape. Granite domes and knobs, forests of lodgepole and subalpine fir, small meadows, numerous pothole tarns (the Toboggan Lakes), and no high country views characterize this segment of the trail.

The trail, with minor ups and downs, follows a pleasant but circuitous course through the Toboggan Lakes basin, passing within view of seven of the shallow lakes—the only source of water until reaching Little Divide Lake at 6.2 miles.

After passing the last of the Toboggan Lakes, climb briefly through forest that now includes Engelmann spruce. Then drop down a minor draw to a narrow, willow-clad meadow draining Scab Creek, and follow its north bank

SCAB CREEK

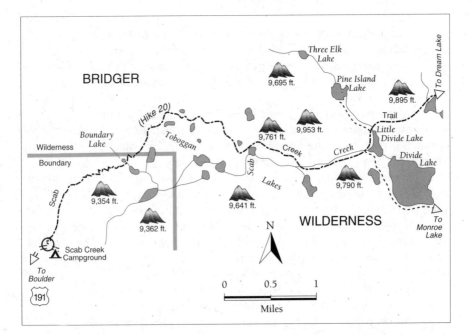

upstream. Rock-hop to the creek's south bank, and continue an east-bound ascent along the forested margins of the meadow to a low saddle overlooking Little Divide Lake.

Here a diversion ditch emanates from Divide Lake, supplementing the headwaters of Scab Creek. Jump across the ditch, splash through a soggy meadow, and then descend to an unsigned junction among the willows on the shore of Little Divide Lake at 9,623 feet. The right-branching trail—the Lowline—leads southeast past good camping areas above Little Divide Lake's west shore to huge Divide Lake, and beyond to numerous mid-elevation lakes that are visited primarily by outfitters. Both Divide Lakes host cutthroat, brook, and rainbow trout.

Little Divide Lake lies in a pleasant setting, surrounded by lodgepole and whitebark pine forest and boulder-dotted meadows. The trail follows the lakeshore northward, soon reaching an easy rock-hop crossing of the lake's small outlet stream. Immediately before the crossing a faint path branches left (northwest), climbing at first, then descending the small valley of Divide Creek to Pine Island Lake in 0.3 mile, and Three Elk Lake 0.6 mile beyond. Both lakes offer secluded camping areas and fishing for rainbow and cutthroat trout.

After crossing the lake's outlet the trail ascends moderately, gaining 100

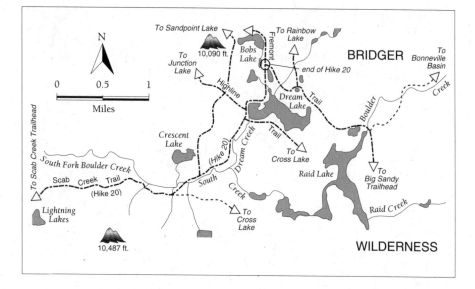

feet of elevation in 0.3 mile, while winding eastward among meadows, boulders, and a forest of spruce and whitebark pine. Surmounting a low, grass- and tree-fringed saddle at 9,750 feet, enjoy your first glimpse of the Wind River high country, including Raid Peak, Mount Bonneville, and Pronghorn Peak.

The trail then descends gently to the north shore of lower Lightning Lake, where views stretch northward across the meadow beyond the lake to the broad, massive peaks in the middle reaches of the range, notched by the prominent gaps of Hay and Europe passes.

The next 1.75 miles are an undulating traverse leading through timber- line forest, and from beneath the shady canopy there are few inspiring views. At length the trail emerges from the forest above the South Fork Boulder Creek, and a memorable panorama unfolds.

The vast rolling meadows of the South Fork spread out to the east, and above that spread rises an impressive array of broad, lofty summits, with the serrated profile of Mount Bonneville forming the centerpiece.

The trail dips down to cross a minor stream, then climbs slightly into spruce forest, soon descending into the meadows above the willow-fringed South Fork. Here a sign marks a fork in the trail. The east-bound fork, labeled Scab Creek Trail on the topo map, follows the southwest margin of the meadows to Cross Lake. To reach Dream Lake, take the left fork (Dream Lake Trail).

Just ahead the trail reaches the banks of the wide South Fork Boulder Creek, where hikers will be forced to wade through its modest current across one or more of the creek's three channels. The creek is seldom more than shin-deep, and in late summer hikers may be able to rock hop-across.

With every step along the creek's north banks, grand views of alpine

Upper Pipestone Lake and Mount Victor.

Dream Lake.

peaks are enjoyed from the trail. About 0.2 mile beyond the ford a well-worn trail forks left, north-bound, climbing a low rocky slope and leading past Crescent Lake in 0.25 mile, and ending on the Fremont Trail 2.3 miles ahead, at Sandpoint Lake.

Bearing right, the trail winds gently up the open valley of first the South Fork, then Dream Creek, through boulder-dotted meadows and a scattering of stunted lodgepoles. At the outlet of 9,850-foot Dream Lake is a signed junction. Here the obscure Highline Trail branches right, bound for Raid and Cross lakes, and left toward Junction Lake (see hike 22).

Dream Lake, as its name suggests, is one of the gems of the Wind Rivers. Rolling grassy hills embrace the lake's sprawling waters, and only a scattering of stunted conifers hug the lake's outlet, forming a narrow band above the south shore. A broad panorama of bold alpine peaks fills the sky beyond the lake, from Mount Geikie in the southeast to distant Mount Baldy in the northwest. The lake is a productive cutthroat and brook trout fishery, but camping areas in the grassy hills around the lake are exposed and austere.

The trail proceeds northwest from the junction with the Highline, following the shore of the western arm of the lake. The trail is well-defined at first, but after leaving the lakeshore it fades into obscurity as the route climbs grassy slopes above the lake, heading northeast. Maps show a trail here, but as with many Wind River trails, it doesn't exist on the ground.

To reach the Fremont Trail plot a visual course using either Dream Creek's small canyon northeast of the lake or the summit of Pronghorn Peak as a landmark. Follow either of these "handrails" to hit the Fremont Trail north of Dream Lake. To follow the Fremont Trail north, see hike 21. To go south on the Fremont, see hike 25.

General description:	A backcountry segment of the Fremont Trail, useful as part of an extended trip.
Distance:	7.6 miles.
Difficulty:	Moderate.
Traffic:	Moderate.
Elevation gain and loss:	+880 feet, -960 feet.
Maximum elevation:	10,291 feet.
Topo maps:	USGS: Raid Lake, Halls Mountain, Horseshoe Lake; Earthwalk: Southern Wind River Range.

Key points:

0.0	Junction of Dream Lake and Fremont trails; turn north.
0.9	Junction with Crescent Lake Trail.
1.4	Ford Middle Fork Boulder Creek.
1.6	Junction with lower segment of Middle Fork Trail.
2.9	Ford Halls Creek.
4.9	Junction with Lake Isabella Trail; stay right.
5.5	Junction with Europe Canyon Trail; bear left.
7.2	Ford North Fork Boulder Creek at inlet of North Fork Lake.
7.6	Junction with southwest-bound spur trail leading to Highline Trail.

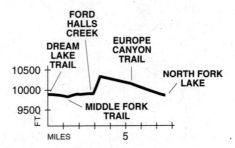

Finding the trail: This segment of the Fremont Trail begins at the signed junction 0.8 mile north of Dream Lake's outlet (11.3 miles from Scab Creek Trailhead) and ends above the northwest shore of North Fork Lake, 12.1 miles from Boulder Lake Trailhead.

The trail: This pleasant, attractive segment of the Fremont Trail traces a northwest-trending fault zone as it undulates over the Wind Rivers' western benchland just below timberline. The route passes half a dozen lakes, with many more lying a short distance off the trail, and offers access via spur trails to remote alpine valleys and lake basins lying beneath the lofty peaks of the Continental Divide.

FREMONT • HIGHLINE

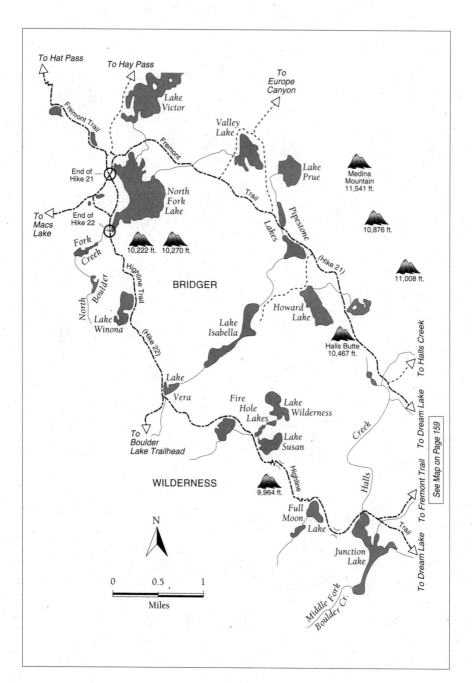

To Hat Pass

To Hay Pass

To Europe Canyon

Fremont Trail

Lake Victor

Valley Lake

Fremont

Lake Prue

Medina Mountain 11,541 ft.

End of Hike 21

North Fork Lake

Trail

Lakes

Pipestone

10,876 ft.

To Macs Lake

End of Hike 22

Fork Creek

10,222 ft.   10,270 ft.

(Hike 21)

11,008 ft.

North Boulder

Highline Trail

BRIDGER

Howard Lake

Lake Winona

Lake Isabella

Halls Butte 10,467 ft.

To Halls Creek

(Hike 22)

Lake Vera

Fire Hole Lakes

Lake Wilderness

Creek

To Dream Lake

See Map on Page 159

To Boulder Lake Trailhead

Lake Susan

WILDERNESS

9,964 ft.

Highline

Halls

To Fremont Trail

Full Moon Lake

Trail

To Dream Lake

N

Junction Lake

0   0.5   1

Miles

Middle Fork Boulder Cr.

FREMONT • HIGHLINE • MIDDLE FORK • RAINBOW LAKE

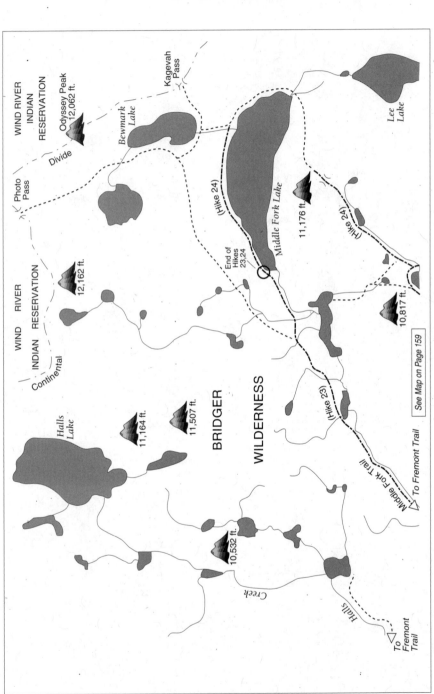

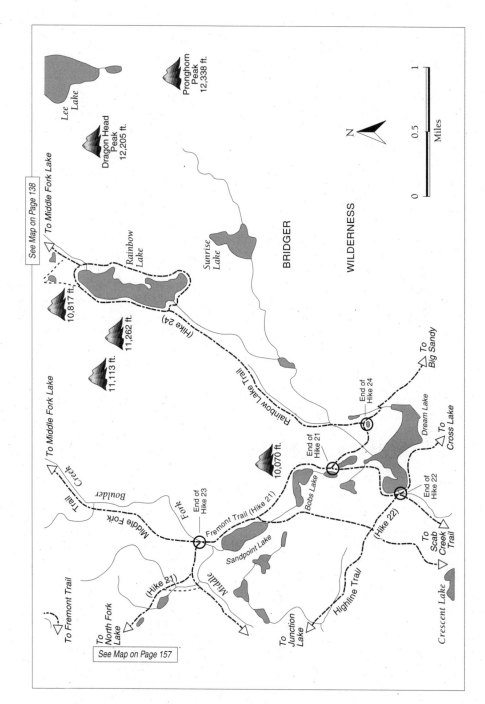

See Map on Page 138

Lee Lake

Dragon Head Peak 12,205 ft.

Pronghorn Peak 12,338 ft.

To Middle Fork Lake

Rainbow Lake

10,817 ft.

11,262 ft.

11,113 ft.

Sunrise Lake

BRIDGER

WILDERNESS

(Hike 24)

Rainbow Lake Trail

To Big Sandy

End of Hike 24

To Middle Fork Lake

Boulder Creek

Trail

Middle Fork

Fork

End of Hike 23

Fremont Trail (Hike 21)

10,070 ft.

Bobs Lake

End of Hike 21

Dream Lake

To Cross Lake

End of Hike 22

To Fremont Trail

(Hike 21)

Sandpoint Lake

To North Fork Lake

Middle

(Hike 22)

To Scab Creek Trail

Highline Trail

To Junction Lake

Crescent Lake

See Map on Page 157

N

0   0.5   1
Miles

159

From the junction with the Dream Lake Trail (signed for Scab Creek Trailhead) at the north end of a long, narrow tarn, the Fremont Trail gently descends north, soon skirting the east and north shores of Bobs Lake, which holds brook trout. Good camping areas can be found inside the forest fringe above the lake.

Beyond Bobs Lake, the vast meadows of South Fork Boulder Creek give way to a landscape dominated by granite domes and timberline stands of whitebark pine and Engelmann spruce. A brief stint of undulating trail leads from Bobs Lake to the shores of larger Sandpoint Lake (also hosting brookies). Just before reaching the lake's sandy point, the unmaintained but easy to follow Crescent Lake Trail branches left (south), crosses the creek between Bobs and Sandpoint lakes, and leads 2.3 miles, via beautiful Crescent Lake, to the Dream Lake Trail along the South Fork Boulder Creek (see hike 20).

Sandpoint Lake also offers numerous good camping areas. As the trail continues along its eastern shores, enjoy views north to Medina Mountain and Mount Victor—broad, rubbly massifs typical of the central Bridger Wilderness.

The inlet of Sandpoint Lake, the wide but shallow Middle Fork Boulder Creek, requires a ford. Immediately beyond this crossing, the Middle Fork Trail branches right, bound 3.3 miles northeast to Middle Fork Lake (see hike 23).

The Fremont Trail then quickly crests a low rise and turns west in open forest above the grassy banks of the Middle Fork below Sandpoint Lake. A trail forks left 0.2 mile beyond the ford, quickly dropping to the meadows along the creek below. This trail leads 1.2 miles to the Highline Trail at Junction Lake.

The Fremont Trail ahead bends into several meadow-covered pockets, then ascends a minor, northwest-trending valley, fringed by spruces and whitebark pines. The trail passes a fish-filled tarn, and then crests a 9,916-foot saddle above a soggy meadow shown as a tarn on the Halls Mountain quad.

From the saddle descend easily into a lovely little valley bisected by Halls Creek and encircled by tree-crested domes and low ridges. Several yards before the trail dips down to a ford of Halls Creek, the unsigned Halls Lake Trail branches right (northeast)

Despite its name, the Halls Lake Trail doesn't lead to the broad waters of 10,602-foot Halls Lake, and its tread becomes obscure after 1 mile at Lake 9,987. Yet the terrain beyond that lake beckons to wanderers and offers exceptional opportunities for solitude. It is a trailless expanse of lakes and tarns, alpine basins, granite domes, and lofty peaks.

The ford of Halls Creek, about 100 feet wide and shallow, is trouble-free after the height of the melt. Once you dry your feet, be prepared for the greatest ascent in this segment, which gains 500 feet of elevation in 1 mile.

The trail rises gradually through meadows brightened by the yellow blooms of groundsel. Then enter a timberline forest and begin climbing in earnest. Approaching the head of the ascent, the trees briefly part, affording fine views to the southeast that include the South Fork meadows and the summits of Bonneville, Pronghorn, Geikie, and distant Temple peaks.

The trail crests a rocky ridge at 10,291 feet, the apex of this segment, and continues north, descending slightly. Occasional breaks in the sparse timberline forest allow glimpses down the west slopes of the range to the upper Green River basin and to the distant Wyoming Range. Threading among granite knolls, watch for an inviting lake below to the east. The trail descends past it to its small outlet stream in a narrow meadow. The forest opposite the stream was burned in the large Fayette Fire in 1988, and it's easy to see where the fire burned itself out at timberline on the flanks of the rocky domes to the east.

The trail then winds among small meadows, scattered and in places charred timberline forest, and rocky knolls on the downhill course to the larger of the pair of Pipestone Lakes, 2 miles from the crossing of Halls Creek. Here a signed trail branches left, bound for Lake Isabella via Howard Lake. Granite domes encircle this pretty lake, its waters the foreground to a fine view north of an array of pyramidal alpine peaks.

The Fremont Trail continues along the rocky east shore of this lake, leading to a rock-hop crossing of Pipestone Creek at the outlet of the second lake in the chain. Follow the rocky trail as it ascends from the lake to a junction with the north-bound Europe Canyon Trail, located among the charred skeletons of whitebark pines.

Europe Canyon is well worth a detour. Alpine lakes, ice-polished domes, and 12,000-foot peaks make Europe Canyon one of the most starkly beautiful alpine valleys reached by a trail in the central Bridger Wilderness. To get there, leave the Fremont Trail at the junction described above and proceed north to a minor ridge. Then wind down into a broad timberline basin, passing between circular Lake Prue (cutthroat trout) and long Valley Lake (barren). Beyond those lakes, the trail ascends rocky slopes above timberline and into Europe Canyon. The tread becomes obscure at times, but the route through the rocky tundra is obvious. The route passes six more lakes on the way to 11,459-foot Europe Pass, on the crest of the range, 4.5 miles from the Fremont Trail. To continue north of the pass toward Milky Lakes, on the Wind River Indian Reservation, travelers need a tribal fishing permit (see the chapter Wilderness Regulations).

The Fremont Trail continues northwest from the Europe Canyon Trail junction, and the following stretch of undulating trail is delightful, dipping into a succession of meadow-draped bowls and crossing wildflower-decorated slopes. Look for the blooms of elephanthead, mountain bluebells, and bracted lousewort.

About 0.75 mile from the Europe Canyon Trail a large cairn in a meadow marks the beginning of an indistinct route leading northeast to Valley Lake to intersect the trail in Europe Canyon.

A gradual 400-foot descent to North Fork Lake begins here, leading down through a forest of increasingly large spruces and lodgepole and whitebark pines. Opening up into the rock-studded meadows above the lake, the grade abates and the trail crosses the meadows to a 100-foot wide, knee-deep ford of North Fork Boulder Creek.

Drying your feet on the opposite bank allows ample time to appreciate the lovely setting of this large lake at 9,754 feet. The lake spreads out along the floor of a broad, shallow bowl encircled by meadows, rocky domes, and scattered forest. North Fork Peak looms overhead to the north, and Mount Victor rises to the northeast, their flanks guarding the portal of North Fork Canyon. The burned trees on the domes south of the lake are the only evidence of the 1988 fire.

Good campsites can be found all along the east shores of the lake, south and east of the ford. The lake's deep waters support a healthy population of cutthroat trout. Abundant feed in the grassy meadows fringing the lake make this a popular destination for stock parties.

West of the ford, the trail stays above the lake's north shore. It leads 0.4 mile to an unsigned trail that branches northwest, offering a shortcut to August Lake for north-bound Fremont Trail travelers.

The "official" course of the Fremont Trail soon crosses a small stream, curves south around the lakeshore, then turns west, briefly ascending a minor draw. At the head of the draw is a four-way junction.

The south-bound trail, signed for Lake Vera, leads 0.5 mile to the Highline Trail near the ford of North Fork Lake's outlet. The west-bound trail, signed for Macs Lake, goes 0.3 mile to its junction with the Highline Trail. North-bound, the Fremont Trail is signed for Lake Victor (see hike 19).

22 HIGHLINE TRAIL—DREAM LAKE TO NORTH FORK LAKE

General description:	A backcountry segment of the Highline Trail, useful as part of an extended trip.
Distance:	8.1 miles.
Difficulty:	Moderate.
Traffic:	Light to moderate.
Elevation gain and loss:	+900 feet, -1,100 feet.
Maximum elevation:	9,960 feet.
Topo maps:	USGS: Raid Lake, Halls Mountain, Horseshoe Lake; Earthwalk: Southern Wind River Range.

See Maps on
Pages 157 & 159

Key points:
0.0 Junction at Dream Lake's outlet; turn northwest onto Highline Trail.
0.4 Junction with Crescent Lake Trail; continue straight ahead.
1.9 Ford Middle Fork Boulder Creek at Junction Lake.
2.1 Ford Halls Creek.
2.9 Full Moon Lake.
4.2 Lake Susan.
6.0 Junction with Boulder Canyon Trail at Lake Vera; turn right (north).
7.0 Lake Winona.
8.1 Ford North Fork Boulder Creek at North Fork Lake's outlet.

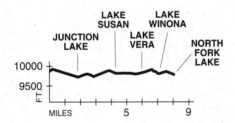

Finding the trail: This segment of the Highline begins at the signed junction next to Dream Lake's outlet, 10.5 miles from Scab Creek Trailhead, and ends at the outlet of North Fork Lake, 12.3 miles from Boulder Lake Trailhead.

The trail: This pleasant segment of the Highline Trail leads from the large grasslands of South Fork Boulder Creek to sprawling North Fork Lake— one of the largest lakes in the central Bridger Wilderness. The route traverses a rolling, lake-dotted landscape cloaked in timberline forests.

Ample opportunities for side trips to remote alpine valleys and hidden lake basins, abundant camping areas, and good fishing are among the reasons for including all or part of this Highline segment in an extended trip beginning at either the Boulder Lake or Scab Creek trailheads.

163

Lake Susan, in the Fire Hole Lakes chain, and broad Medina Mountain, from the Highline Trail.

At the outlet of Dream Lake, follow the Highline northwest; the sign points to Junction Lake. The trail through the grassy hills is obscure, but widely spaced cairns show the way. Soon the trail reaches an open bench and intersects the well-worn but unmaintained Crescent Lake Trail. Continue straight ahead, descending a northwest-trending draw. The tread becomes more evident as it descends alongside the narrow meadows in the draw, and a light forest of Engelmann spruce and lodgepole pine begins to cloak the slopes above.

At length an arm of Junction Lake comes into view below. Exit the draw and follow an undulating course among granite knobs to a ford of willow-bordered Middle Fork Boulder Creek, which is shin deep and about 20 feet wide, with a modest current. A few yards beyond the ford is a junction with the seldom-used Middle Fork Trail, signed for Halls Lake (which no trail leads to).

That trail is a scenic and convenient 1.2-mile shortcut between the Highline and Fremont trails. It joins the Fremont 0.2 mile west of the Middle Fork ford and the upper segment of the Middle Fork Trail, or 3.3 miles from Middle Fork Lake and 1 mile south of the Halls Lake Trail. Both trails offer rewarding side trips into peak-rimmed, alpine lake basins.

Beyond that junction, the Highline carves a swath through meadows enlivened by the blooms of cinquefoil, American bistort, Parry's townsendia, and whorled penstemon, staying north of Junction Lake and soon reaching a ford of Halls Creek. Be prepared to get your feet wet once again, as you must wade the wide, shin-deep stream.

Sprawling Junction Lake, at 9,576 feet, lies in a scenic open bowl, its meadow-fringed shores encircled by low, tree-crested domes. Numerous good camping areas can be found around the shoreline, and brook trout inhabit its waters.

The trail ahead curves south around the west shore of the lake and then ascends a boulder-studded draw. Vistas from this stretch of the trail reach southeast beyond the lake's broad waters to an alpine crest punctuated by the 12,000-foot summits of Dragon Head, Pronghorn, Bonneville, and Raid peaks.

At the head of the draw, the trail is funneled between a shallow tarn and a soggy meadow. Then it descends beneath the shade of spruce boughs to the forest-fringed shores of Full Moon Lake at 9,567 feet. At the north end of the lake the trail cuts across a wet meadow, and hikers are likely to emerge from the bog with wet feet.

The trail then begins the most vigorous climb in this segment, an ascent of 300 feet in the following 0.6 mile. A series of switchbacks helps to ease the grade as you tackle the west wall of the valley above the lake. Openings in the spruce and lodgepole forest offer infrequent glimpses of the peaks surrounding Mount Bonneville to the southeast.

Above the switchbacks a more gentle uphill grade through subalpine forest leads to a rocky saddle. The trail descends steadily, losing 200 feet en route to the meadows bordering the rock-studded waters of Lake Susan. This is the southernmost lake in the beautiful Fire Hole Lakes chain. All of the lakes here offer fine camping areas in timberline forest and good fishing for cutthroat trout. Medina Mountain, the broad 11,541-foot massif rising on the northeastern skyline, is composed of 3.8-billion year old rocks—some of the oldest rocks on Earth.

The trail ahead is a pleasant, gentle stretch, winding through the basin in predominantly lodgepole pine forest among ice-polished domes and slabs. Skirt the north shore of Lake 9,584, then wind westward, eventually descending to the log footbridge at the outlet of Lake Vera. Immediately beyond the footbridge, the Boulder Canyon Trail comes up from Boulder Lake Trailhead (see hike 17).

Bear right, staying on the Highline, and begin following Lake Vera's west shore. Here the trail enters forests consumed in the 1988 Fayette Fire; much of the remainder of this segment passes through the burn.

The trail undulates through a landscape of snag-studded granite domes beyond Lake Vera, eventually descending to the shores of 9,688-foot Lake Winona, where anglers will find a population of cutthroats. Above Winona the rocky trail rises 150 feet, then winds northward beneath the bedrock of Dome 10,222. It then descends to the wide ford of North Fork Boulder Creek at the outlet of North Fork Lake, and the end of this segment.

Fair campsites can be found on either side of the ford. To continue on either the Highline or Fremont trails, see hikes 16, 19, and 21.

23 MIDDLE FORK TRAIL—SANDPOINT LAKE TO MIDDLE FORK LAKE

General description:	A short backcountry spur trail useful as part of an extended trip.
Distance:	3.4 miles, one way.
Difficulty:	Moderately easy.
Traffic:	Light.
Elevation gain:	450 feet.
Maximum elevation:	10,252 feet.
Topo maps:	USGS: Halls Mountain, Roberts Mountain; Earthwalk: Southern Wind River Range.

See Maps on Pages 158 & 159

Key points:

0.0 Junction with Fremont Trail.
2.0 West end of Lake 10,048.
2.8 Signed junction with obscure northeast-bound trail to Bewmark Lake; continue following obvious trail to the east.
3.4 West end of Middle Fork Lake.

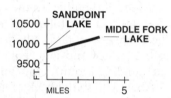

Finding the trail: This trail begins at an unsigned junction with the Fremont Trail, a few yards northwest of the ford of Middle Fork Boulder Creek, just upstream from the inlet of Sandpoint Lake.

The trail: This spur trail to Middle Fork Lake is used most frequently by backpackers as part of a backcountry circuit originating at Dream Lake and ascending past Rainbow Lake or Bonneville Basin to the upper Middle Fork basin. Others use this trail to reach Middle Fork Lake and establish a base camp. From here numerous remote lake basins can be explored or peaks climbed; routes range from technical ascents to class 2 walkups.

Middle Fork Lake and the two lakes below it are all productive brook trout fisheries. The high lakes both north and south of Middle Fork Lake offer outstanding alpine scenery but are barren of fish.

Sheep may be encountered at any time along this trail during summer, and they are sometimes found grazing the steep grassy slopes around Middle Fork Lake. Contact the Forest Service office in Pinedale for information regarding the location of sheep in the backcountry.

From the junction with the Fremont Trail at 9,840 feet, the trail to Middle Fork Lake briefly follows the meadow's edge along the Middle Fork Boulder Creek, then begins a gentle to moderate ascent away from the creek and into a subalpine forest of Engelmann spruce, and lodgepole and whitebark pine.

Views from the outset reveal only a scattering of tree-crested domes up the canyon, with no intimation of the bold crags that lie beyond.

The first mile of trail stays west of the Middle Fork, winding among a few tarns, open meadows, and a steadily thinning timberline forest. Views soon begin to open up in the meadow clearings, revealing an array of massive alpine summits embracing the remote Halls Lake cirque. The highest and most prominent of those peaks is 12,475-foot Halls Mountain, notable for its splintered crest and fluted walls.

After the 1-mile point, the trail follows the northwest margin of the willow-fringed meadows bisected by the Middle Fork, a large, noisy stream coursing over its boulder-strewn bed. The trail ahead rises gently through the meadows, soon reaching a spreading basin littered with glacial erratics and surrounded by domes of ice-polished bedrock, next to Lake 10,048.

The grass-fringed lake foregrounds dramatic views of some of the lofty summits that encircle the Middle Fork basin, including 12,062-foot Odyssey Peak in the northeast. The notch south of Odyssey is Kagevah Pass, above which rises 12,127-foot Kagevah Peak. Farther south along the crest of the range are the pinnacles that form the summit of 12,166-foot Bailey Peak. To the southeast, the exceedingly steep northwest flanks of Dragon Head Peak punctuate the skyline.

The trail soon leaves that inviting basin and ascends moderately, gaining 150 feet of elevation to the level terrain of a broad bench next to a pair of tarns. About 250 yards beyond the tarns, an old sign points to Middle Fork and Sandpoint lakes, and to Halls Lake. Although there has never been a trail to massive Halls Lake, adventurous travelers can easily plot a route to that remote lake with the aid of the Halls Mountain quad.

The topo map shows a trail from this "junction" that leads northeast over the undulating bench to Bewmark Lake and Photo and Kagevah passes. That trail is obscure and receives very little use, but the route along the bench is obvious and leads to Bewmark Lake in less than 2 miles. Travelers ascending to either Photo or Kagevah passes should not cross the Continental Divide into the Wind River Indian Reservation without a Tribal Fishing Permit in their possession.

From the bench, the trail descends briefly to traverse slopes above Lake 10,100, lying on the valley floor below, 0.25 mile away. Soon the trail inclines moderately, passing through a typical timberline landscape of stunted conifers, boulders, grass, and willows, and staying north of the Middle Fork.

At length it reaches the narrow outlet end of 1.5-mile-long Middle Fork Lake. The Continental Divide, which here forms the crest of the Wind Rivers, rises abruptly via broken cliffs from the east shore of the lake to Kagevah Peak. Grand views of Mount Bonneville and the upper Middle Fork basin, encircled by towering walls and spires, open up from midway around the lake's north shore.

For a lake of Middle Fork's size, and with its miles of shoreline, it is surprising that there are few possible camping areas here. Slopes clad in grasses and willows rise steadily from the lake's shores. Near the lake's outlet, though, a tarn-dotted bench to the north offers suitable camping areas among stunted timberline trees.

To continue around Middle Fork Lake, and to circle back to the Fremont Trail via Rainbow Lake, see hike 24.

24 RAINBOW LAKE TRAIL—DREAM LAKE TO RAINBOW & MIDDLE FORK LAKES

General description:	A backcountry spur trail useful as part of an extended trip.
Distance:	6.4 miles, one way.
Difficulty:	Moderate.
Traffic:	Light.
Elevation gain and loss:	+900 feet, -550 feet.
Maximum elevation:	10,800 feet.
Topo maps:	USGS: Raid Lake, Halls Mountain, Roberts Mountain; Earthwalk: Southern Wind River Range.

See Maps on Pages 158 & 159

Key points:

0.0   Junction with Fremont Trail.
1.9   Junction at Rainbow Lake's outlet; hikers stay left, stock users bear right.
3.9   10,800-foot pass above Middle Fork Lake.
4.7   Inlet of Middle Fork Lake.
6.4   Outlet of Middle Fork Lake.

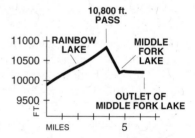

Finding the trail: The signed trail to Rainbow Lake begins next to a tarn on the Fremont Trail, 0.25 mile east of the Dream Creek ford above Dream Lake and 1 mile northwest of the South Fork Boulder Creek ford above Raid Lake.

The trail: This scenic route, part cross-country, ascends to beautiful Rainbow Lake at timberline, crosses an alpine divide, then descends into the upper Middle Fork basin above immense Middle Fork Lake, one of the largest backcountry lakes in the Bridger Wilderness.

Experienced backpackers can cross the Middle Fork divide at one of two obvious passes and return to the Fremont Trail at Raid Lake via Bonneville Basin. Others, either on foot or horseback, can follow the shores of Middle Fork Lake to its west end, where the trail begins the descent to Sandpoint Lake and the Fremont Trail. Whether you choose the Middle Fork Lake environs as a backcountry base camp, or use this trail as part of a high country circuit, this trip will be a memorable and rewarding excursion.

The trail to Rainbow Lake, marked by an obscure sign, begins just north of a pair of tarns at 9,920 feet. The trail heads generally north up a shallow draw, passing two more tarns en route to a crossing of Dream Creek, an easy rock hop for hikers.

Beyond the crossing, the trail follows a grassy, willow-bordered tributary of Dream Creek northeast on a moderate grade. The trailside slopes that embrace this lovely valley are clothed with a scattering of stunted spruce and whitebark pine. Enjoy exciting views of the soaring western flanks of Ambush, Raid, Pronghorn, and Dragon Head peaks, and the bold towers of Mount Bonneville looming on the southeastern skyline.

The trail arrives at the southwestern shore of Rainbow Lake at 10,369 feet, where two trails diverge. The slightly longer trail, at 1.3 miles, follows the southwest and east shores of the lake to the inlet stream, and is most often used by stock parties. The 1-mile trail around the west shore is a more direct route to the lake's inlet, but that route is more obscure than the longer one, and there are more boulders en route.

Rainbow Lake is a scenic gem, nearly 1 mile in length. It lies in a shallow bowl just below timberline, its shores fringed with meadows and boulders. Soaring alpine peaks background the lake in three directions. But there are few suitable camping areas near the lake. As the name suggests, Rainbow Lake is a productive rainbow trout fishery.

Travelers following the west shore will pass a generally north-trending draw near the head of the lake. The topo map shows a trail ascending that draw, and another trail ascending the draw beyond the lake. In fact, only traces of a path can be found. If the outlet area of Middle Fork Lake is your goal, follow either draw through a tarn-dotted saddle and then down to Lake 10,100 (see hike 23) and to the trail in the Middle Fork. Avoid a boulder field by staying west of it in the spruce forest.

Both lakeshore trails converge at Rainbow Lake's inlet, and the trail then follows the northwest bank of the small stream in a narrow timberline valley. The broad, boulder-covered northwest slopes of Dragon Head Peak loom overhead to the southeast, and peakbaggers can visualize a variety of non-technical routes to the summit.

The gradual ascent levels off alongside Tarn 10,575. From its grassy and rocky shore look to the skyline ahead for the pass, less than 0.5 mile away. The grade inclines more steeply to gain the broad pass, ascending 300 feet in 0.4 mile. Only a few stunted spruces and whitebarks cling to existence here, and just above this windswept pass the trees are reduced to a ground-hugging cushion of krummholz.

Proceed 250 yards through the pass to its rim above the yawning valley of the upper Middle Fork basin, and follow the now poor trail as it descends east. The trail is soon lost on the rocky slopes, so pick your way carefully down the steep rocky and grassy slopes. Descend 450 feet in 0.75 mile to the valley floor, south of the inlet of Middle Fork Lake.

The final part of the descent reveals views into the head of the Middle Fork basin—one of the classic views in the range. Embracing the basin is an

Nylon Peak and Mount Bonneville, seen from the alpine basin above Middle Fork Lake, are among the most spectacular peaks in the central Wind Rivers.

array of steel-gray peaks and exceedingly steep mountain walls. These peaks aren't as high as those in the northern reaches of the range; not one summit exceeds 13,000 feet. But what these peaks lack in height is compensated for by their stark profiles.

To the southeast, the smooth, massive walls and hornlike summit of 12,392-foot Nylon Peak pierce the sky. The splintered crest of 12,585-foot Mount Bonneville rises boldly to the south, and the fluted eastern walls of Dragon Head and Pronghorn peaks rise 2,000 feet above and bound the west side of the basin. These peaks will remain in view for much of the remaining distance around the shores of Middle Fork Lake.

Only a scattering of small conifers dot the meadows above Middle Fork Lake, meadows that stretch southward up to Lee Lake and the alpine boulder fields beyond. Two prominent passes above the basin's headwall offer cross-country routes to Bonneville Basin—for hikers with ample off-trail experience.

Enormous, curving Middle Fork Lake is an awe-inspiring expanse of alpine water. It is so large, you won't see the opposite end until you've traveled midway around it. The northeast shore of the lake is trailless until you reach the cascading outlet stream emanating from Bewmark Lake.

From the lake's inlet make your way around the northeast shore through a tangle of willow thickets and a maze of sheep trails. Try to visually plot a course that stays high above the lake and avoids most of the willows.

Proceeding from the outlet stream plunging down the basin wall from Bewmark Lake there are fewer willows, more grass, and a trail (of sorts) along the lake's north shore.

A short but steep scramble to Bewmark Lake, gaining 550 feet in 0.3 mile, follows the east side of Bewmark's outlet.

The path continues over rocky knolls, through meadows, and past more frequent groves of stunted trees to the outlet of Middle Fork Lake. Here the grand backdrop of the Middle Fork basin fades from view, and the beautiful valley and granite domes of the lower Middle Fork appear to the southwest. To continue down to the Fremont Trail, see hike 23.

BIG SANDY OPENING TRAILHEAD

OVERVIEW

The Big Sandy Trailhead is the most remote and isolated trailhead in the Wind Rivers, lying some 25 miles from the nearest paved road. Its remoteness notwithstanding, Big Sandy attracts a disproportionate number of visitors and bears the distinction of being the second most heavily used Bridger Wilderness trailhead.

The trailhead's setting is unlike any other on the west slope of the range. The trailhead and campground rest at the northern edge of the expansive grasslands of Big Sandy Opening at 9,080 feet, deep in the interior of the Wind Rivers' west slope benchland. Rocky alpine summits jut skyward above the trailhead, and access to some of the most spectacular peak-rimmed lake basins in the range is gained in a matter of hours, rather than the usual two or more trail-days typical of a trip in the Bridger Wilderness.

The Big Sandy Trailhead offers access to a greater variety of trails and backcountry destinations than any other trailhead in the range. Because the majority of Big Sandy visitors follow the trails to Big Sandy Lake and the Cirque of the Towers, other trails, such as the Fremont, Hailey Pass, and numerous spur trails and informal routes offer opportunities for solitude and a rewarding variety of extended backcountry trips.

Four gravel roads leading from various directions converge 10 miles south of Big Sandy. Those remaining 10 miles are unquestionably the roughest, rockiest, and poorest major trailhead access road in the range. Whether you're driving to the trailhead from Lander, Boulder, or Farson, be sure to top off your gas tank before leaving those outposts of civilization.

Travelers arriving late in the day will find numerous undeveloped camping areas located off the road, between the national forest boundary near Dutch Joe Guard Station and the trailhead. The 12-site Big Sandy Campground is located at the trailhead and offers tables, fire pits, and toilets, but no potable water (no fee).

Finding the trailhead: Route 1: Probably the most popular route to the trailhead follows Wyoming Highway 353 east from the town of Boulder. Find Boulder by driving 11.5 miles south of Pinedale, or 88 miles north of Rock Springs, via U.S. Highway 191. Follow this narrow, two-lane highway southeast from Boulder for 18 miles to the end of the pavement, after which the road becomes wide and sandy, often with rough washboard stretches.

About 0.7 mile south of the pavement's end, at **Junction 1,** a dirt road branches right, leading back to US 191 (see Route 2). Bear left at that junction, and then bear right after another 2.9 miles (a left fork leads to the Muddy Feedground, where elk herds are fed hay during snowy winters).

The road ahead crosses a vast, empty, high desert landscape, beyond the view of the Wind Rivers' high peaks. After driving 27.4 miles from Boulder, just beyond a crossing of Big Sandy River, you reach **Junction 2**. The road straight ahead, County Road 118, leads to Farson and Wyoming Highway 28 (see Route 3), but bear left (east) instead; the sign points to Big Sandy. This road becomes increasingly rough and rocky as it ascends moraines, and the high southern peaks of the range finally come into view.

Bear right after another 4.6 miles, where a ranch road forks left. You'll reach another prominently signed junction (**Junction 3**), 32 miles from Boulder. The road straight ahead (see Route 4) leads to South Pass and WY 28.

Turn left here onto the Big Sandy Road; the sign points to various Big Sandy destinations. The remaining distance to the trailhead has steep grades, is rough, rocky, and narrow, and receives minimal maintenance.

Pass the turnoff to Dutch Joe Guard Station 4.4 miles from Junction 3. After you reach the spreading meadows of Big Sandy Opening, avoid the turnoff to Temple Creek Summer Homes and bear right at 10 miles, where the signed left fork branches off toward Mud Lake and Big Sandy Lodge. Follow the right fork another 0.75 mile to the large trailhead parking area and campground.

The unloading and parking area for stock parties lies west of the road, 200 yards south of the trailhead.

Route 2: Drivers approaching from points west and south can follow Sublette County Roads 23-113 and 23-139 to reach **Junction 1** above.

This turnoff from US 191 is 14.7 miles south of Boulder and 3.6 miles south of the US 191/Wyoming Highway 351 junction; or 33 miles north of Farson and 73 miles north of Rock Springs. The turnoff is signed for Bridger Wilderness, Big Sandy Entrance.

This east-bound county road has a wide sandy bed, and it leads 7.4 miles to the junction with CR 23-139, upon which you turn right, reaching **Junction 1** after another 3.4 miles. Here turn right onto CR 23-118 and follow the directions for **Route 1** above.

Route 3: Drivers approaching from the south will find a long but good sand and gravel road leading from Farson to **Junction 2.**

Find the turnoff from WY 28, 4.5 miles east of the junction with US 191 in Farson. This road, Farson 4th East Road, is signed for Bridger Wilderness, Big Sandy Entrance.

Follow the road north, passing alfalfa fields at first, and avoid a left-branching road after 1.9 miles and another, signed for Eden Reservoir, after 5.1 miles. The road dips and climbs over the vast high desert landscape for 32.2 miles to **Junction 2,** where you turn right and follow **Route 1** to the trailhead.

The only confusing junction lies about 18 miles from WY 28. The right fork bears signs pointing to Big Sandy, and it leads 7 miles to the Lander Cutoff Road (see **Route 4**), at a point 6 miles east of **Junction 3**. The left fork at this junction, County Road 23-118, is the better of the two roads, and it leads past Midland Ranch (for which it is signed) en route to **Junction 2.**

Route 4: To reach Big Sandy from the direction of Lander, follow WY 28 to the Lander Cutoff Road, signed for Bridger Wilderness, Big Sandy Entrance, and for Sweetwater Gap Ranch. The turnoff is 44 miles from Lander, 10.2 miles west of the turnoff to the ghost town of South Pass City, and 0.7 mile west of a rest area and a bridge over the Sweetwater River.

Follow this good, wide county road 15 miles to the signed junction with the Sweetwater Road (see Trailhead 8), and stay left. Continue straight ahead for another 10 miles to **Junction 3,** where you turn right (north), and follow **Route 1** to the trailhead.

THE TRAILS

- Fremont Trail (to Dream Lake)
- Big Sandy Trail
- Jackass Pass Trail
- Shadow Lake Trail
- Pyramid Lake Trail
- Hailey Pass-Bears Ears-Washakie trails

SUGGESTED EXTENDED TRIPS

1) Big Sandy Lake base camp; round trip, 10 miles, 3 to 5 days.

2) Cirque of the Towers base camp, round trip, 16 to 19.4 miles, 4 to 6 days.

3) Shadow Lake base camp; round trip, 21.6 miles, 4 to 6 days.

4) Dream Lake or Raid Lake base camp; round trip, 31 to 35.8 miles, 5 to 7 days.

5) Pyramid Lake base camp; round trip, 24.4 miles, 5 to 7 days.

6) Hailey Pass-Washakie Pass loop; 33.5 miles, 5 to 8 days.

PLACES TO AVOID IF YOU'RE LOOKING FOR SOLITUDE

- Big Sandy, Clear, Deep, and Black Joe lakes
- Cirque of the Towers
- Pyramid Lake
- Shadow Lake

25 FREMONT TRAIL—BIG SANDY OPENING TO DREAM LAKE

General description:	An extended trip along the southernmost segment of the Highline, or Fremont, Trail.
Distance:	17.1 miles, one way.
Difficulty:	Moderate.
Traffic:	Heavy to Meeks Lake Trail junction, moderate to Dream Lake.
Elevation gain and loss:	+2,500 feet, -1,600 feet.
Trailhead elevation:	9,080 feet.
Maximum elevation:	10,560 feet.
Topo Maps:	USGS: Big Sandy Opening, Mount Bonneville, Raid Lake; Earthwalk: Southern Wind River Range.

Key points:

0.0 Big Sandy Trailhead.
0.6 Junction of Big Sandy and Meeks Lake trails; bear left toward Meeks Lake.
1.4 Junction with V Lake Trail; stay left.
1.5 Junction with Fremont Trail; turn right.
3.6 Enter Fish Creek Park.
4.9 Junction with Donald Lake Trail; bear left.
5.1 Dads Lake.
6.3 Marms Lake.
6.8 Junction with Hailey Pass Trail; stay left.
8.8 Ford East Fork River.
10.3 Surmount 10,560-foot pass.
11.9 Junction with trail to Cross Lake; bear right.
12.9 Ford Sheep Creek.
15.5 Ford South Fork Boulder Creek above Raid Lake.
16.5 Junction with north-bound trail to Rainbow Lake.
16.7 Ford Dream Creek above Dream Lake.
17.1 Junction of Fremont Trail and signed but obscure trail to Scab Creek; end of segment.

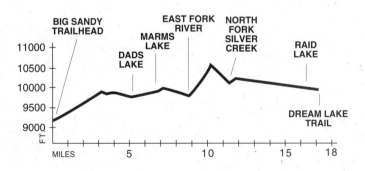

FREMONT • BIG SANDY • JACKASS PASS
• BIG SANDY TO SHADOW & PYRAMID LAKES
• HAILEY PASS-WASHAKIE PASS LOOP

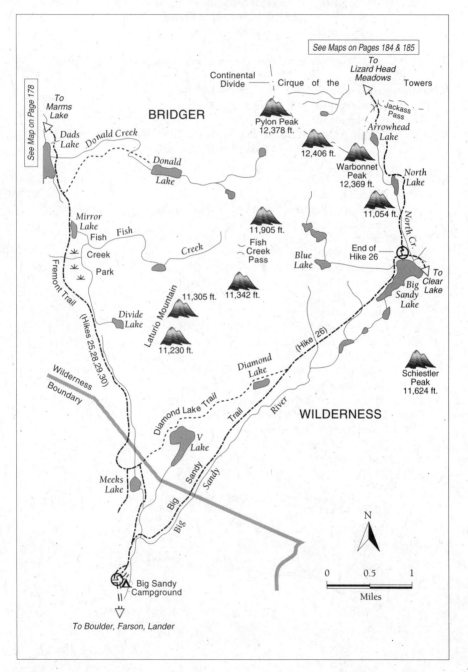

See Maps on Pages 184 & 185

To Lizard Head Meadows

Towers

Continental Divide

Cirque of the

See Map on Page 178

To Marms Lake

BRIDGER

Dads Lake

Donald Creek

Donald Lake

Pylon Peak 12,378 ft.

Jackass Pass

Arrowhead Lake

12,406 ft.

Warbonnet Peak 12,369 ft.

North Lake

Mirror Lake

Fish Creek

Fish Creek

11,905 ft.

11,054 ft.

North Cr.

Fish Creek Park

Fish Creek Pass

Blue Lake

End of Hike 26

To Clear Lake

Fremont Trail

Laturio Mountain

11,305 ft.

11,342 ft.

Big Sandy Lake

Divide Lake

11,230 ft.

(Hikes 25,28,29,30)

Diamond Lake

(Hike 26)

Schiestler Peak 11,624 ft.

Wilderness Boundary

Diamond Lake Trail

Trail

River

WILDERNESS

V Lake

Meeks Lake

Big Sandy

Big Sandy

Big

N

Big Sandy Campground

0   0.5   1

Miles

To Boulder, Farson, Lander

Best day hike destination: Meeks Lake, at 1.2 miles, features brook trout fishing in a forested setting. V Lake, 2 miles from the trailhead, also lies in forest and boasts a population of rainbow trout. Dads Lake, 5.1 miles from the trailhead, makes a fine all-day trip and offers fishing for brook and cutthroat trout in a scenic subalpine setting surrounded by ice-polished granite domes.

The trail: The Fremont Trail, from Big Sandy Opening to North Fork Lake in the Boulder Creek drainage, shown as the "Old Highline" on some maps, is the preferred trail of Highline travelers. In fact, the "official" Highline Trail in this area is often obscure and difficult to follow.

The Fremont Trail stays closer to timberline and the high peaks of the range, and it offers access to a variety of spur trails, informal trails, and cross-country routes into the alpine high country beneath the crest of the range.

This segment of the Fremont, or Highline, Trail, is also one of the most scenic, second only to the segments between Pole Creek and Summit Lake (see hike 11). Vistas are panoramic, encompassing scores of lofty summits from the Temple peaks to the west flanks of the Cirque of the Towers, and also peaks surrounding the crest as far north as Mount Lester.

If you enjoy traveling through broad meadows, this trail traverses the most expansive grasslands in the Wind Rivers. From the alpine pass above East Fork River to Dream Lake, a distance of 6.5 miles, this trail passes through vast meadows beneath towering crags, and it passes numerous lakes, both large and small.

The lakes that sprawl across the meadows of South Fork Boulder Creek—Cross, Raid, and Dream—are convenient places to establish a base camp from which to explore high lake basins, to fish, or to pioneer non-technical routes to such nearby prominences as Mount Geikie and Ambush, Raid, Pronghorn, and Dragon Head peaks.

The trail begins at the north end of the campground and trailhead parking lot and heads north through lodgepole pine forest, quickly reaching the banks of Big Sandy River. After 0.3 mile it opens up into a dry meadow with a trail register and information sign. Shortly thereafter, along the banks of the river, is a signed junction.

The right fork is the most heavily used trail, leading to Big Sandy Lake and the Cirque of the Towers (see hikes 26 and 27). But bear left instead; the sign points to Meeks Lake. Climb easily upon an open hillside below an old burn, where young lodgepoles are pioneering the slopes among gray snags. The trail follows the sluggish outlet stream from Meeks Lake; hop across it then proceed nearly on the level through shady lodgepole forest and pass above the east shore of 9,303-foot Meeks Lake. Numerous side trails lead to its shores for those who want to fish this shallow lake (for brookies).

The trail proceeds northwest and emerges into the meadow above the lake, where it meets the northeast-bound Diamond Lake Trail, heading for V Lake and Big Sandy Lake. Continue on the signed Meeks Lake Trail and

FREMONT

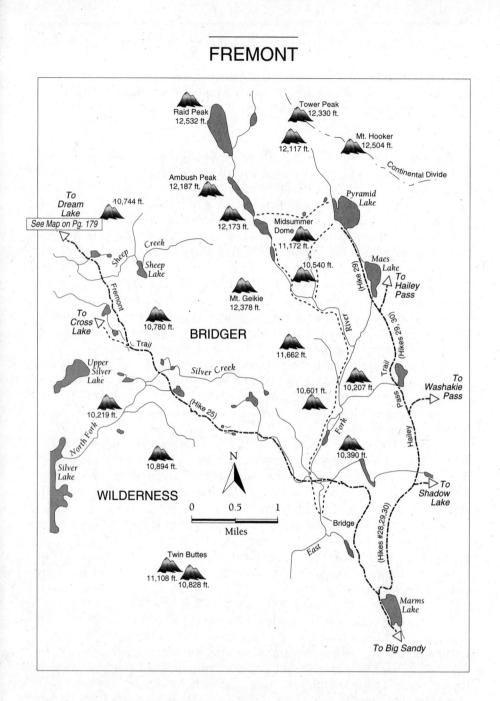

curve west heading across the meadow and hopping across Meeks Lake's inlet stream. The open expanse of the meadow affords fine views to the steely gray ramparts of 11,305-foot Laturio Mountain to the east.

A brief climb above the meadow's western margin leads to the junction with the signed Fremont Trail. Turn right (west) and follow the Fremont

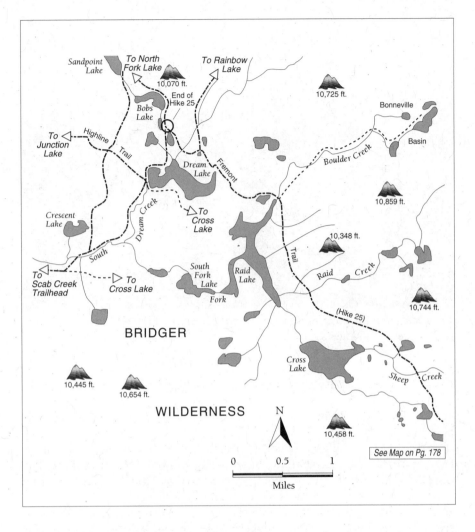

To North Fork Lake
Sandpoint Lake
To Rainbow Lake
10,070 ft.
End of Hike 25
Bobs Lake
10,725 ft.
Bonneville
To Junction Lake
Highline Trail
Dream Lake
Basin
Boulder Creek
Fremont
10,859 ft.
Crescent Lake
To Cross Lake
Dream Creek
10,348 ft.
Trail
To Scab Creek Trailhead
South
South Fork Lake
Raid Lake
Raid Creek
To Cross Lake
Fork
10,744 ft.
BRIDGER
(Hike 25)
10,445 ft.
10,654 ft.
Cross Lake
Sheep Creek
WILDERNESS
N
10,458 ft.
See Map on Pg. 178
0   0.5   1
Miles

Trail as it inclines moderately into an aspen stand and across the Bridger Wilderness boundary. The grade ahead, alleviated by some minor switchbacks, varies from gentle to moderate and soon enters lodgepole forest. Higher upslope Engelmann spruce dominates the forest.

Trailside trees inhibit views along this stretch, but occasional vignettes of high peaks to the east, most notably Laturio Mountain and Temple Peak, help to pass the time. At length the trail skirts a sloping, boulder-dotted meadow, enlivened by the blooms of cinquefoil, American bistort, and one-flower daisy. At the meadow's head the trail tops out on a broad, grassy flat, and from here a grand view unfolds to the north. Mounts Geikie, Bonneville, Tower, and Hooker rise to the distant horizon, embracing the alpine cirque at the head of the East Fork River. Divide Lake, lying only 0.25 mile east of this high point, offers good camping areas and fishing for brook trout.

The trail then dips to skirt the southwest margin of forest-rimmed Fish

View east from the pass above East Fork River on the Fremont Trail. Spires of the Cirque of the Towers lie at right.

Creek Park and an easy rock-hop crossing of Fish Creek. Topo maps show two trails heading west from Fish Creek Park and leading to Francis Lake and the East Fork River, but the routes are obscure and difficult to follow here in the meadows.

Ascend the grassy slopes north of Fish Creek to meadow- and forest-fringed Mirror Lake, a shallow lake hosting rainbows and brookies. The trail follows above the west shore, where the grasslands are decorated by the blooms of lupine, groundsel, cinquefoil, one-flower daisy, and yarrow. The trail tops a barely perceptible rise beyond Mirror Lake and then descends a meadowed draw toward the irregular shores of island-studded Dads Lake, at 9,741 feet. About 0.3 mile beyond Mirror Lake, the trail to Donald Lake (1.3 miles) forks right, ascending forested slopes to the north.

The undulating Fremont Trail wanders above the east shores of Dads Lake, hosting a population of brook and cutthroat trout. Low ice-polished domes rise west of the lake, and good camping areas can be found around its irregular west shores. Midway around the lake is wide but shallow Donald Creek, an easy rock-hop crossing.

The trail soon climbs north away from Dads Lake, dips into the meadow above, and crosses the shallow, sand-bottomed inlet stream. Soon it enter a narrow draw alongside the small stream, and ascends its rocky confines. A careful study of the Big Sandy Opening and Mount Bonneville quads reveals that this draw is part of a northwest-trending series of draws and minor saddles extending from near Meeks Lake in the southeast to the head of East Fork River in the northwest. This is a fault zone, where fractured

180

bedrock has been exfoliated by the erosive action of glaciers and running water, facilitating a relatively easy course for the trail. The streamside grade soon ends alongside Marms Lake at 9,878 feet, a brook trout fishery with limited potential for camping.

The trail leads along the boulder- and meadow-fringed west shore, among spruce and whitebark pine, to a signed junction just beyond the lake. The right-forking Hailey Pass Trail leads to Shadow Lake, Washakie Creek, and Washakie and Hailey passes (see hikes 28, 29, and 30). But stay left on the Fremont Trail, ascending gently through a forest-rimmed subalpine meadow, topping out in a small but lovely basin dotted by shallow tarns. At the north end of the basin the trail begins a mild descent toward Washakie Creek, a wide, slow-moving stream meandering in the meadows below. From here the vista that spreads out from the north to the southeast is grand, the last good view of these lofty summits on your north-bound trip. From Tower Peak to Mount Hooker, Pyramid Peak, Dike Mountain, Bernard Peak, and two northern horns on the west side of the Cirque of the Towers—Overhanging Tower and Shark's Nose—the panorama is one of the classic vistas in the southern Bridger Wilderness.

The trail soon becomes rocky as it descends moderately into a forest of increasingly large spruces and whitebarks. But it soon reaches the meadow floor of the East Fork River, a beautiful subalpine valley. American bistort, cinquefoil, dandelion, groundsel, and one-flower daisy, color the grasslands in shades of white, yellow, and lavender.

A major ford of the East Fork River lies ahead. When the water is low, you can rock-hop Washakie Creek or wade across to reach the banks of the river. The waters here are at least knee-deep, but with a modest current. Travelers on foot who wish to avoid this ford can follow the east bank of the river downstream for 0.4 mile. There a sturdy steel sheep bridge spans a narrow gorge. From the bridge hikers must then double back along the west bank to find the trail.

West of the ford, begin a steady ascent, at first upon grassy slopes, gaining 800 feet in 1.2 miles. The uphill grind is made more pleasant by only occasional moderate grades and stretches of meadows and an open timberline forest that allow good views of the East Fork valley and the peaks beyond. The trail follows a small stream for much of the way to the pass above.

Approaching the pass, the trees rapidly thin out, becoming stunted and restricted to growing on nearby hummocks and rocky outcrops. The final climb leads to a vast alpine meadow at 10,560 feet, stretching for 2 miles from the foot of Mount Geikie to the rocky knobs of Twin Buttes. The views of the peaks surrounding the East Fork River, particularly of the western flanks of the Cirque of the Towers, now reach an appropriate crescendo.

Mount Geikie looms closely above to the north, and farther east the crest of the range stretches from Dike Mountain to the distant dome of Wind River Peak. In the heat-hazy distance to the south, broad mesas and buttes stretch to the horizon, contrasting their high desert landscape with the alpine grandeur of the Wind Rivers.

As the trail descends moderately from the high meadow it affords glimpses of several small, unnamed lakes sprawling across the broad basin of North Fork Silver Creek below. The view also stretches northwest along the wide bench that abuts the high peaks of the range, offering a view of the western flanks of the range in cross-section. Peaks as far north as Mount Lester can be seen, and on the far northwest skyline are the southeastern summits of the Gros Ventre Range.

Upon reaching the ice-scoured, meadow-covered floor of the North Fork Silver Creek basin, travelers can see its tarn-dotted expanse stretching south-west, nearly at the same level, for 2 miles. An easy rock-hop crossing of the North Fork soon follows, after which the grade climbs gently up the opposite slope, passing through meadows and timberline forest to a 10,342-foot saddle. Here the trail forks: left to Cross Lake, and right to Raid Lake.

Ahead, the view stretches across vast boulder-littered meadows below a crest of serrated peaks. About 5 miles to the northwest the meadows merge with timberline forests, and a landscape of tree-fringed rocky knobs stretches to the northwest horizon.

Taking the right fork at the junction, still on the Fremont Trail, enter the sprawling treeless basin of the South Fork Boulder Creek. The trail heads northwest above two tarns and south of massive Mount Geikie. Soon it crosses small Sheep Creek, 1 mile from the last junction. There may be logs in place to afford a dry crossing, or rock-hop the stream.

The trail ahead is faint in places as it proceeds generally west across the nearly level grasslands north of Cross Lake. Enjoy the views of vast meadows foregrounding the distant Wyoming Range on the western horizon. At length the trail curves northwest into open subalpine forest and dips to a rock-hop crossing of Raid Creek between deep pools. The trail then meanders across a corrugated landscape among boulders, scattered conifers, and meadow openings.

You won't see massive Raid Lake until you emerge from the forest and cross the South Fork Boulder Creek above the lake's northeast arm. An informal trail leading 3 miles to Bonneville Basin follows the east bank of the South Fork upstream. The crossing is 15 to 20 feet wide, but shallow.

From the South Fork, curve west, briefly climb to a tarn, follow its north shore, and continue through meadows to a gentle descent. A curious aspect of these meadows is the reversal of timberline tree habits. Below the trail spruces and whitebarks are stunted and scattered, as they would be near timberline. But above the trail there grows a narrow band of thick subalpine forest.

The descent leads down to the northeast arm of Dream Lake, but then the trail quickly ascends beyond the shore to gain a broad saddle and skirt a tarn, where it passes the unobvious junction with the trail to Rainbow Lake (see hike 24). The trail descends for 0.25 mile to a ford of Dream Creek, 20 feet wide but shallow. Dream Lake's grassy shores lie just below to the south.

Beyond the ford, climb quickly to a broad, grassy bench, reaching a sign that points to Scab Creek Trailhead, at the end of this trail segment. There are fair campsites to the south near Dream Lake's outlet, or continue north toward Bobs and Sandpoint lakes (see hike 21), where a canopy of subalpine forest offers more sheltered camping areas.

26 BIG SANDY TRAIL—BIG SANDY TRAILHEAD TO BIG SANDY LAKE

General description:	A long day hike, or extended trip to a backcountry base camp.
Distance:	5.2 miles.
Difficulty:	Moderately easy.
Traffic:	Heavy.
Elevation gain:	610 feet.
Trailhead elevation:	9,080 feet.
Maximum elevation:	9,690 feet.
Topo maps:	USGS: Big Sandy Opening, Temple Peak; Earthwalk: Southern Wind River Range.

Key points:

0.0   Big Sandy Trailhead.
0.6   Junction with Meeks Lake Trail; bear right.
3.2   Junction with Diamond Lake Trail; stay right.
4.6   West end of Big Sandy Lake.
5.2   Junction with Jackass Pass Trail.

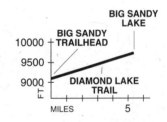

The trail: This scenic, relatively easy trail offers the quickest access of any trail into the Bridger Wilderness high country. Grades are gentle, the tread is smooth for much of the way, and views of the alpine peaks that embrace the upper Big Sandy valley are enjoyed from the start.

But the ease of backcountry access and grand scenery combine to make this trail one of the most heavily used in the Bridger Wilderness. If you're looking for solitude, avoid this trail.

Most visitors establish a base camp at Big Sandy Lake and take day trips to Black Joe, Clear, and Deep lakes, or to the Cirque of the Towers. As a result, campsites at Big Sandy Lake are numerous, and many bear the impacts of overuse.

Black bears have also discovered the Big Sandy Lake environs, and their nightly visits into campsites are routine. Two bear-resistant food storage containers have been installed at Big Sandy Lake—use them, or bear-bag

BIG SANDY • JACKASS PASS

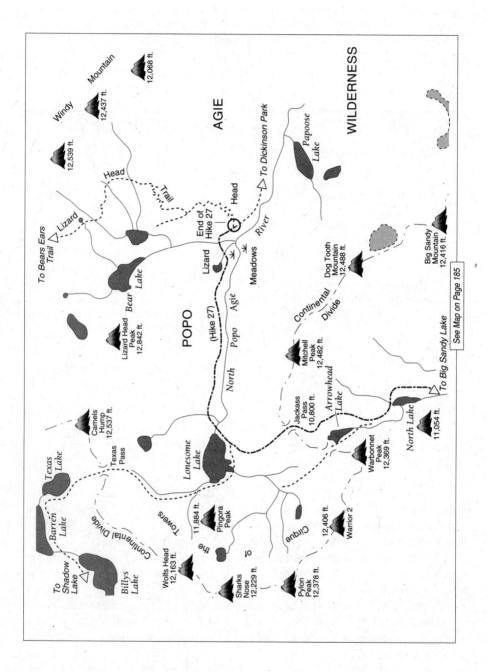

Windy Mountain 12,539 ft.

12,437 ft.

12,068 ft.

Head Trail

To Bears Ears Trail

Lizard

AGIE

Head

To Dickinson Park

Papoose Lake

WILDERNESS

End of Hike 27

Lizard

Meadows

River

Bear Lake

Lizard Head Peak 12,842 ft.

POPO

(Hike 27)

North Popo Agie

Continental Divide

Dog Tooth Mountain 12,488 ft.

Big Sandy Mountain 12,416 ft.

See Map on Page 185

Mitchell Peak 12,482 ft.

Camels Hump 12,537 ft.

Texas Pass

Jackass Pass 10,800 ft.

Arrowhead Lake

To Big Sandy Lake

Texas Lake

Lonesome Lake

Warbonnet Peak 12,369 ft.

North Lake

11,054 ft.

Barren Lake

Continental Divide

the Towers

11,884 ft.

Pingora Peak

of

Cirque

12,406 ft.

Warrior 2

To Shadow Lake

Billys Lake

Wolfs Head 12,163 ft.

Sharks Nose 12,229 ft.

Pylon Peak 12,378 ft.

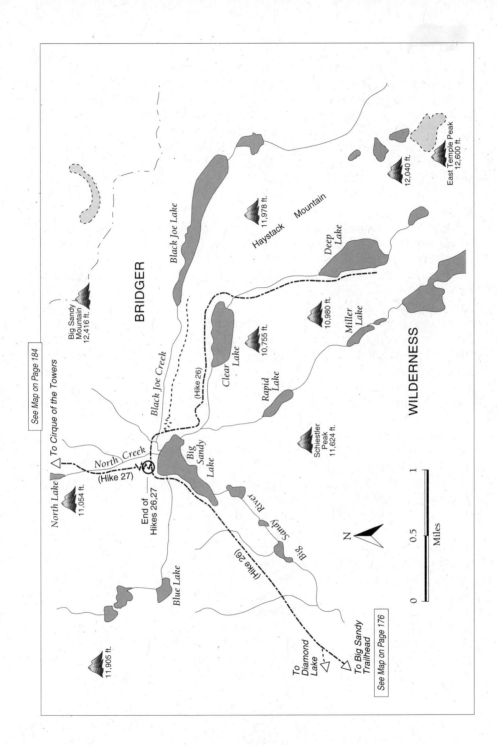

BRIDGER

WILDERNESS

See Map on Page 184

To Cirque of the Towers

Big Sandy
Mountain
12,416 ft.

Black Joe Lake

Haystack   Mountain

11,978 ft.

12,040 ft.

East Temple Peak
12,600 ft.

Deep
Lake

Black Joe Creek

(Hike 26)

Clear
Lake

10,980 ft.

Miller
Lake

10,755 ft.

Rapid
Lake

North Creek

North Lake

(Hike 27)

End of
Hikes 26,27

11,054 ft.

Big
Sandy
Lake

Schiestler
Peak
11,624 ft.

Big
Sandy
River

Blue Lake

(Hike 26)

11,905 ft.

N

0   0.5   1

Miles

To
Diamond
Lake

To Big Sandy
Trailhead

See Map on Page 176

your food supply (see the introductory section *Backcountry Travel*). Big Sandy bears know all the tricks for stealing food; store food out of reach of bears so you won't be forced to unexpectedly abandon your trip.

The trails over Jackass and Temple passes are extremely rough and rocky and are not recommended for stock parties. Consequently, the majority of Big Sandy Trail users are backpackers and climbers.

From the trailhead parking lot at Big Sandy Campground, follow the Big Sandy Trail north along the banks of Big Sandy River 0.6 mile to the junction with Meeks Lake Trail (see hike 25), and bear right. The trail follows a horseshoe bend in the river; midway around the bend rock-hop the small stream draining Meeks Lake.

The trail ahead briefly ascends a moderate grade through lodgepole pine forest—the only significant grade en route to Big Sandy Lake. Then begin the protracted, gradual ascent of Big Sandy valley.

The route alternates between shady stands of lodgepole pines and meadows adorned with the blooms of cinquefoil, yarrow, mountain dandelion, subalpine daisy, and lupine. The character of the river also varies along the way, ranging from slow meanderings over a sandy bed to boulder-choked rapids. Views open up from trailside meadows, reaching up the canyon to Warbonnet, Mitchell, Dog Tooth, Big Sandy, Schiestler, and Temple peaks.

After the junction with the Diamond Lake Trail at 9,500 feet, Engelmann spruce and whitebark pine join the ranks of the lodgepole forest, and the terrain becomes increasingly rocky.

At length, a footbridge affords a dry crossing of a minor creek. Then the trail ascends a rocky draw, crests a low rise, then ascends another draw to a minor saddle overlooking Big Sandy Lake, backdropped by the broad pyramid of 12,416-foot Big Sandy Mountain.

Descend toward the lake, soon passing a right-branching path leading to lakeside campsites and one of the two bear-resistant food storage boxes at the lake. The trail continues on around the north shore of the large, 9,690-foot lake. Don't be surprised if a succession of tents are perched upon the lightly forested bench above the trail.

This picturesque lake, fringed by an open subalpine forest, meadows, and abundant granite bedrock, lies in a broad bowl encircled by an exciting array of bold peaks. To the northeast are Mitchell, Dog Tooth, and Big Sandy; to the east the sheer walls of Haystack; to the southeast the north faces of East Temple and Temple; and to the south the rocky cone of Schiestler juts skyward from the lakeshore. Campsites here are heavily used, so expect plenty of company. The lake also sustains heavy fishing pressure, so fishing for brook and cutthroat trout may not be as productive here as in other parts of the range.

Some travelers, attempting to avoid the overused campsites at Big Sandy Lake, continue up the trail to Black Joe, Clear, and Deep lakes. Consequently, campsites at those lakes are often just as congested as they are at Big Sandy Lake.

Pass the spur trail leading to the second food box, indicated by a sign, just before the trail curves north into an expansive meadow. At the northern

Big Sandy Lake, East Temple, and Temple peaks.

of the meadow, you meet the north-bound Jackass Pass Trail (see
7), leading to the incomparable Cirque of the Towers.

The right fork leads to the aforementioned lakes, and it is frequently used by visitors on day hiking forays from Big Sandy Lake. To reach those lakes, continue following the trail, known as the Little Sandy Trail, as it curves through the meadow above Big Sandy Lake. Rock-hop North Creek, then Black Joe Creek. About 0.4 mile from the junction, above the east shore of the lake, the trail meets the Black Joe Trail, where it branches left (east). That trail rises 550 feet in 1 mile as it climbs through the timberline forest to the outlet of long and narrow Black Joe Lake, at 10,258 feet. Look for campsites near the creek below the outlet and above the south shore. The lake harbors cutthroats, and fishing from the creek can also be productive.

To reach Clear and Deep lakes, continue south through the tree-fringed meadow for 0.2 mile from the Black Joe Trail junction. There the trail turns east, skirts the northern margin of a soggy meadow, then steadily ascends an east-trending draw cloaked in a timberline forest of whitebark pine and spruce.

The trail gains 250 feet while ascending this draw, reaching scenic Clear Lake after another 0.5 mile. The trail follows the north shore of the 10,012-foot lake, where inspiring views reach eastward to the big walls of Haystack Mountain and up-canyon to the bold, 1,000-foot north face of 12,600-foot East Temple Peak.

The trail bends around Clear Lake's east shore, crosses its inlet stream, then ascends above timberline via the tundra and bedrock of an alpine valley, gaining 500 feet in 0.75 mile, to the shores of 10,502-foot Deep Lake. Haystack Mountain and East Temple Peak overshadow the lake's broad waters in this grand alpine basin.

Haystack Mountain and the Temple peaks are second only to the Cirque of the Towers as a premier rock climbing area in the Wind Rivers. Deep Lake has become increasingly popular in recent years as a climber's base camp, and backpackers in this majestic alpine basin are usually in the minority.

27 JACKASS PASS TRAIL—BIG SANDY TO CIRQUE OF THE TOWERS, LIZARD HEAD MEADOWS

General description:	An extended trip, or day hike from a Big Sandy Lake base camp.
Distance:	19.4 miles, round trip.
Difficulty:	Strenuous from Big Sandy Lake to Cirque.
Traffic:	Heavy.
Elevation gain and loss:	+2,100 feet, -1,725 feet.
Trailhead elevation:	9,080 feet.
Maximum elevation:	10,800 feet.
Topo maps:	USGS: Big Sandy Opening, Temple Peak, Lizard Head Peak; Earthwalk: Southern Wind River Range.

See Maps on
Pages 176, 184 & 185

Key points:
- 0.0 Big Sandy Trailhead.
- 0.6 Junction with Meeks Lake Trail; bear right.
- 3.2 Junction with Diamond Lake Trail; stay right.
- 5.2 Junction of Little Sandy and Jackass Pass trails; bear left.
- 6.5 North Lake.
- 6.8 Junction with climber's route to pass above Arrowhead Lake; bear right.
- 7.3 Jackass Pass.
- 8.0 Outlet of Lonesome Lake.
- 9.7 Junction with Lizard Head Trail at Lizard Head Meadows.

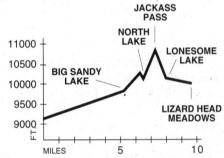

The trail: Much like Titcomb Basin in the northern Bridger Wilderness, the Cirque of the Towers is a mecca for climbers and backpackers in the southern reaches of the Wilderness. Although the Cirque is much smaller in area than Titcomb Basin, it harbors the greatest concentration of big walls and granite spires in the range. The summits here are lower than those farther north; the highest—12,842-foot Lizard Head Peak—lies nearly 1,000 feet lower than Gannett Peak.

The Cirque of the Towers is the preeminent rock climbing area in the American Rockies, and each year climbers in great numbers flock to its few campsites and its many challenging climbs. But the Cirque is not the exclusive domain of the rock climber. Backpackers, and day hikers from their Big Sandy Lake base camps, seize the opportunity to visit one of the most dramatic landscapes in the Rockies.

Travelers should expect much company between the trailhead and the Cirque. The impact of too many backpackers in the past has led to a prohibition of camping within 0.25 mile of Lonesome Lake, at the foot of Pingora Peak in the Popo Agie Wilderness.

Climbers and many backpackers camp in the alpine basin above and southwest of the lake. Although small in size, the intricate nature of the terrain in that basin affords modest privacy between campsites on ledges, among boulders, in small meadows, and next to groves of krummholz trees. Others may wish to continue east from Lonesome Lake toward Lizard Head Meadows in search of more shelter and privacy there in the timberline forest.

Be sure to protect your food supply from the black bears that frequent this area (see *Backcountry Travel*).

The rugged, rock-bound trail over Jackass Pass is impassable to stock parties, though sure-footed llamas should be able to traverse the trail. The section of the trail from North Creek to the pass involves much scrambling over boulders and across bedrock slabs. Novice hikers should avoid the trail until they gain more confidence and experience.

From the Big Sandy Trailhead, follow the Big Sandy Trail (see hikes 25 and 26) for 5.2 miles to the junction with the Jackass Pass Trail above the north shores of Big Sandy Lake and turn left (north). At once the trail begins a steep ascent, via switchbacks, beneath an open canopy of whitebark pines. The meadow-draped slopes here host a diversity of colorful wildflowers, including subalpine daisy, goldenrod, cinquefoil, mountain dandelion, American bistort, yarrow, lupine, hairy arnica, mountain bluebells, and larkspur.

Fine views unfold after the first switchback, stretching across Big Sandy Lake to the broad walls of Haystack Mountain, and to the shadowed north faces of Temple and East Temple peaks. Those bold peaks, and farther on the dome of Wind River Peak, offer splendid over-the-shoulder views along much of the trail to Jackass Pass.

Above the switchbacks, the grade abates where it enters a lovely bowl with meadows fringed by groves of Engelmann spruce and whitebark pine. A traverse of this bowl leads to a rock-hop crossing of North Creek, its channel choked with car-sized boulders.

The "trail" ahead, more of a route than an obvious path, rises steeply over ice-polished slabs and around huge boulders. This extremely rough and rocky stretch is marked by cairns where it crosses bedrock. After climbing high above North Lake, it eventually descends nearly 200 feet to the meadow fringing the lake's north shore. There are a few poor campsites at the lake, and nightly visits from hungry black bears are common.

Above North Lake the trail ascends very steeply upon slopes clothed in an increasingly stunted conifer forest. A minor basin marks timberline, where hikers can enjoy a brief respite from the grinding ascent. Here a path forged by climbers leaves the main trail, branching left.

This route ascends to the outlet of Arrowhead Lake, then traverses its western shoreline. Midway around the lake is a jumble of large boulders

Pingora Peak looms above Lonesome Lake.

Warbonnet and the Warrior peaks, Cirque of the Towers.

that must be carefully negotiated. Beyond that obstacle, tundra slopes lead up to a 10,600-foot pass on the crest of the range. On the Cirque side of that pass follow rock and tundra slopes down into the basin above Lonesome Lake.

From that obscure junction, the main trail ascends a very steep and rocky course, passing the last few persistent clumps of krummholz trees en route to a rocky knob high above Arrowhead Lake. To the north, the grassy notch of Jackass Pass foregrounds the first good views of the spires of the Cirque.

To reach Jackass Pass, though, requires a steep descent of 200 feet into the draw above Arrowhead Lake, then another very steep ascent of tundra slopes. Alpine cushion plants begin to appear in the tundra along the final ascent to the pass. Look for the yellow blooms of Gordon's ivesia, alpine cinquefoil, bracted lousewort, and alpine sunflower; the white blossoms of cushion phlox, alpine bistort, and alpine pussytoes; and the lavender flowers of sky pilot, lupine, and Parry's townsendia.

At length the trail arrives on the Continental Divide at 10,800-foot Jackass Pass. The Cirque of the Towers spreads out in a grand array of sheer granite walls and splintered spires. Here the trail enters the Popo Agie Wilderness and descends the grassy north slopes of the pass. It quickly becomes a steep and deeply eroded trench as it drops toward Lonesome Lake. Those looking to stay overnight here may wish to leave the trail about midway down this grade and head west to camping areas in the Cirque's upper basin.

The grade eases upon reaching the basin floor south of Lonesome Lake. Bear in mind that this point is within 0.25 mile of the lake, where camping is not allowed. Fishing, however, is allowed for the cutthroats that inhabit the lake's waters. The trail ahead winds among groves of large spruces and whitebarks to the lake's south shores. The trail follows the shoreline eastward, carving a swath through thickets of willow and huckleberry to the lake's outlet—the North Popo Agie River.

After snowmelt runoff subsides, it is possible to boulder-hop across this large stream. In early season, travelers must wade the river here, when its waters may be thigh deep with a modest current. The trail beyond the crossing curves northeast through a soggy, willow-clad meadow with inspiring views of the sweeping granite walls of Mitchell Peak to the south, and of the majestic amphitheater of the Cirque to the west.

A dense band of spruce and whitebark pine fringes the northern margin of the meadow, and the trail soon turns east and follows the forest's edge. Midway between Lonesome Lake and the eastern reaches of the meadow, you will pass beyond the 0.25-mile camping restriction, and you may begin searching for a campsite.

The trail continues its eastward course through the forest north of the river, descending nearly 200 feet to the low moraine that forms the notch in Lizard Head Meadow's V-shaped spread. Cross a sluggish stream draining a minor tarn, then curve through the northern reaches of the grassy expanse to a crossing of the creek draining Bear Lake. Soon thereafter, above the meadow's eastern margin at 10,000 feet, the trail meets the north-bound Lizard Head Trail.

The Lizard Head Meadows environs offers good camping areas in the timberline forest around its margins. Fine views of Dog Tooth Peak, Mitchell Peak, and the Cirque provide an inspiring backdrop. The meadows make a good base camp, and day hiking forays to nearby Bear Lake and into the Cirque can keep you busy for several days.

The Lizard Head Trail can be used as part of a long-distance, extended trip that loops back to the trailhead via Washakie or Hailey passes (see hike 30). That trail—faint, rough, and rocky in places—ascends the slopes of Windy Mountain above timberline, then winds northward through the tundra, reaching the Bears Ears Trail after 5.5 miles.

General description:	An extended trip to a timberline base camp.
Distance:	21.6 miles, round trip.
Difficulty:	Moderate.
Traffic:	Moderate.
Elevation gain and loss:	+1,550 feet, -400 feet.
Trailhead elevation:	9,080 feet.
Maximum elevation:	10,287 feet.
Topo maps:	USGS: Big Sandy Opening, Mount Bonneville, Lizard Head Peak; Earthwalk: Southern Wind River Range.

Key points:

0.0	Big Sandy Trailhead.
0.6	Junction of Meeks Lake and Big Sandy trails; bear left.
1.4	Junction with Diamond Lake Trail; bear left.
1.5	Junction with Fremont Trail; bear right.
4.1	Fish Creek Park.
4.4	Mirror Lake.
4.9	Junction with Donald Lake Trail; stay left.
5.1	Dads Lake.
6.8	Junction with Hailey Pass Trail at Marms Lake; bear right.
8.7	Junction with Shadow Lake Trail; bear right.
9.7	Ford Washakie Creek.
10.8	Shadow Lake.

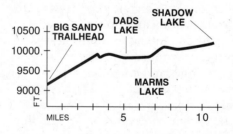

The trail: Following the Fremont Trail north from Big Sandy offers travelers the chance to escape the throngs of backpackers en route to Big Sandy Lake and the Cirque of the Towers. This trail leads over a rolling, lake-dotted landscape to the high valley of Washakie Creek, and on up to scenic Shadow Lake, resting in a timberline basin beneath the western flanks of the Cirque's spires.

This "backside" of the Cirque offers comparative solitude, and establishing a base camp here affords the opportunity to explore the peak-rimmed basin above the lake. Anglers will appreciate that Shadow, Billys, and Barren lakes all support populations of brook trout. Good camping areas can be

BIG SANDY TO SHADOW LAKE
• BIG SANDY TO PYRAMID LAKE

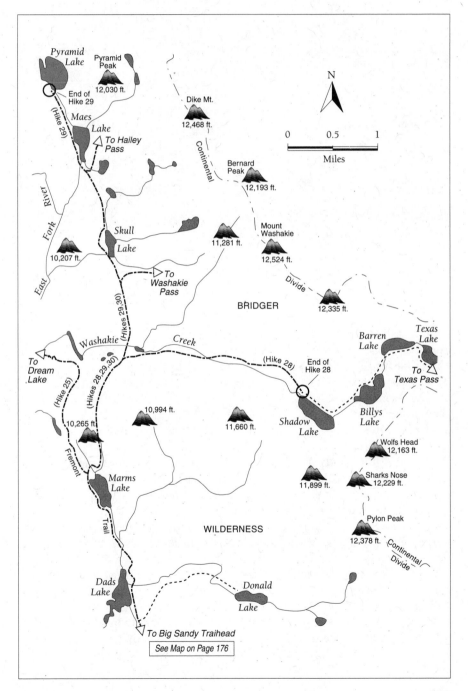

Marms Lake.

found in timberline groves of spruce and pine at both Shadow and Billys lakes.

A cross-country route of moderate difficulty, recommended for experienced backpackers only, ascends to Texas Lake at the head of the Washakie Creek basin, then rises over steep talus (and usually snow) to 11,640-foot Texas Pass on the crest of the range. Steep slopes of talus and tundra, and snow in some years, lie on the south slopes of the pass. The route leads down to the west shores of Lonesome Lake in the Cirque of the Towers, and from there the Jackass Pass Trail (see hike 27) can be used to loop back to the trailhead.

From the Big Sandy Trailhead follow the route of hike 25 north for 6.8 miles past Meeks Lake, Fish Creek Park, and Dads Lake to the junction signed for Shadow Lake above the northwest shore of Marms Lake. Bear right here onto the Hailey Pass Trail.

This trail heads northeast, curves around a knoll, then descends into the wide meadow fringing Marms Lake's north shore. Soon you bend north into a minor draw—an extension of the fault-controlled valley the trail has followed from its beginning. Grassy trailside slopes in the draw host wildflowers such as Parry's townsendia, cinquefoil, dandelion, and American bistort, and a scattering of timberline trees dot the higher slopes.

Climbing gently at first, the trail soon inclines steeply uphill to a narrow gap on the edge of the broad, rock-studded meadows that reach northward to Washakie Creek. Enjoy the splendid views that stretch north into the upper valley of the East Fork River, a valley embraced by soaring walls and one half dozen bold, 12,000-foot peaks: Geikie, Raid, Bonneville, Tower, Hooker, and Pyramid.

The trail descends into the grasslands from the gap, then curves northeast, following an undulating course. The East Fork peaks fade from view as you approach Washakie Creek, and you soon reach a junction on a bench above its grassy banks. Take the right fork, signed for Shadow Lake, and part company with north-bound travelers en route to Pyramid Lake (see hike 29), and to Hailey and Washakie passes (see hike 30).

Our trail descends eastward to the willow-bordered banks of broad, meandering Washakie Creek. Views up-canyon reach to broad peaks composed of massive granite, to towering domes, and to an exciting array of spires—the backside of the Cirque of the Towers—including Wolfs Head, Overhanging Tower, Sharks Nose, and Block Tower.

After 1 mile of pleasant travel from the previous junction, ford the shallows of Washakie Creek. Then continue eastward up the increasingly narrow valley, crossing more meadows and entering occasional timberline groves of Engelmann spruce and whitebark pine.

Eventually you reach 10,287-foot Shadow Lake, resting in a timberline bowl at the very foot of the western flanks of the Cirque's spires. Erratic boulders and meadows fringe the shoreline, and groves of stunted conifers cloak the slopes above.

Travelers will surely want to spend several days exploring this splendid basin. Good camping areas dot the conifer groves north of the lake. Billys Lake, 300 feet above and 0.5 mile away, also offers a number of camping areas, but there are fewer trees there and campsites are more austere.

29 *BIG SANDY TRAILHEAD TO PYRAMID LAKE*

General description:	An extended trip to an alpine base camp.
Distance:	24.4 miles, round trip.
Difficulty:	Moderate.
Traffic:	Moderate.
Elevation gain and loss:	+2,050 feet, -600 feet.
Trailhead elevation:	9,080 feet.
Maximum elevation:	10,570 feet.
Topo maps:	USGS: Big Sandy Opening, Mount Bonneville; Earthwalk: Southern Wind River Range.

See Map on Page 195

Key points:

0.0	Big Sandy Trailhead.
0.6	Junction of Meeks Lake and Big Sandy trails; bear left.
1.4	Junction with Diamond Lake Trail; bear left.

1.5	Junction with Fremont Trail; turn right.
4.1	Fish Creek Park.
4.4	Mirror Lake.
4.9	Junction with Donald Lake Trail; stay left.
5.1	Dads Lake.
6.8	Junction of Fremont and Hailey Pass trails; turn right.
8.7	Junction with Shadow Lake Trail; stay left.
8.8	Ford Washakie Creek.
9.7	Junction with Washakie Pass Trail; stay left.
10.0	Skull Lake.
11.1	Junction of Pyramid and Hailey Pass trails; bear left.
12.2	Pyramid Lake.

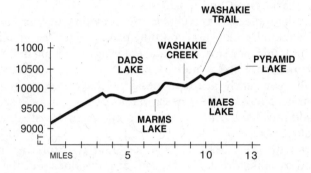

The trail: The East Fork River, one of the principal drainages of the southern Bridger Wilderness, gathers its waters in a lake-dotted basin lying in the shadow of the Continental Divide. Several 12,000-foot peaks embrace this high valley, of which 12,585-foot Mount Bonneville—a Wind River landmark—is the highest. Lying on a bench above the upper East Fork valley is a chain of three splendid lakes, and these are the goal of this memorable journey.

This trail climbs into this lofty realm via a two-day trip, though strong backpackers and stock parties can make the trip in one long day. Many good campsites can be found at Skull and Maes lakes in timberline forest. Pyramid Lake also offers good, but austere, camping in the tundra above its shores.

Anglers will find good fishing for several varieties of trout in these lakes. The lakes in the upper basin of East Fork River, accessible via cross-country routes from Pyramid Lake, harbor golden trout.

Skull, Maes, and Pyramid lakes are popular destinations. Solitude seekers may wish to continue into the East Fork, where they're likely to have a lake in the basin to themselves.

The trip begins at Big Sandy Trailhead, following the Meeks Lake and Fremont trails north (see hike 25) for 6.8 miles to Marms Lake. At this point leave the Fremont and follow the Hailey Pass Trail, signed for Shadow Lake (see hike 28), for another 1.9 miles to the junction with the Shadow Lake Trail. Bear left and descend northeast for 300 yards to a ford of Washakie

Skull Lake, with Midsummer Dome, Mount Bonneville, Tower Peak, and Mount Hooker in the background (from left to right).

Creek. There is a good stock ford here, and backpackers can either wade the creek's shin-deep waters or boulder-hop the creek just upstream from the ford.

There are good views northeast from the ford to the high, grassy notch of Washakie Pass, wedged between the dark, rubbly slopes of Bernard Peak and the ramparts of pyramidal Mount Washakie.

The trail leads north from the ford, ascending 300 feet in 0.9 mile via a minor draw, passing beneath a canopy of Engelmann spruce, whitebark pine, and subalpine fir. Here the forest floor is mantled with a green carpet of grouse whortleberry, a diminutive shrub that bears a crop of small, tart red berries that typically ripen by mid to late August.

Near the head of the draw small meadow openings appear, decorated by the blooms of American bistort and cinquefoil. The grade ends at 10,392 feet above a grassy notch at a junction with the east-bound Washakie Pass Trail (see hike 30).

Bear left here, and continue north while descending a grassy draw among scattered clumps of stunted timberline conifers. The grade soon abates on the shores of 10,282-foot Skull Lake, its waters foregrounding a grand view of the peaks encircling the upper East Fork River basin. Especially striking are the soaring east walls of Mount Geikie and Ambush and Raid peaks, to the northwest.

The lake's inlet is easily crossed via a rock hop, and the trail ahead undulates above the west shore. Brook trout inhabit the lake's waters, and travelers seeking campsites will find several to choose from above these shores.

Beyond Skull Lake, ascend another minor draw to an open, grassy saddle at 10,400 feet, then gradually descend to a signed junction a few hundred yards south of Maes Lake. Here the Hailey Pass Trail (see hike 30) branches right, but bear left instead, quickly descending to an easy crossing of Maes Lake's outlet stream. Tower Peak, the broad flanks of flat-topped Mount Hooker, and aptly named Pyramid Peak jut skyward north of the 10,343-foot lake.

The well-worn Pyramid Lake Trail follows above the west shore of Maes Lake, staying in the rocky, willow-studded meadows below a narrow ribbon of timberline forest. Rainbows and brookies lurk in the depths of the lake, as do a few heavy lake trout. The better campsites lie south of the lake atop a tree-crested moraine and near the lake's inlet stream.

A final ascent of the draw northwest of the lake leads above timberline to the broad, circular waters of Pyramid Lake at 10,570 feet. This alpine jewel lies at the very foot of a triad of lofty summits: 12,330-foot Tower Peak to the north, 12,504-foot Mount Hooker to the northeast, and 12,030-foot Pyramid Peak to the east-northeast. Good but austere campsites can be found in the boulder-dotted tundra, where scattered clumps of krummholz trees offer minimal shelter.

Many travelers will want to establish a base camp at Pyramid Lake and spend several days, perhaps exploring the East Fork basin, scaling the summits of Tower and Pyramid (via class 2 scrambles), or sampling the golden trout fishing in the lake.

Two straightforward cross-country routes to the East Fork basin begin at Pyramid Lake. One route descends a southwest-trending draw into the basin from the lake's west shore. Another route ascends the tarn-dotted draw west of the lake, staying north of ice-polished Midsummer Dome (Point 11,172), then descending rocky tundra to the basin floor.

30 HAILEY PASS-WASHAKIE PASS LOOP, FROM BIG SANDY TRAILHEAD

General description:	A long-distance, multi-day trip.
Distance:	33.5 miles.
Difficulty:	Moderately strenuous.
Traffic:	Moderate to Maes Lake, light over Hailey and Washakie passes.
Elevation gain and loss:	+5,000 feet, -4,700 feet.
Trailhead elevation:	9,080 feet.
Maximum elevation:	11,611 feet.
Topo maps:	USGS: Big Sandy Opening, Mount Bonneville, Lizard Head Peak; Earthwalk: Southern Wind River Range.

Key points:

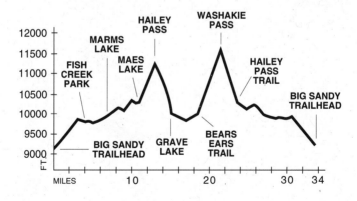

The hike: This five- to seven-day trip is one of the most rewarding and memorable trips in the Wind Rivers. The trail follows the range's western benchland in the Bridger Wilderness to timberline, then crosses the Continental Divide into the Popo Agie Wilderness, and finally circles back to the Divide via high lake basins and the valley of the South Fork Little Wind River.

HAILEY PASS-WASHAKIE PASS LOOP

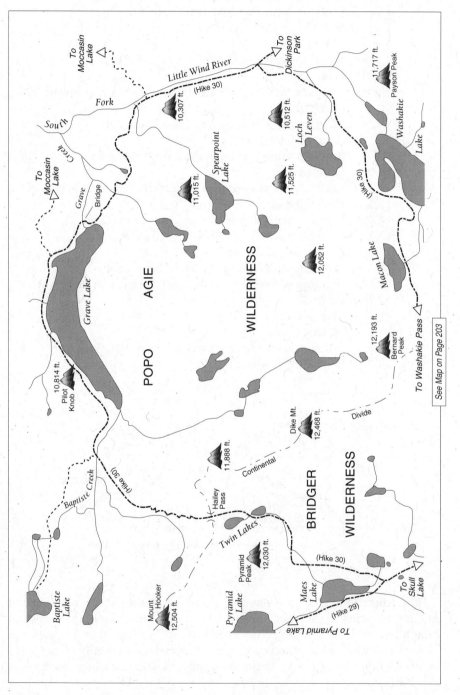

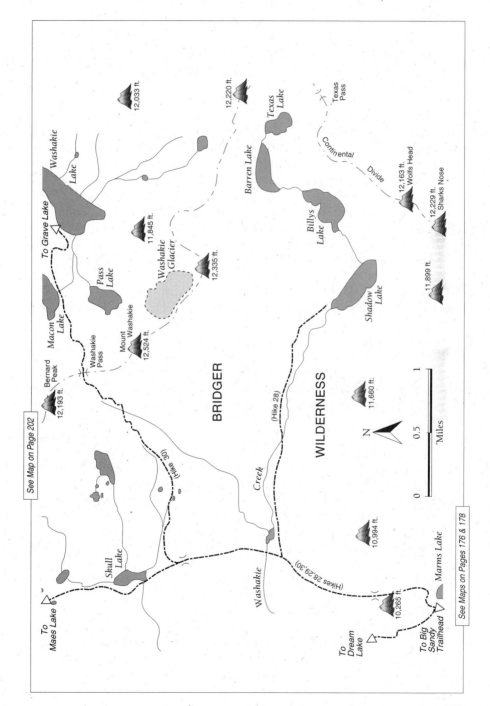

To Grave Lake

Washakie
Lake

12,033 ft.

12,220 ft.

Texas
Lake

Texas
Pass

Continental

Divide

Barren Lake

12,163 ft.
Wolfs Head

11,845 ft.

Billys
Lake

12,229 ft.
Sharks Nose

Washakie
Glacier

12,335 ft.

11,899 ft.

Pass
Lake

Macon
Lake

Mount
Washakie

Shadow
Lake

Bernard
Peak

Washakie
Pass

12,524 ft.

12,193 ft.

BRIDGER

11,660 ft.

To
Maes Lake

(Hike 30)

(Hike 28)

WILDERNESS

N

Skull
Lake

Creek

0.5   1

Miles

0

10,994 ft.

Washakie

(Hikes 28,29,30)

To
Dream
Lake

10,265 ft.

Marms Lake

To Big
Sandy
Trailhead

Although the loop part of the trip can be reached via the Bears Ears Trail from Dickinson Park (see hike 36), beginning the trip at Big Sandy involves much less climbing. It is also 5 miles shorter.

The loop can be done in either direction. But persistent snowfields on the east slopes of Washakie (pronounced WASH-a-key) Pass, lingering through summer in some years, are more safely ascended than descended. When the passes are snow-free, the trails are passable to pack and saddle stock. When snow is present, the trail is safely traversed by experienced backpackers only.

From the Big Sandy Trailhead proceed north on the Fremont Trail 6.8 miles to Marms Lake (see hike 25) and the junction with the Hailey Pass Trail. Bear right onto The Hailey Pass Trail (signed for Shadow Lake). Continue 1.9 miles to the junction with the Shadow Lake Trail in the Washakie Creek valley (see hike 28). Bear left (see hike 29), ford Washakie Creek, and ascend 1 mile to the junction with the Washakie Pass Trail.

Travelers who opt to first ascend Washakie Pass should bear right, while others should continue north (left) toward Hailey Pass. Let's go left. The trail ahead skirts Skull Lake en route to the junction above Maes Lake. Turn right here; the sign points to Hailey Pass.

The trail rises into an Engelmann spruce and whitebark pine forest, soon crossing a minor stream draining a tarn to the east. A gently ascending traverse follows, leading north through timberline forest high above Maes Lake. Inspiring views encompass the bold peaks and soaring cliffs that surround the upper valley of the East Fork River. Hop across the small stream draining Twin Lakes, then bend eastward at the southern foot of Pyramid Peak, its rocky slopes rising 1,400 feet above the trail.

After climbing above timberline, the trail crosses the stream two more times and eventually enters the Twin Lakes basin, a small, high cirque resting just below the Continental Divide. Cross the creek one final time between the two icy Twin Lakes at 11,000 feet, then briefly ascend tundra slopes to crest the Divide at 11,200-foot Hailey Pass. Vistas both north and south from the pass are somewhat restricted by intervening mountain slopes, but the view reaches north into the tundra of the Baptiste Creek valley and beyond to flat-topped 12,000-foot summits. Especially striking is Mount Hooker to the northwest. Its broad summit plateau is a dramatic contrast to its sheer, 1,000-foot east face.

North of the pass the trail enters the Popo Agie Wilderness; the trail ahead is the Bears Ears Trail. Descend the rocky headwall of a cirque north from the pass, losing 900 feet of elevation in the 1.25 miles to Baptiste Creek. The trail is ill-defined in places but the route is straightforward, dropping off the headwall and into a confined alpine valley. There may be lingering snowfields on the headwall, necessitating minor detours.

At length the trail leads beyond the confines of the alpine valley and into the tundra of the broad Baptiste Creek basin. Views from the open expanse of the basin are dramatic, dominated by the towering north face of 12,504-foot Mount Hooker—a 1,600-foot near-vertical wall of granodiorite. This

Macon and Washakie lakes, and the South Fork Little Wind River valley from Washakie Pass.

face of Hooker is the highest unbroken wall in the Wind Rivers, and its rock-climbing routes are the most challenging in the range.

Approaching the eastern reaches of Baptiste Creek's hanging valley, cross the creek and meet the left-forking Baptiste Lake Trail at 10,280 feet. This trail gains 500 feet in 1.3 miles to reach the alpine shores of Baptiste Lake. The Wind River Indian Reservation boundary lies just north of the lake's twin outlets. Travel beyond that point requires a tribal fishing permit (see the section on *Wilderness Regulations*).

From the junction descend steadily into an increasingly heavy timberline forest, losing 300 feet of elevation en route to Grave Lake. At first the trail traverses well above the lakeshore, passing beneath the 500-foot walls of Pilot Knob, a prominent dome rising above the northwest shore. Then the trail drops toward the north shore of the 1.5-mile-long, 9,964-foot lake and some of the many good camping areas in the surrounding spruce and whitebark pine forest. Cutthroat and lake trout lurk in Grave Lake's deep waters, and some travelers pack in an inflatable raft or float tube.

Cross Grave Creek midway around the lake. Soon thereafter meet the Onion Meadows Trail, branching left (north), bound for the Wind River Indian Reservation. Meanwhile, the main trail leaves the lakeshore and briefly descends to the footbridge spanning large Grave Creek below the lake's outlet. Follow the creek upstream along the opposite bank, and soon the trail is funneled between the lakeshore and a rocky dome.

Leaving Grave Lake behind, the trail leads east through a shady subalpine forest. Cross the stream draining the hidden waters of Lake 10,490, then begin a 200-foot ascent that leads past a tarn and crests a ridge at 10,200 feet.

A steady descent ensues, dropping below the 10,000-foot contour to the banks of the South Fork Little Wind River. There the Moss Lake Trail branches left (east, bound for Moss and Gaylord lakes, and ultimately to the Moccasin Lake Trailhead on the Reservation). From this point on, the trail is uphill all the way to Washakie Pass.

Follow the South Fork upstream along the valley floor, soon entering a rock-studded, tree-fringed meadow. From this spread views open up to reveal the bold cirque headwalls that bound the upper end of the valley. Payson Peak, the north summit of a monolithic massif variously known as Buffalo Head and Big Chief Mountain, rises from the center of the valley.

At the southern reaches of the meadow the trail meets the junction of the Bears Ears and Washakie trails. Here the Bears Ears Trail forks left, crosses the wide South Fork (which can be a knee-deep ford), and ascends past Valentine Lake en route to the Dickinson Park Trailhead (see hike 36).

Instead, bear right onto the Washakie Trail, an ancient Indian route over the range. It begins a 400-foot ascent into the expansive Washakie Lake basin. Midway up the ascent, cross Loch Leven's outlet stream, then continue the uphill grade to the rim of the basin. Here the trail opens up into boulder-dotted meadows, above which timberline groves of stunted trees cling to the rubbly flanks of trailside moraines.

Skirt the shores of a tarn before curving around the north shore of large Washakie Lake at 10,363 feet. This lake is the logical choice for an overnight stay before tackling the steep slopes of Washakie Pass. Many fine camping areas can be found in the gentle terrain north of the lake, sheltered by groves of spruce and whitebark pine. Golden-rainbow hybrids in the lake should keep anglers busy during their stay here.

The trail ahead curves around the lakeshore, then begins a steady 400-foot ascent to the timberline bench harboring Macon Lake at 10,771 feet. As you labor up the grade watch for Pass Lake in the basin below, its waters opaque with sediments from Washakie Glacier, one of the southernmost glaciers in the range. Macon Lake, brimming with brookies, offers some of the most productive fishing in the basin.

After rock-hopping Macon Lake's outlet, the trail begins a very steep ascent of rocky tundra, gaining 800 feet of elevation over the next 0.8 mile to 11,611-foot Washakie Pass. Steep snowfields en route may force hikers to detour onto unstable talus slopes.

From the pass, the apex of this memorable circuit, travelers are rewarded with some of the best vistas this trail offers. Bernard Peak, accessible via an easy class 2 scramble northeast from the pass, and Mount Washakie to the south, a more challenging class 3 scramble via its northwest ridge, both offer far-ranging vistas encompassing a vast stretch of the range.

At the pass your gaze stretches east over the route you followed to get here—a high landscape of cliff-bound alpine plateaus, massive, rubbly peaks, and timberline lake basins. On the southeastern skyline looms the square-edged summit of Lizard Head Peak, which, at 12,842 feet, is the loftiest peak in view. To the west views reach past the valleys of Washakie Creek and East Fork River and across the range's western benchland to the sprawling upper Green River basin, bounded on the west by the Wyoming Range.

Head west from the pass, reentering the Bridger Wilderness, and descend tundra slopes into a small, confined valley. Here grow some of the fragrant and colorful blooms of the cushion plants that enliven the tundra. Look for the yellow blooms of alpine sunflower and alpine cinquefoil; the white flowers of cushion phlox, alpine bistort, and arctic-alpine daisy; and the lavender blossoms of sky pilot, moss campion, shooting star, alpine laurel, and Parry's townsendia.

The trail descends steeply, crosses a small, cold stream, then plunges into the wet meadows of a minor basin. Here the grade moderates, and the trail leads past rocky knobs cloaked with clumps of krummholz spruce and whitebark pine—the first trees since Macon Lake, 2 miles behind.

The trail continues its downhill course, winding through minor basins, and across benches, meadows, over slabs, and around erratic boulders. Stunted conifers begin to dot the landscape as the descent continues, until they form a discontinuous forest at the junction with the Hailey Pass Trail. From there, turn left (south) and proceed 9.7 miles back to Big Sandy Trailhead.

SWEETWATER TRAILHEAD

OVERVIEW

From Togwotee Pass at the northern end of the Wind Rivers to Mount Nystrom in the south, the Continental Divide forms the crest of the range. But at Mount Nystrom, the Wind River crest and the Continental Divide diverge, spreading out to the southeast and southwest, respectively. This V-shaped ridgeline embraces the headwaters of the Sweetwater River, one of the most peculiar drainage systems in the range.

The river gathers its waters from the soggy meadows at Sweetwater Gap and flows south, east of the Continental Divide, tumbling and meandering through a broad, forested valley before exiting the range. It then threads its way across Wyoming's high desert to offer its waters to the North Platte River.

The Sweetwater Trailhead lies in the upper Sweetwater valley at 8,900 feet, and it is one of the most infrequently used Bridger Wilderness trailheads. Two trails begin here. The Little Sandy Trail, obscured by deadfall following the 3,447-acre Ann Fire of 1988, is seldom-used and difficult to follow.

The Sweetwater Gap Trail also passes through part of the burn, but it is well-maintained and easy to follow. Although this trail passes through the Bridger Wilderness, it offers access to few Wilderness destinations suitable for an extended stay. The trail is most useful as a means to access the Tayo Creek region of the Popo Agie Wilderness.

This trailhead lies two valleys east of Big Sandy—reach the trailhead turnoff by following the same roads. (Refer to Big Sandy Opening Trailhead). The final 1.9 miles of the road to the trailhead is a narrow, rocky track passable only to high-clearance vehicles. Be sure to top off your gas tank before leaving the towns of Lander, Boulder, or Farson.

Finding the trailhead: Reach the trailhead by following either of the four routes described in the section on the Big Sandy Opening Trailhead. Drivers approaching from the west or south will find the turnoff to the trailhead located 10 miles east of **Junction 3**. If approaching from the east, via the Lander Cutoff Road, the turnoff is 15 miles west of the junction with Wyoming Highway 28. It is prominently signed for White Acorn Ranch, Sweetwater Ranch, Sweetwater Campground, and Sweetwater Guard Station.

Follow Sweetwater Road north. This road is rougher and narrower than the county roads, and it grows worse. After 3.4 miles, avoid a left turn leading to Block and Tackle Hill on the Continental Divide, and bear right, passing the turnoff to White Acorn Ranch after 4.5 miles.

After 5.8 miles, bear left where another road forks right to the site of Sweetwater Guard Station and the campground. After 7.2 miles, avoid the spur to Sweetwater Gap Ranch. One mile farther is a T-intersection.

An old national forest sign here points right to the campground and guard station and left to "Sweetwater Wilderness," apparently indicating the Bridger Wilderness.

Drivers of stock trailers and low-clearance vehicles are strongly advised to park near the intersection. Those with high-clearance vehicles can turn left. The unmaintained road ahead initially has a high center, and is very narrow and rocky farther on.

After 1 mile, avoid a left-forking track signed for Lowline Trail. The road ahead is extremely poor, its bed full of roots, rocks, and sawed-off stumps. The road ends in 0.9 mile, in burned-over lodgepole pine forest. The trail begins behind the trail register at the end of the road.

Travelers arriving late in the day can stay the night at the Sweetwater Campground or in one of several undeveloped camping areas located along the final 1.9 miles to the trailhead.

THE TRAILS

- Sweetwater Gap Trail

SUGGESTED EXTENDED TRIPS

1) Sweetwater Gap base camp; round trip, 12.6 miles, 3 to 5 days.

2) Tayo Park base camp; round trip, 17 miles, 4 to 5 days.

31 SWEETWATER GAP TRAIL—SWEETWATER RIVER TO TAYO PARK, MIDDLE POPO AGIE RIVER

General description:	A long day trip or an extended trip.
Distance:	17 miles, round trip.
Difficulty:	Moderate.
Traffic:	Light.
Elevation gain and loss:	+1,450 feet, -630 feet.
Trailhead elevation:	8,890 feet.
Maximum elevation:	10,327 feet.
Topo maps:	USGS: Sweetwater Needles, Sweetwater Gap; Earthwalk: Southern Wind River Range (map does not cover trailhead area).

Key points:
0.0   Sweetwater trailhead.
0.1   Junction with Little Sandy Trail to Little Sandy Lake; bear right.
1.2   Wilderness boundary.
6.3   Sweetwater Gap.
8.5   Junction with Middle Fork Trail in Tayo Park.

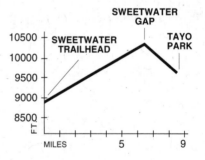

Best day hike destination: Strong day hikers will enjoy the 12.6-mile round trip to the crest of the range at Sweetwater Gap.

The trail: This scenic and seldom-traveled trail, the southernmost trail in the Bridger Wilderness, ascends the broad headwaters valley of Sweetwater River. The valley is flanked by massive, rubbly alpine ridges and ends in the meadows of Sweetwater Gap—the lowest elevation pass on the crest of the range in the Bridger Wilderness. Tayo Park, a lovely forest-fringed meadow on the Middle Popo Agie River, lies just 2 miles north of the gap, within the Popo Agie Wilderness.

Although this trail lacks the dramatic mountain scenery the Wind Rivers are noted for, it offers an uncrowded alternative route into the backcountry, and once you reach Tayo Park numerous other trails afford opportunities to reach alpine lakes and to scale lofty peaks. Both Sweetwater Gap and Tayo

SWEETWATER GAP

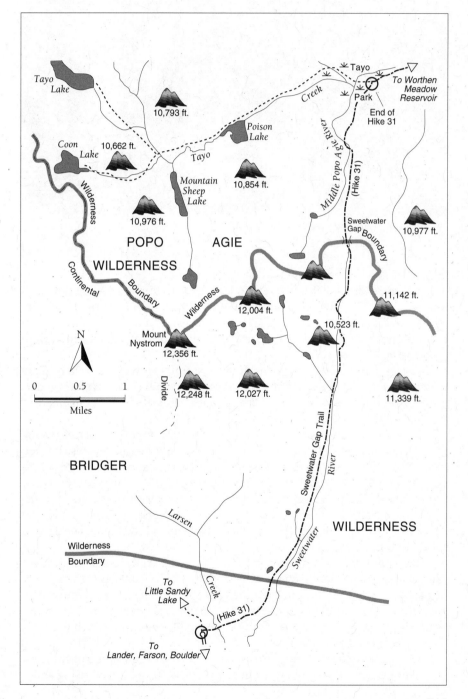

Tayo Lake

10,793 ft.

Poison Lake

Coon Lake

10,662 ft.

Tayo

Mountain Sheep Lake

10,854 ft.

10,976 ft.

Tayo Creek

Park

Tayo

To Worthen Meadow Reservoir

End of Hike 31

Middle Popo Agie River

(Hike 31)

Sweetwater Gap Boundary

10,977 ft.

POPO AGIE

WILDERNESS

Wilderness

Continental

Boundary

Wilderness

12,004 ft.

11,142 ft.

10,523 ft.

N

Mount Nystrom

12,356 ft.

0   0.5   1

Miles

Divide

12,248 ft.

12,027 ft.

11,339 ft.

Sweetwater Gap Trail

River

BRIDGER

Larsen

Sweetwater

WILDERNESS

Wilderness Boundary

Creek

To Little Sandy Lake

(Hike 31)

To Lander, Farson, Boulder

Wind River Peak from Sweetwater Gap.

Park offer good camping areas.

From the trailhead at 8,890 feet follow the trail north, heading downhill through burned lodgepole pine forest. After 200 yards, bear right onto the trail signed for Sweetwater Gap. (The left fork, signed for Little Sandy Lake, becomes obscure in the burned forest after about 0.5 mile and is difficult to follow.)

The rocky trail skirts a soggy meadow as it quickly descends to a bridged crossing of Larsen Creek. It then ascends gently to moderately over a boulder-covered moraine, heading northeast through charred forest consumed in the 3,447-acre Ann Fire in the summer of 1988.

A profusion of lodgepole saplings grow on the forest floor in places among the blackened snags. Lodgepole pines are well adapted to reforest burned areas, as the trailside saplings attest. These trees bear a number of serotinous, or closed, cones that open to release the seeds within only after being exposed to the high temperatures of a forest fire. Forest fires release nutrients tied up in trees and in dead forest litter, and open up the once-shady forest floor to the sun. In this enriched post-fire soil lodgepole seeds soon sprout and grow rapidly.

After about 1 mile the grade abates. Soon the trail enters the Bridger Wilderness and a shady lodgepole forest. The trail ahead stays primarily in forest but at times passes through the charred fringes of the old burn. The monotony of the forest is interrupted occasionally by small meadows and tarns. In places it follows the banks of the small Sweetwater, a fine stream that cascades and meanders by turns.

The trail crosses a few minor tributaries and offers glimpses of the massive boulder piles of Mount Nystrom and the Atlantic peaks, all rising above

12,000 feet. At 4.2 miles rock-hop across a larger tributary that drains a half-dozen alpine lakes to the northwest. Here at 9,600 feet the character of the landscape begins to change. Engelmann spruce and whitebark pine dominate the timberline forest, ice-scoured granite walls embrace the canyon, and the alpine ridges loom closely above.

Ahead, hop across more small streams, including the much diminished Sweetwater, then begin a 400-foot ascent on the rocky, moderately rising trail. The ascent levels off at the edge of a lovely oval meadow at 10,021 feet, enlivened by the blooms of yarrow, subalpine daisy, one-flower daisy, pussytoes, hairy arnica, and northern goldenrod. Prominent Peak 11,139 points skyward to the northwest, and a narrow, wooded draw leads north from the meadow toward still-invisible Sweetwater Gap.

The trail ahead skirts the eastern margin of the meadow. The opening affords the first good view of alpine terrain to the west, including one of the many cirques carved into the flanks of Mount Nystrom. Beyond the meadow the trail ascends the draw along the banks of the infant Sweetwater River to its source in the long, narrow meadows of the gap, fringed by a forest of stunted timberline conifers.

The 10,327-foot gap divides not only the Sweetwater and Middle Popo Agie river drainages, but forms the boundary between the Bridger and Popo Agie wilderness areas. The Sweetwater originates where seeps in the meadow coalesce at its southern margin. The gap is arguably one of the prettiest and most pleasant of Wind River passes. A fairly dense timberline forest surrounding the meadow, and the availability of water makes the gap an attractive place for an overnight stay.

Descending north from the gap, views briefly open up to reveal a host of 11,000-foot alpine peaks to the north. Look northwest to the snow-streaked dome of 13,192-foot Wind River Peak. The smooth, ice-polished walls of Peak 11,500 rise 1 mile west, above the head of the Middle Popo Agie River.

Upon entering a thickening timberline forest the sweeping views begin to fade. The trail ahead alternates between rocky and swampy stretches, and 1.1 miles from Sweetwater Gap it reaches the Middle Popo Agie River, here only a 12-foot wide stream. This crossing is an easy rock-hop in low water, but it can be a shin-deep wade early in the season. The trail rock hops back across after 150 yards, and then continues descending through increasingly large forest trees to the broad spread of Tayo Park. Here Tayo Creek and the Middle Popo Agie converge to create a sizable stream that meanders through the rich grasslands. Good camping areas lie in the forest fringing the park, and ridges clad in timberline forest, punctuated by granite domes, rise above.

The Tayo Creek and Ice Lakes trails head west from the park midway across its expanse, at 9,720 feet. To use those trails you must wade the broad, but slow-moving Middle Popo Agie in water that may be waist-deep.

CHRISTINA LAKE TRAILHEAD

OVERVIEW

The paved and graveled Sinks Canyon-Louis Lake Road, connecting Lander with Wyoming Highway 28 near South Pass, offers a popular scenic drive through the southeastern reaches of the Wind Rivers. A variety of national forest campgrounds, lakes, and trailheads combine to make this region a popular recreational getaway.

The Christina Lake Trailhead at Fiddlers Lake, resting high on the flanks of the southeastern Wind Rivers, bears the distinction of being the highest elevation trailhead in the range, at 9,411 feet. (Cold Springs Trailhead, on the Wind River Indian Reservation, is actually higher, but is closed to the public.)

Only one trail begins at Fiddlers Lake, but that route divides 1.8 miles from the trailhead. The left branch is the Christina Lake Trail, leading to a four-wheel-drive road at large Christina Lake. The right branch is the Silas Canyon Trail, which heads into the Popo Agie Wilderness.

Few backcountry travelers brave the crowds and noise common to Christina Lake, unless they are en route to the high lakes of Atlantic Canyon, which lies behind the protective vail of the wilderness boundary. The trail to Silas Canyon, by contrast, offers fast and easy access to the Wilderness.

Travelers accustomed to trails in the Bridger Wilderness know that to reach the high country typically requires an investment of two days on the trail. But the Silas Canyon Trail offers a condensed version of a typical Wind River excursion over its modest 4.5-mile length.

Finding the trailhead: This trailhead (and Worthen Meadow Reservoir Trailhead) lies alongside the 36.2-mile-long Sinks Canyon-Louis Lake Road (Forest Road 300 within the boundaries of the Shoshone National Forest).

To reach the trailhead from the south, via Wyoming Highway 28, look for a sign indicating Louis Lake, just east of a large turnout featuring a kiosk with area information, and restrooms. The turnoff for FR 300 lies just east of the turnout. Find the turnoff 45.7 miles east of Farson and U.S. Highway 191.

Follow FR 300 generally north from WY 28 as it ascends low ridges and dips into minor draws. The roadbed can be quite rocky and rough in places.

Pass the Christina Lake four-wheel-drive road at 5.1 miles and the turn-off to Louis Lake Campground at 7.9 miles. After 12.7 miles the road arrives at Fiddlers Lake. The large trailhead parking area, signed for the Christina Lake Trail, lies next to the road 100 yards south of the southeast shore of the lake.

You can also reach the trailhead from Lander; signs on the main street downtown point to Sinks Canyon and Wyoming Highway 131. Follow the west-bound road through a residential area of Lander, making a number of right-angled turns, all signed for WY 131. After 0.6 mile, exit Lander and continue east on the two-lane paved highway. About 8.9 miles from downtown Lander the pavement ends, and the gravel road ahead becomes FR 300.

Pass the turnoff to Sinks Canyon Campground at 9.2 miles, and shortly thereafter reach the Bruce Picnic Ground and the large Middle Fork Trailhead parking area at 9.4 miles.

The road ahead climbs out of the Middle Popo Agie River canyon via switchbacks, leveling off above the shores of Frye Lake at 16.4 miles, where memorable views open up to include Roaring Fork Mountain and Wind River Peak.

The signed, west-bound road to Worthen Meadow Reservoir (see the next section) branches right after 17.7 miles, but bear left instead, following the road's ascending, south-bound course to its 9,600-foot summit at Blue Ridge. The road then begins a long descent, passing the turnoff to Fiddlers Lake Campground after 23.8 miles. Continue south for another 0.7 mile to the trailhead.

Travelers arriving late in the day can find numerous undeveloped camping areas along FR 300 south of the trailhead. Or spend the night in the 20-site Fiddlers Lake Campground (fee area), or in the popular, 9-site Louis Lake Campground (also a fee area), 4.8 miles south of the trailhead.

THE TRAILS

- Christina Lake Trail-Silas Canyon Trail

SUGGESTED EXTENDED TRIPS

1) Upper Silas Lake base camp; round trip, 7 miles, 3 to 4 days.

32 SILAS CANYON TRAIL—FIDDLERS LAKE TO SILAS CANYON, ISLAND LAKE

General description:	A day trip or overnighter.
Distance:	9 miles, round trip.
Difficulty:	Moderate.
Traffic:	Light.
Elevation gain and loss:	+1,200 feet, -150 feet.
Trailhead elevation:	9,411 feet.
Maximum elevation:	10,600 feet.
Topo maps:	USGS: Cony Mountain, Christina Lake (trail to Silas Canyon not shown on maps).

Key points:

   0.0   Fiddlers Lake Trailhead.

   1.8   Junction with Christina Lake Trail;
         bear right.

   2.3   Junction with trail to Lower Silas Lake;
         stay right.

   3.2   Upper Silas Lake.

   4.5   Island Lake.

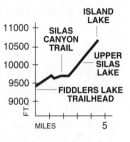

Best day hike destination: Both Lower and Upper Silas lakes offer scenic destinations and good fishing for brook and cutthroat trout. If you have an entire day, consider taking the trip to Island Lake or to the upper lakes in the basin.

The trail: The landscape in the southeastern reaches of the Wind Rivers, in the southern Popo Agie Wilderness, is dominated by rolling alpine plateaus exceeding 12,000 feet in elevation. The summit areas of these plateaus are unglaciated, but on their flanks glaciers carved deep cirque basins, with near-vertical headwalls, that now harbor numerous alpine lakes. Geologists refer to the resulting terrain as "biscuit board" topography.

The short trail to Silas Canyon visits one of the classic cirques deeply gouged into the eastern flanks of Roaring Fork Mountain. Unlike its counterparts in the Bridger Wilderness, Silas Canyon offers travelers who are budgeting their time and energy the opportunity to reach an alpine lake basin in a matter of hours, rather than spending at least two days on the trail.

From the trailhead on the southeast shore of Fiddlers Lake at 9,400 feet the signed Christina Lake Trail heads south beyond a trail register and a destination and mileage sign. Soon the trail curves west, following a small moraine that dams the lake. It winds among boulders in the open lodgepole pine forest. After 0.3 mile, the old trail coming down from the Fiddlers Lake Campground joins the main trail. Curve southwest here, soon reaching a rock-hop crossing of small Fiddlers Creek (there are logs in place to afford a dry crossing in high water).

The rocky trail ahead winds through lodgepole forest, with occasional minor grades. The shady forest floor is covered with a green carpet of low-growing grouse whortleberry shrubs. About 1 mile from the trailhead, rock-hop three small creeks in quick succession, then ascend a moderate grade to the signed junction of the Christina Lake and Silas Canyon trails, at 9,700 feet. The left-branching Christina Lake Trail leads southwest across forested Little Popo Agie Basin for 2.3 miles to Gustave Lake and the Christina Lake four-wheel-drive road.

Instead, bear right at the junction, quickly entering the Popo Agie Wilderness, and ascend a moderate grade through whitebark pine forest for 0.5 mile. The trail then briefly dips down to the banks of Silas Creek, where it meets a south-bound trail leading to Lower Silas Lake in 0.2 mile, visible through the forest just below.

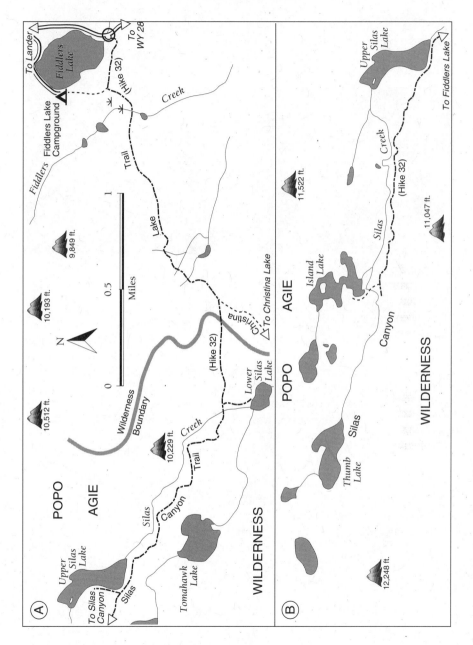

Continue straight ahead (west) and boulder-hop the cascading stream. The boulder-choked streambed is a difficult crossing for stock parties. The trail ahead rises moderately on slopes littered with granite boulders and

217

Island Lake in Silas Canyon.

studded with whitebark pines. After climbing for 0.4 mile from the crossing the trail levels out along the willow-bordered banks of Silas Creek. It then follows the tree-fringed margin of a meadow to 10,100-foot Upper Silas Lake.

This scenic timberline lake offers many fine camping areas above its rock- and tree-studded shoreline, and also good fishing for brook and cutthroat trout. The broad dome of Peak 11,522 rises west of the lake, and the rubbly cone of 11,109-foot Cony Mountain punctuates the skyline to the north.

The trail follows the south shore beneath a canopy of tall, spreading whitebark pines, and upon reaching the west end of the lake, the trail forks. The north-bound trail follows the west shore to the north, leading past numerous campsites.

To reach upper Silas Canyon follow the west-bound trail as it ascends a draw at a moderate grade. Beyond the grade the sometimes faint, infrequently used trail winds among boulders and a stunted timberline forest of Engelmann spruce and whitebark pine. About 1.3 miles from Upper Silas Lake, 10,600-foot Island Lake comes into view, sprawling out across the basin floor to the north. To get to the lake's rocky, irregular shoreline, leave the faint path and head north, avoiding the boggy meadow at the lake's inlet.

Good timberline camping areas, sheltered by stunted and wind-flagged spruces and whitebarks, can be found all around the lake's rocky shoreline. Fishing for cutthroats can be productive. The 0.5-mile-wide basin of Silas Canyon harbors five more lakes above Island Lake, the highest of which lies at 11,200 feet. Gentle alpine ridges flank the basin to the north and south, and the soaring 600-foot headwall of the cirque, 1.5 miles west of Island Lake, is as sheer as any wall in the range.

WORTHEN MEADOW RESERVOIR TRAILHEAD

OVERVIEW

Midway along the Sinks Canyon-Louis Lake Road, between Lander and Wyoming Highway 28 at South Pass, Worthen Meadow Reservoir lies at 8,800 feet, high above the forested confines of the Middle Popo Agie River. This large, artificial lake features a pleasant 28-site campground and a major trailhead to the middle reaches of the Popo Agie Wilderness.

The Middle Popo Agie River is the principal drainage in the southern half of the Wilderness. Gathering its waters from dozens of high lakes beneath the Continental Divide and from the high plateaus east of the Divide, the river flows through a prominent, forested canyon for 25 miles to the eastern foot of the range near Lander. Dominating the Divide at the head of the canyon is the snow-streaked dome of 13,192-foot Wind River Peak. This is the southernmost 13,000-footer in the range, and no other peak exceeds that elevation for 40 miles to the north.

This trailhead offers access to a network of backcountry trails via the Middle Popo Agie River canyon and the alpine tableland of Roaring Fork Mountain. Whether you enjoy the bucolic atmosphere of meadows and forests or the high landscapes of ice-carved cirques, you'll find what you are looking for on trails originating at Worthen Meadow Reservoir.

Finding the trailhead: Worthen Meadow Reservoir is at the end of a west-bound spur road that branches off the Sinks Canyon-Louis Lake Road (Forest Road 300).

From WY 28 to the south, follow FR 300 (see the Fiddlers Lake Trailhead) north 19.5 miles to the signed turnoff for Worthen Meadow Reservoir and the Fremont County Youth Camp.

From Lander, follow Wyoming Highway 131 and FR 300 17.7 miles to the same turnoff.

At the reservoir turnoff turn west on the good gravel road and drive 2.2 miles to a junction. Right goes to the campground and picnic area; left goes to the trailhead. Bear left and pass the *No Parking* sign at the Stough Creek Basin trailhead in 0.1 mile. Continue another 0.1 mile to the spacious trailhead parking area above the west shore of the reservoir.

Travelers arriving late in the day will find some undeveloped camping areas along FR 300, primarily south of Fiddlers Lake. Or stay the night in the 28-site campground near the trailhead (a fee is charged).

THE TRAILS

- Sheep Bridge Trail
- Middle Fork Trail
- Stough Creek Basin Trail

1) Stough Creek Basin base camp; round trip, 16.2 miles, 3 to 5 days.

2) Stough Creek Basin to Bills Park via Stough Creek Basin Trail, return to the trailhead via Middle Fork and Sheep Bridge trails; loop trip, 21 miles, 3 to 5 days.

3) Tayo Park base camp; round trip, 23 miles, 4 to 6 days.

33 STOUGH CREEK BASIN TRAIL—WORTHEN MEADOW RESERVOIR TO STOUGH CREEK BASIN

General description:	A rigorous extended trip offering one-day access to a large alpine lake basin in the southern Popo Agie Wilderness.
Distance:	16.2 miles, round trip.
Difficulty:	Moderately strenuous.
Traffic:	Moderate.
Elevation gain and loss:	+2,100 feet, -400 feet.
Trailhead elevation:	8,840 feet.
Maximum elevation:	10,550 feet.
Topo maps:	USGS: Cony Mountain, Sweetwater Gap (trailhead and trail to Stough Creek Basin not shown on maps); Earthwalk: Southern Wind River Range (only Stough Creek Basin and points west shown on map).

Key points:

0.0 Worthen Meadow Reservoir trailhead parking lot.
0.1 Trailhead.
0.8 Roaring Fork Lake, ford of the Roaring Fork.
4.8 10,550-foot pass.
7.0 Junction with Stough Creek Basin Trail; turn left.
8.1 Lower Stough Creek Lake (Lake 10,484).

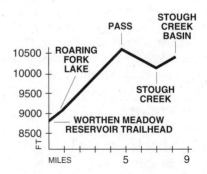

STOUGH CREEK BASIN
• SHEEP BRIDGE & MIDDLE FORK

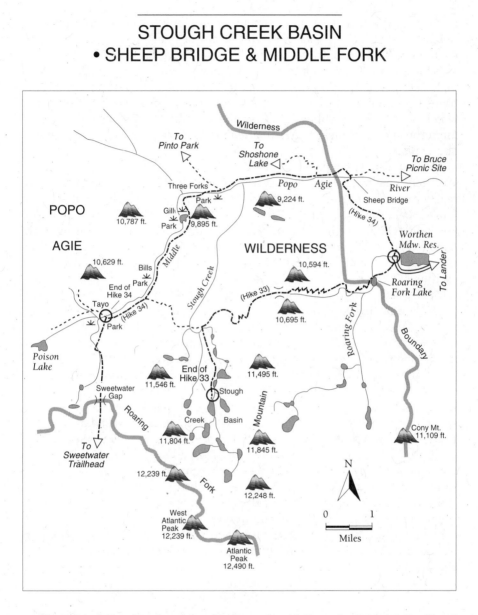

Best day hike destination: Anglers often follow the initial 0.7 mile of the trail to Roaring Fork Lake, which hosts a brook trout fishery.

A day hike to the 10,550-foot pass at 4.8 miles is a strenuous but rewarding trip, offering grand vistas into the upper reaches of the Middle Popo Agie River and of towering Wind River Peak.

The hike: This trail, a longer version of hike 32 to Silas Canyon, also visits an alpine lake basin carved into the flanks of Roaring Fork Mountain in the southern reaches of the Popo Agie Wilderness. Grand vistas of the rugged peaks of the Popo Agie country accompany travelers for the final 3 miles to vast Stough Creek Basin, a broad cirque encompassing more than 3 square miles on the north slope of Roaring Fork Mountain.

No less than 30 lakes dot this basin, ranging in elevation from 10,300 feet to 11,000 feet and many of them harboring populations of cutthroat and brook trout. A person could spend a week's time exploring just half of them. Hikers who enjoy rambling for miles above timberline will be attracted by numerous non-technical routes that lead to Roaring Fork Mountain's stony alpine plateau.

From the spacious parking area at 8,840 feet, above the west shore of Worthen Meadow Reservoir, backtrack down the road 0.1 mile to the trail register and the beginning of the trail. The wide rocky trail, a long-closed four-wheel-drive road, ascends gradually through shady lodgepole pine forest, gaining 200 feet in 0.7 mile. Here at 9,023 feet it skirts Roaring Fork Lake, a pleasant lake fringed with meadows and forest. The broad alpine slopes and sheer cirque headwalls on Roaring Fork Mountain provide an exciting backdrop.

At the lake's outlet ford the wide, shallow Roaring Fork. Travelers have forged a trail that leads north, downstream, to dry crossings via boulders and log jams, but from those crossings be sure to double back upstream to the lake's outlet to relocate the trail. (The trail from Roaring Fork Lake to the Stough Creek Basin Trail is not shown on the topo map.)

From the ford the trail ascends moderately southwest through a forest of small pines to a large meadow—the boggy remains of a silted-in lakebed. Bridges lead across two small streams, and a boardwalk stretches across the wet eastern end of the meadow. The trail then threads westward into an increasingly steep draw, ascending 1,100 feet for 2.5 miles at a moderate grade. As elevation is gained whitebark pine and spruce begin to supplant the lodgepole forest. Occasional views open up to the northeast, past the series of hogback ridges on the eastern flanks of the range to the distant Wind River Basin and the Owl Creek Mountains.

As the trail switchbacks up the draw it approaches a small stream at convenient intervals, allowing travelers to slake their thirst (after treating the water) on the steady climb. At length the trail emerges from the draw and enters a timberline pass at 10,550 feet, embraced by stunted conifers. A grand panorama unfolds, offering ample reward for the long climb.

The snow-streaked dome of 13,192-foot Wind River Peak dominates the westward view. The alpine ridges of Roaring Fork Mountain rise to the southwest, and beyond lies Mount Nystrom with deep cirques and towering headwalls on its flanks. The heavily forested Middle Popo Agie and Tayo Creek beyond lie in the gulf between this lofty viewpoint and the crest of the range far to the west.

From the pass follow the trail as it contours southwest, briefly crossing a rocky slope where an even broader panorama unfolds, now including the bold peaks rising above the North Fork Popo Agie River. Lizard Head Peak, Windy Mountain, and Mount Chauvenet are especially prominent.

Wind River Peak from pass west of Stough Creek Basin.

The trail enters an increasingly thick stand of whitebark pine and descends gradually, curving into a minor basin. Switchbacks lead down to the basin's floor and a hop across a small stream. A descending traverse through spruce forest follows, leading to a small meadow and past a trio of tarns. Presently back in pine forest, follow the banks of Stough Creek and reach the junction with the Stough Creek Basin Trail.

Turn left (south) onto that trail, cross a bridge spanning the large creek, and follow the streambank briefly downstream. Then begin a moderate, rocky ascent, gaining 400 feet in 1 mile through a whortleberry-carpeted forest of spruce and whitebark pine. The trees quickly diminish in size and numbers as the trail climbs a broad ridge above Lake 10,484, where Stough Creek Basin spreads out below. The trail quickly drops to the willow-bordered shores of the lake, then continues up the basin, passing two more lakes before dividing into boot-worn paths leading to the larger lakes in the middle reaches of the basin.

This classic cirque basin is embraced by the spreading arms of Roaring Fork Mountain, which rises above in grassy and rocky slopes, ledges, and cliffs to a series of 11,000- and 12,000-foot prominences that punctuate the plateau. Travel is easy between most of the lakes in the basin. Those lying below 10,600 feet have a modest forest cover of stunted trees. Higher lakes are surrounded by rock and tundra.

34 SHEEP BRIDGE & MIDDLE FORK TRAILS— WORTHEN MEADOW RESERVOIR TO MIDDLE POPO AGIE RIVER, TAYO PARK

General description:	An extended trip in the southern Popo AgieWilderness.
Distance:	23 miles, round-trip.
Difficulty:	Moderate.
Traffic:	Moderate.
Elevation gain and loss:	+1,500 feet, -700 feet.
Trailhead elevation:	8,840 feet.
Maximum elevation:	9,733 feet.
Topo maps:	USGS: Cony Mountain, Sweetwater Gap; Earthwalk: Southern Wind River Range (shows only Three Forks Park and points west).

See Map on Page 221

Key points:

0.0	Worthen Meadow Reservoir trailhead parking lot.
1.5	Surmount Roaring Fork/Middle Popo Agie divide.
2.9	Sheep Bridge spanning Middle Popo Agie.
3.1	Beaver ponds.
3.8	Junction with northwest-bound Shoshone Trail; stay left.
6.0	Junction with Pinto Park Trail; bear left.
6.4	Ford Middle Popo Agie River in Three Forks Park.
7.4	Enter Gill Park.
9.7	Enter Bills Park.
10.4	Junction with Stough Creek Basin Trail; stay right.
11.5	Tayo Park, junction with Sweetwater Trail.

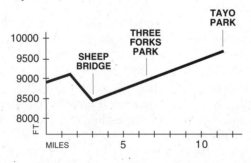

Best day hike destination: Sheep Bridge, at 2.9 miles, offers a pleasant destination along the wide Middle Popo Agie River.

The trail: The Sheep Bridge Trail, beginning at Worthen Meadow Reservoir, offers a high-elevation alternative trailhead for a trip up the Middle Popo Agie. This eliminates the long climb from the traditional trailhead far down the canyon at Bruce Picnic Area, near Sinks Canyon State Park.

The Middle Popo Agie River flows through a long, meandering canyon that is heavily forested but occasionally interrupted by large, wet meadows. Gently contoured forested ridges and granite domes embrace the long canyon, offering infrequent glimpses of alpine country. At Tayo Park, a long one-day journey from the trailhead, the high country finally comes into view.

This trail is used by anglers who enjoy forest-sheltered camping and fly fishing on the river for rainbow and brook trout. It's also favored by long-distance trekkers who can choose a variety of spur trails to design rewarding loop trips to grand alpine lake basins. The Middle Fork Trail gains minimal elevation en route to Tayo Park, and camping areas and water are abundant.

The trail to Sheep Bridge, and down-canyon to Bruce Picnic Area, lies outside the boundaries of the Popo Agie Wilderness. That part of the trail is open to bicycles, and is a favorite trip of mountain bikers.

From the large trailhead parking area at 8,840 feet, the trail heads north into the lodgepole pine forest, quickly dipping down to a bridged crossing of the Roaring Fork. The trail ahead is rocky as it ascends gently to moderately up the south-facing slopes, passing through stands of lodgepole pine and groves of aspen. Occasional vignettes of the sheer headwalls of the Roaring Fork cirque to the southwest are revealed between trailside trees.

Soon the trail gains a minor ridge, curves into a shallow basin, then begins the steep, rocky descent toward the Middle Popo Agie. A moderate forest cover of small lodgepoles obscures views into the canyon below. At length you reach open lodgepole forest on a bench above the river. Instead of heading northwest to Sheep Bridge, as shown on the outdated Cony Mountain quad, turn east and follow the river downstream for 0.2 mile to the sturdy bridge spanning the wide Middle Popo Agie River. There is a fine spot to rest along the river just south of the bridge before continuing up the canyon.

The trail quickly rises from the bridge to join the Middle Fork Trail (7 miles from Bruce Picnic Area on the Sinks Canyon-Louis Lake Road). Turn left on the Middle Fork Trail, heading up-canyon. At first the trail curves northwest away from the river, passing between a chain of terraced beaver ponds. The trail ahead follows the north side of the river up-canyon, through open forests of lodgepole pine and aspen groves intermingled with sagebrush.

Rounded ridges punctuated by granite knolls and clad in lodgepole and aspen forest rise both to the north and south of the open canyon. Occasional glimpses of Wind River Peak and its alpine environs lure you onward up the pleasant canyon. The trail follows the riverbank at times, and its waters range from silent meanders in willowy meadows to a brawling torrent in boulder-choked channels.

Bear left at the signed Shoshone Lake Trail at 3.8 miles, and continue up the increasingly confined canyon to the junction with the signed Pinto Park Trail, at 9,040 feet. Bearing left again, the trail soon emerges into the narrow meadow of Three Forks Park. Good camping areas lie nearby in the open lodgepole forest.

At the west end of the park hikers must ford the Middle Popo Agie over its sand and cobble bed, 10 yards wide, shin-deep, and with a modest current. The undulating trail ahead curves around a southward bend in the river, passing the swampy meadows of Gill Park, an ancient lakebed on the river, 1 mile from the ford. Here the river widens and silently meanders through the wet spread. Granite knobs and domes loom above the east and west flanks of the canyon.

At the south end of the park hop across a minor stream and ascend 200 feet up its shallow, forested draw to mount a narrow saddle. The trail then quickly drops down to the ponds and marshy grasslands of Bills Park, another former lakebed in the river, and skirts the meadow's eastern margin. Approaching the south end of Bills Park, the trail meets the east-bound Stough Creek Basin Trail at 9,500 feet.

The final 1.1 miles to Tayo Park leads through predominantly lodgepole forest, across two minor streams, and finally to the junction with the Tayo Creek and Ice Lakes trail alongside the rich, spreading grasslands of Tayo Park. Good camping areas lie around the forested fringes of the park. To continue up the Tayo Creek Trail, wade the deep, slow-moving river.

DICKINSON PARK TRAILHEAD

OVERVIEW

Although the Bridger Wilderness trailheads at Green River Lakes, Big Sandy, and Sweetwater are farther removed from civilization, Dickinson Park *feels* like the most remote trailhead in the range. From the Wind River Valley you drive up and up, rising over a seemingly endless series of steep slopes and ridges. When views of civilization are far behind, with nothing but a vast expanse of mountainous terrain ahead and in the rear view mirror, the road emerges into the meadows of Dickinson Park. Here boulder-heaped ridges and alpine plateaus reach to the western skyline.

Even more remote than the trailhead, of course, is the backcountry of the northern Popo Agie Wilderness, a land of large lakes, rugged peaks, alpine cirques, and vast tracts of treeless tundra.

Several good trails begin here, including the incomparable Bear Ears Trail, one of the classic alpine routes in the range. This trail offers access to a vast stretch of backcountry, both in the Popo Agie Wilderness and in the Wind River Roadless Area (permit required) on the Wind River Indian Reservation. Surprisingly few travelers use this trail, however. Instead, many opt to join the throngs in such places as Big Sandy, Elkhart Park, and Green River Lakes.

The Bears Ears Trail is suitable for travelers planning an extended long-distance trip into the Wilderness. Those who wish to budget their time and energy will find that the Smith Lake Trail suits their needs nicely.

The long, tortuous road to Dickinson Park, ascending the range's eastern slope, allows ample time for contemplating the forces of uplift that created the Wind Rivers. Here you can plainly see how the sedimentary strata that once covered the region were tilted upward at a moderate angle, broken, and eroded by streams and glaciers. The road climbs through a succession of layers of sandstone, dolomite, and limestone stacked against the flanks of the range like so many slices of bread.

Each layer of rock breaks off in a west-facing cliff band, and each crest forms a long hogback ridge. You ascend one layer of sedimentary rock only to dip into a minor valley and then ascend the next layer. Only as you approach the national forest boundary near Dickinson Park, about 20 miles from the Wind River Valley, do the granitic rocks that compose the range's core begin to appear.

Finding the trailhead: This remote trailhead is easy to find once you locate the obscure turnoff for the road leading to it. Find the turnoff on U.S. Highway 287 near the south end of the small town of Fort Washakie on the Wind River Indian Reservation. It is 13 miles north of Lander, or 17 miles south of the junction of US 287 and 26, or 60 miles southeast of Dubois.

From Fort Washakie drive south on US 287 to the turnoff, 1 mile past the Wind River Agency and just north of the Wind River Trading Post and Hines General Store. The road is signed as Trout Creek Road, and it branches west at the only four-way intersection on the south end of town.

Follow this paved road west for 5.1 miles, then bear right onto the good gravel road signed for Moccasin Lake. A spur road branches left in another 0.3 mile; bear right. The road ascends to the eastern foot of the range, then climbs steadily on switchbacks. The roadbed becomes narrow and rocky and turns quite slippery during or after heavy rains.

After gaining 4,200 feet in 19.1 miles the road meets the Moccasin Lake Road. Bear left toward Dickinson Park. In another 0.4 mile the road leaves the Wind River Indian Reservation and enters Shoshone National Forest.

The rocky tread winds through the meadows of Dickinson Park, passing the turnoff to a guest ranch. At 20.7 miles from US 287 watch for the signed spur road on the right to the Bears Ears Trailhead.

To reach that trailhead, turn right, pass the Dickinson Park Guard Station, and follow the rough one-lane road as it skirts the meadows of Ranger Creek. Pass corrals after 0.25 mile and slow down for the final 200 yards of rocky road leading to the trailhead parking area, 0.6 mile from the main road.

To reach Smith Lake Trailhead, stay left at the turnoff to the Bears Ears Trailhead and continue south another 1.4 miles to the entrance to Dickinson Creek Campground (15 sites, no water, no fee). Turn left here; the sign points to the trailhead. The road ahead is narrow and rough with potholes and rocks. Pass a horse corral and unloading ramp 0.4 mile from the camp-ground. Hikers should go another 0.3 mile to the spacious trailhead parking area.

There are few undeveloped camping areas inside the national forest near Dickinson Park. The best bet for finding a place to stay for the night is at the campground.

THE TRAILS
- Smith Lake Trail
- Bears Ears Trail

SUGGESTED EXTENDED TRIPS

1) Smith Lake base camp; round trip, 11 to 13 miles, 3 to 4 days.

2) Washakie Lake base camp; round trip, 27.4 miles, 5 to 7 days.

3) Grave Lake base camp; round trip, 29.6 miles, 5 to 7 days.

4) Valentine Lake base camp; round trip, 22.6 miles, 5 to 7 days.

5) Washakie Pass-Hailey Pass loop; 38.6 miles, 5 to 7 days.

PLACES TO AVOID IF YOU'RE LOOKING FOR SOLITUDE
- Smith Lake
- Valentine Lake

35 SMITH LAKE TRAIL—DICKINSON PARK TO SMITH LAKE

General description:	A long day hike or overnight trip.
Distance:	12 miles, round trip.
Difficulty:	Moderate.
Traffic:	Moderate.
Elevation gain and loss:	+1,100 feet, -500 feet.
Trailhead elevation:	9,360 feet.
Maximum elevation:	9,900 feet.
Topo maps:	USGS: Dickinson Park, Lizard Head Peak; Earthwalk: Southern Wind River Range.

Key points:

0.0   Dickinson Park Trailhead.
0.4   Junction with North Fork Trail; bear right.
4.2   Junction with High Meadow Trail; stay right.
5.5   Smith Lake.
5.8   Junction with Cook Lake Trail; bear right.
6.0   Middle Lake.

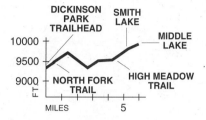

The trail: In the northern reaches of the Popo Agie Wilderness, between the high granite plateaus east of the Continental Divide and the long limestone ridges on the eastern flanks of the range, numerous large, deep cirques reach back into the interior of the Wind Rivers.

The Smith Lakes chain, west of Dickinson Park, lies beneath a broad alpine plateau where three large cirques converge. Eight lakes dot this basin, and five of these can be reached within a few hours from the trailhead by following the scenic Smith Lake Trail.

The trip to the lakes can be completed in one long day, but the basin, with its backdrop of soaring cirque headwalls, many good campsites, and productive fishing, is better suited for an extended stay. Brook and a few large lake trout inhabit the waters of Smith, Middle, and Cathedral lakes, while Cook and Cloverleaf lakes host only brookies.

Be sure to protect your food supply from the black bears that frequent this area (see the introductory section on *Backcountry Travel*).

The trail begins 250 yards east of the parking area, next to a trail register and large information sign. Follow the boardwalk south across the soggy spread of Dickinson Park, then bear right, avoiding a left-branching cattle trail. Climb the slopes of a dry, boulder-dotted meadow, decorated by the blooms of stonecrop and bitterroot.

A junction with the infrequently used North Fork Trail marks the meadow's southern margin, after which the trail rises gently over boulder-studded slopes beneath a canopy of lodgepole pines. After passing the signed boundary of the Popo Agie Wilderness begin a descent via switchbacks, curving around the shoulder of a ridge high above the forested depths of the North Popo Agie River canyon.

Splendid views stretch beyond the canyon to craggy Mount Chevo and to the snow-streaked dome of 13,192-foot Wind River Peak. The rocky trail descends 400 feet through an open lodgepole forest, eventually crossing a small stream along the fringes of a willow-mantled meadow. Blocky Dishpan Butte rises 1,000 feet above to the northwest.

The rocky and sandy trail then begins a moderate to steep ascent up a confined, rock-bound draw, where subalpine fir and Engelmann spruce join

SMITH LAKE

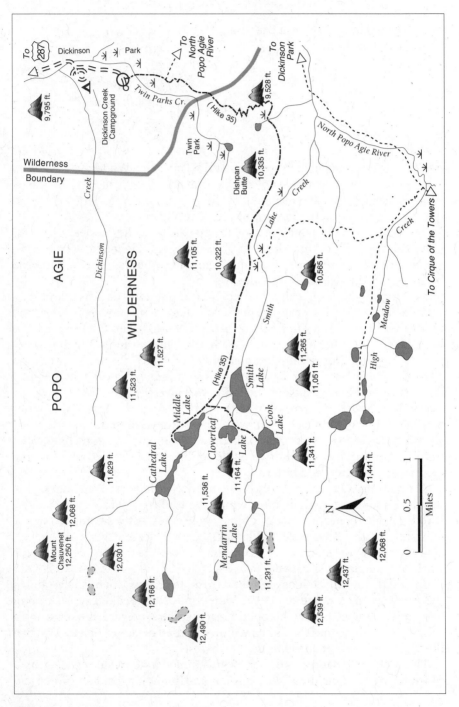

To 287

Dickinson Park

To North Popo Agie River

To Dickinson Park

9,795 ft.

Dickinson Creek Campground

Twin Parks Cr.

(Hike 35)

9,528 ft.

North Popo Agie River

Wilderness Boundary

Twin Park

Dishpan Butte

10,335 ft.

Lake Creek

Dickinson Creek

POPO AGIE WILDERNESS

11,105 ft.

10,322 ft.

To Cirque of the Towers

Smith Creek

10,565 ft.

Meadow

11,527 ft.

11,265 ft.

11,523 ft.

High

(Hike 35)

11,051 ft.

Middle Lake

Smith Lake

Cook Lake

Cloverleaf Lake

11,629 ft.

11,341 ft.

12,068 ft.

11,536 ft.

11,164 ft.

11,441 ft.

Cathedral Lake

N

Mount Chauvenet 12,250 ft.

12,030 ft.

Mendarrin Lake

11,291 ft.

0   0.5   1
Miles

12,166 ft.

12,068 ft.

12,490 ft.

12,539 ft.

12,437 ft.

the ranks of the lodgepole forest. After cresting the notch at the head of the draw, views open up that reach westward into the deep, glacier-gouged cirques ahead. The trail descends briefly to the valley of Smith Lake Creek, then begins a long, gentle ascent along the valley floor.

At about 3.9 miles ignore an unsigned, left-forking trail at the point where the Smith Lake Trail becomes extremely rocky. Soon thereafter enter the northern margin of a soggy, willow-studded meadow, and bear right again at the junction with the signed High Meadow Trail. (That trail offers access to the North Fork Trail at Sanford Park, after 2.75 miles. It is the preferred route of North Fork Trail users, since it avoids two of the four deep fords of the North Popo Agie River.)

Enjoy a final, splendid view of Dishpan Butte from the junction before the trail returns to the forest, continuing the gradual ascent. The trail then traverses above the north shore of 9,748-foot Smith Lake, passing several fair campsites in the shade of the spruce and lodgepole forest.

Ice-polished granite slopes, slabs, and knolls bound the lake, and a host of alpine summits—some exceeding 12,000 feet—reach to the skyline in the background. A towering dome juts above the south shore of the lake to an elevation of 11,100 feet. From the lake you can see erratic boulders scattered on a high ledge just below the dome's summit—boulders that were left behind by a retreating glacier that buried this cirque beneath more than 1,000 feet of ice.

The traverse above Smith Lake rises at a moderate grade through mixed conifer forest to a signed junction 25 yards west of a rock-hop crossing of a minor stream. Here trails lead south for 0.75 mile to Cook Lake, and northwest for 0.2 mile to Middle Lake and 0.8 mile to Cathedral Lake.

To reach Cook Lake, turn left at the junction, descend to the rock-hop crossing of Middle Lake's outlet stream, then ascend moderately for 0.2 mile to a crossing of the outlet of Cloverleaf Lake. That 9,940-foot lake, offering good campsites, lies about 150 yards west of the trail in a shallow bowl beneath the bold cliffs of Point 11,164.

The trail rises 150 feet above Cloverleaf Lake to crest a rocky knoll just east of its summit, then quickly descends to the north shore of 10,055-foot Cook Lake, backdropped by a sheer 600-foot cliff. The dead-end, cliff-bound cirque extends 1.5 miles west of Cook Lake to timberline, where wanderers will find two scenic but barren lakes.

If Middle and Cathedral lakes are your goal, bear right at the aforementioned junction. Within minutes you will reach the meadow-fringed shores of Middle Lake, one of the gems of the Smith Lake basin. Good camping areas can be found above the 9,919-foot lake's north and west shores, shaded by an open forest of whitebark and lodgepole pine, subalpine fir, and spruce. The lake lies in a spacious cirque flanked by towering cliffs and alpine ridges. Especially striking is the 1,200-foot face of the southeast buttress of the Cathedral Peak massif.

Mount Chauvenet, the conical peak on the northwest skyline, is the highest summit in view, rising to 12,250 feet. In the west, look to the blocky,

Middle Lake in the Smith Lake basin.

12,160-foot east summit of Cathedral Peak.

The trail continues around the north and west shores of Middle Lake, then follows the stream connecting it to the long and narrow waters of Cathedral Lake, where the trail ends. Cathedral Lake's shores are more confined by steep, rocky slopes and offer fewer opportunities for camping than Middle Lake.

36 BEARS EARS TRAIL—DICKINSON PARK TO SOUTH FORK LITTLE WIND RIVER

General description:	A rigorous multi-day trip.
Distance:	12.4 miles, one way.
Difficulty:	Strenuous.
Traffic:	Moderate.
Elevation gain and loss:	+2,750 feet, -2,100 feet.
Trailhead elevation:	9,300 feet.
Maximum elevation:	11,920 feet.
Topo Maps:	USGS: Dickinson Park, Lizard Head Peak; Earthwalk: Southern Wind River Range.

Key points:

0.0	Bears Ears Trailhead.
1.8	Popo Agie Wilderness boundary.
4.5	Adams Pass.
8.8	Junction with Lizard Head Trail; bear right.
10.9	Junction with Moss Lake Trail; bear left.
11.3	Valentine Lake.
12.4	Junction with Washakie Trail at ford of South Fork Little Wind River.

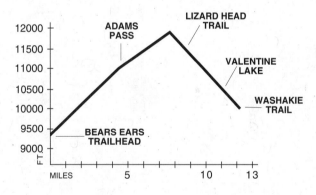

Best day hike destination: A 9-mile round trip to Adams Pass offers the chance to enjoy far-ranging vistas from alpine tundra at 11,000 feet.

The trail: Most Wind River trails pass for miles through subalpine forests, often with few inspiring vistas, while en route to the alpine heights. Many of the range's higher trails only briefly touch the alpine country; most stay at or just below timberline. Much of the Wind Rivers' alpine areas remain trailless and are seldom visited save for occasional rock climbers or cross-country enthusiasts.

One exception, however, is the incomparable Bears Ears Trail. This high trail stays above timberline in alpine tundra, at elevations exceeding 11,000

BEARS EARS

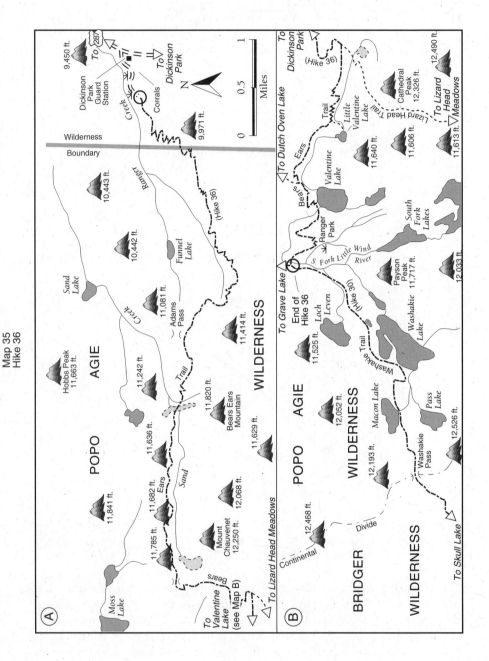

Map 35
Hike 36

Map A:

POPO AGIE WILDERNESS

9,450 ft.

To 287

To Dickinson Park

Dickinson Park Guard Station

Corrals

N

0   0.5   1
Miles

9,971 ft.

Ranger Creek

Wilderness Boundary

10,443 ft.

10,442 ft.

Funnel Lake

Sand Lake

11,081 ft.

Adams Pass

(Hike 36)

11,414 ft.

Hobbs Peak 11,663 ft.

11,242 ft.

Sand Creek

Trail

11,636 ft.

11,820 ft.

Bears Ears Mountain

11,629 ft.

11,841 ft.

11,682 ft.

Bears Ears

Sand

11,785 ft.

11,250 ft.

Mount Chauvenet 12,250 ft.

12,068 ft.

Moss Lake

Bears

To Valentine Lake (see Map B)

To Lizard Head Meadows

A

Map B:

To Dickinson Park

(Hike 36)

12,490 ft.

To Lizard Head Meadows

Cathedral Peak 12,326 ft.

To Dutch Oven Lake

Bears Ears Trail

Little Valentine Trail

Valentine Lake

11,640 ft.

11,606 ft.

Lizard Head Trail

11,613 ft.

To Lizard Head Meadows

South Fork Lakes

Ranger Park

S. Fork Little Wind River

Payson Peak 11,717 ft.

12,033 ft.

To Grave Lake

End of Hike 36

Loch Leven

(Hike 30)

Washakie Lake

11,525 ft.

Washakie Trail

POPO AGIE WILDERNESS

12,052 ft.

Macon Lake

Pass Lake

12,193 ft.

Washakie Pass

12,526 ft.

12,468 ft.

Continental Divide

BRIDGER WILDERNESS

To Skull Lake

B

234

feet, for 6 miles. The route offers splendid vistas into the range's remote interior, and to a dramatic array of ice-encrusted crags.

But the trail is strenuous, rising nearly 3,000 feet in the first 8 miles. The first campsites below timberline, at Valentine and Dutch Oven lakes, lie more than 11 miles from the trailhead. Be sure to get an early start on the trail if you expect to reach Valentine Lake on the first day.

At the far end of the Bears Ears (on the South Fork Little Wind River), backcountry travelers will find trails enough to keep them busy for several more days. Trails lead to the Washakie Lake basin (see hike 30) and to Grave and Baptiste lakes. A rewarding 14.1-mile loop via Washakie and Hailey passes (also see hike 30) can extend this trip into a 39-mile backcountry vacation—for those in top condition.

From the trailhead in the meadows of Ranger Creek, granite knobs punctuate the skyline on the crest of the broad alpine mountain to the west. Adams Pass, at 11,000 feet, is the rocky saddle on the north ridge of that mountain. You can visualize your route to the pass after signing in at the trail register.

The trail immediately heads southwest into the lodgepole pine forest and soon begins a series of tedious, gently ascending switchbacks. Please restrain the urge to shortcut these seemingly unnecessary switchbacks.

There is a noticeable lack of vegetation on the needle-carpeted forest floor, in contrast to the greenery on trailside slopes on the western flanks of the range in the Bridger Wilderness. Lodgepole pines dominate the forest at first, but as elevation is gained, Engelmann spruce, subalpine fir, and whitebark pine join the ranks of the forest.

Shortly after the first series of switchbacks end the trail enters the Popo Agie Wilderness at 10,000 feet, in a forest of spindly whitebark pines. The trail ahead ascends more steadily, crossing boulder-littered slopes to the headwaters bowl of a Ranger Creek tributary. As the trail enters the bowl and approaches timberline, notice that spruce and whitebark pine now dominate the forest, and wildflowers begin to enliven the grassy slopes among the boulders. Look for the yellow, sunflower-like blossoms of hairy arnica; the white, spike-like blooms of American bistort; and the blue and purple flowers of one-flower daisy, Parry's townsendia, mountain bluebells, and the unforgettable Parry's primrose. Colorado columbine, growing here near the northern limits of its range, is cream to pale lavender in color, in contrast to its striking blue blossoms common in the southern Rocky Mountains.

The trail continues on a semi-circuit of the bowl, steadily ascending and passing several cold springs. Exit the bowl to the north, following switchbacks into the last persistent stand of stunted conifers. Follow the curve west around the shoulder of a minor ridge. A few remaining clumps of tenacious krummholz trees are soon left behind as the trail traverses the rocky tundra toward Adams Pass.

Vistas from this stretch of trail are superb, reaching west and northwest to sprawling alpine plateaus studded with granite pinnacles. Look east and down 1,100 feet upon rock-bound Funnel Lake, in the headwaters bowl of

Grave Lake and the peaks of the Continental Divide from the Bears Ears Trail.

Ranger Creek. Beyond the trailhead far below rise the rims of the hogback ridges lapping against the eastern flanks of the range. The vast Wind River Basin spreads out beyond, where the cottonwood-lined Wind River and its tributaries contrast with the basin's mostly empty desert. The Owl Creek Mountains bound the basin to the northeast, and on the far horizon, 80 miles distant, are the Bighorn Mountains.

The tread so far has been remarkably smooth in spite of the rocky terrain. Above timberline, though, the trail is invariably rocky as it weaves among granite slabs and crosses flower-decorated tundra. The following 6 miles of the trail remain above timberline in the rock-studded tundra. Alpine wildflowers here are abundant, fragrant, and colorful, and they include alpine cinquefoil, sky pilot, cushion phlox, boreal sandwort, alpine forget-me-not, alpine lousewort, alpine bistort, mountain bluebells, Parry's primrose, alpine sunflower, moss campion, Parry's townsendia, mat milkvetch, and silky phacelia.

The trail ascends gradually above Adams Pass, soon entering the headwaters valley of Sand Creek, embraced by alpine plateaus and granite knobs. West of Adams Pass, crest a saddle next to a low, slab-stacked knob, then descend 150 feet to a long boardwalk spanning a multitude of small streams in a willow-studded meadow. The Lizard Head Peak quad shows two permanent snowfields, bisected by Sand Creek, flanking the trail above this meadow. In some years these snowfields are joined and travelers may be forced onto the snow to ascend beyond the meadow.

Above the snowfields, rock-hop the cold, cascading waters of Sand Creek and proceed west on a moderate ascent of the starkly beautiful alpine valley. The twin knobs of 11,820-foot Bears Ears Mountain poke up to the south of the valley, and the cone of 12,250-foot Mount Chauvenet rises in the southwest. At the head of Sand Creek, crest an 11,650-foot pass, where dramatic views unfold to the west and northwest in one of the more memorable vistas in the range.

The trail continues climbing above the pass, and after two switchbacks the full breadth of the panorama is revealed. Northwest, long, curving Grave Lake and the alpine gem of Baptiste Lake lie beneath an array of ice-chiseled crags too numerous to name. But seasoned Wind River travelers will recognize, from left to right, the bold cliff-bound dome of 12,504-foot Mount Hooker, 12,330-foot Tower Peak, the 12,623-foot crag of Mount Lander, and the prominent tower of 12,593-foot Musembeah Peak (meaning "bighorn sheep" in the Shoshone language). To the north, 12,767-foot Roberts Mountain, another Mount Hooker-like plateau, is the loftiest summit in this view.

To the south, far above the trail, is the rocky cone of 12,326-foot Cathedral Peak, followed in the distance by the shadowed walls of Lizard Head Peak and Camels Hump. Beyond those summits the very top of the spires of the Cirque of the Towers form a sawtoothed horizon.

And to the west, resting in the broad basin beneath the pyramid of Washakie Peak and the high notch of Washakie Pass, are Macon, Pass, Washakie, and Loch Leven lakes. For an all-encompassing vista, consider scrambling via slabs and tundra to the rocky summit of Mount Chauvenet, an easy class 2 route above the trail.

The trail ahead soon reaches its highest point in the bowl high above Dutch Oven Lake, then begins a steady descent down to a broad, 11,500-foot saddle. Here it meets the southwest-bound Lizard Head Trail, leading faintly across the tundra for another 5.5 miles to Lizard Head Meadows on the North Popo Agie River (see hike 27).

Bears Ears Mountain, Mount Chauvenet, and the upper Sand Creek valley, from the Bears Ears Trail.

Bear right at this junction and descend steadily into an alpine bowl, passing a spur trail that drops to Little Valentine Lake 1.2 miles from the junction, where stunted trees make an appearance. Continue down the valley amid increasing forest to meet the Moss Lake Trail (the route of an ancient Indian trail across the mountains), branching right. That trail leads northeast for 0.4 mile, crossing a minor saddle en route to Dutch Oven Lake, an alternative campsite to popular Valentine Lake.

The Bears Ears Trail continues the descent through the forest for 0.4 mile to the outlet of the large, circular waters of 10,399-foot Valentine Lake.

A subalpine forest of spruce and whitebark pine shades the many good campsites at the lake, which harbors golden and cutthroat trout. The lake foregrounds a fine view of massive Payson Peak, in the southwest.

After crossing Valentine Lake's outlet, a steady 400-foot descent follows, leading through a forest of increasingly large trees to the long, narrow spread of Ranger Park. The trail finally enters the willow-clad meadows that fringe the South Fork Little Wind River, at 9,960 feet. Here you must ford the wide river just downstream from the confluence of multiple channels. The riverbed is filled with slippery rocks, and the waters can be shin- to knee-deep, with a moderate current.

Immediately west of the ford is the junction with the south-bound Washakie Trail, where the Bears Ears Trail turns north. Washakie Lake lies 1.4 miles southwest via the Washakie Trail, and Grave Lake lies 2.5 miles northwest via the Bears Ears Trail (see hike 30).

TORREY CREEK TRAILHEAD

OVERVIEW

Extensive alpine plateaus, deep rock-bound defiles polished smooth by ancient glaciers, immense lakes, large glaciers, and a bold array of jagged, sawtoothed peaks—the highest in the range—characterize the landscape in the northern reaches of the 198,838-acre Fitzpatrick Wilderness. Four good trails offer access to this landscape from the popular Torrey Creek Trailhead, located in the northeastern reaches of the Wind Rivers.

Much of the Wilderness remains trailless, and experienced backcountry travelers will enjoy the prospect of devising a variety of unforgettable cross-country routes over remote passes and alpine plateaus, across glaciers and tundra, and past jewel-like lakes lying in hidden cirques.

Those who have spent any time in the Bridger Wilderness, where the trails are relatively easy, should be prepared for a surprise here. The trails that begin at the Torrey Creek Trailhead, the second lowest elevation trailhead covered in this book, climb steeply and relentlessly for many miles. The Whiskey Mountain and Glacier trails are among the most scenic and rewarding trails in the range, but they require a considerable investment of time and effort during the first day on the trail; each trail gains more than 3,000 feet of elevation.

The road to the trailhead was once the roughest and rockiest trailhead access road in the range. But in the autumn of 1994, the road was rebuilt, widened, and graveled as far as Ring Lake, 6 miles from the highway. Today the road is one of the better roads in the range.

Travelers arriving late in the day can stay in one of three state-administered "parking" areas, with toilets, located at Ring and Trail lakes. The national forest boundary lies just east of the trailhead. Although some people camp around the meadow south of the trailhead, the Forest Service encourages visitors to camp at the lakeshore sites instead.

Finding the trailhead: The Trail Lake Road, Forest Road 411, heads south from U.S. Highway 26/287, 71.5 miles west of Riverton or 3.6 miles east of Dubois (and 0.2 mile east of a bridge spanning the Wind River). The turnoff is signed for Dubois Fish Hatchery and for Whiskey Basin Wildlife Habitat Management Area.

Follow the road south for several yards to a fork just beyond the cattle guard. Take the left fork, which is signed for Ring Lake Ranch and FR 411. Follow the good, wide gravel road south over the moraines that form the range's northeastern foothills. Signs at junctions point the way to the trailhead.

After 6 miles a good road forks left to Ring Lake Ranch, at the end of the reconstructed road. Bear right here; the road ahead is narrow and rough, with rocky stretches and potholes, but it's passable to low-clearance vehicles. After 7.5 miles bear right at the entrance to Whiskey Mountain Wildlife

Conservation Camp and continue another 1.5 miles to the trailhead.

Parking areas are available for both cars and stock trailers. There are corrals, unloading ramps, toilets, an information sign, and trail register at the trailhead.

THE TRAILS

- Lake Louise Trail
- Glacier Trail
- Whiskey Mountain-Ross Lake Trails
- Bomber Lake Trail

SUGGESTED EXTENDED TRIPS

1) Ross Lake base camp; round trip, 12 miles, 3 to 5 days.

2) Dinwoody Lakes base camp; round trip, 20 miles, 4 to 5 days.

3) Ink Wells base camp; round trip, 39 miles, 6 to 8 days.

4) Wilson Meadows base camp; round trip, 38.2 miles, 7 to 8 days.

PLACES TO AVOID IF YOU'RE LOOKING FOR SOLITUDE

- Phillips Lake
- Star Lake
- Wilson Meadows

37   GLACIER TRAIL—TORREY CREEK TRAILHEAD TO DINWOODY GLACIER

General description:	A rigorous extended trip of one week or longer.
Distance:	44.2 miles, round trip.
Difficulty:	Strenuous.
Traffic:	Heavy.
Elevation gain and loss:	+5,300 feet, -3,100 feet.
Trailhead elevation:	7,600 feet.
Maximum elevation:	10,895 feet.
Topo maps:	USGS: Torrey Lake (New Glacier Trail between Torrey Creek and Williamson Corrals not shown on quad), Ink Wells, Fremont Peak North; Earthwalk: Northern Wind River Range.

Key Points:

0.0   Torrey Creek Trailhead.
0.6   Junction with Whiskey Mountain Trail; stay left.
0.8   Junction with Lake Louise Trail; bear left.
3.3   Junction with Bomber Lake Trail; bear left.
6.2   Junction with Old Glacier Trail; stay right.
7.2   Crest 10,895-foot pass.
9.0   Phillips Lake.
9.6   Double Lake.
10.6 Star Lake.
12.4 Junction with spur trail to falls on Dinwoody Creek; bear right.
13.5 Cross Downs Fork.
16.7 Junction with Ink Wells Trail; stay right.
19.1 Wilson Meadows.
22.1 End of trail on Dinwoody Glacier terminal moraine.

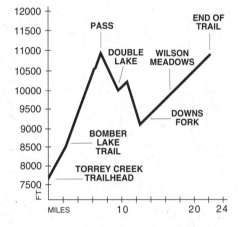

Best day hike destination: The 6.6-mile round trip to the meadows of Bomber Basin, at the foot of the Glacier Trail's switchbacks, is a pleasant, leisurely day trip. Or take the longer trip to Bomber Falls (see hike 39), or the rewarding half-day trip to Lake Louise (see hike 38).

The trail: The Glacier Trail, one of the classic high trails in the Wind Rivers, is an epic journey with no rivals in the Rocky Mountains. This long trail leads from the semi-arid, sagebrush-encircled trailhead to an alpine pass, past a sprawling lake-dotted cirque, and finally ascends a remote valley to its headwaters, born on the glacier-shrouded flanks of the range's highest peaks.

.The trail is popular with mountaineers en route to Gannett Peak and to dozens of other challenging summits, and with backpackers and off-trail wanderers. Anglers are attracted to the area by the fish-filled Dinwoody Lakes and the Ink Wells. In spite of the rigors of this demanding trail, the lofty, remote landscapes it traverses attract large numbers of wilderness travelers from July through mid-September. Don't attempt this trail unless you're in good condition and acclimated to higher elevations.

Although there are camping areas between 5.3 and 6 miles (near the site labeled Williamson Corrals on the topo map), most travelers spend their first night in the backcountry near Phillips, Double, or Star lakes, a trip of at least 9.1 miles, with an elevation gain of 3,300 feet. The small streams draining the north slopes of the pass and Burro Flat may dry up by late summer in some years. Contrary to some reports, cattle *do not* graze the tundra and foul

GLACIER • LAKE LOUISE
• TORREY CREEK TO BOMBER FALLS

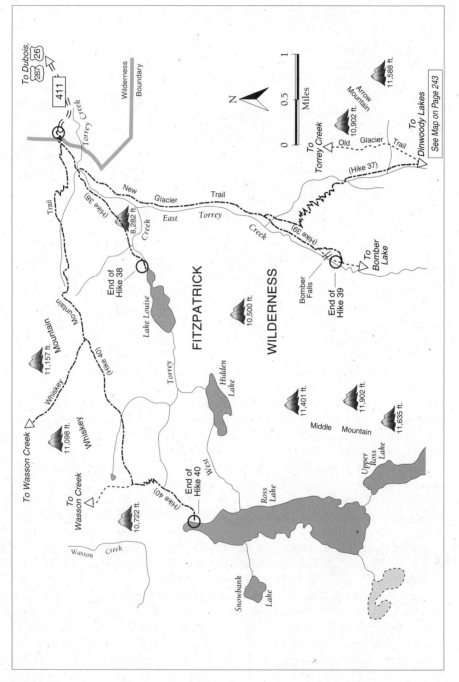

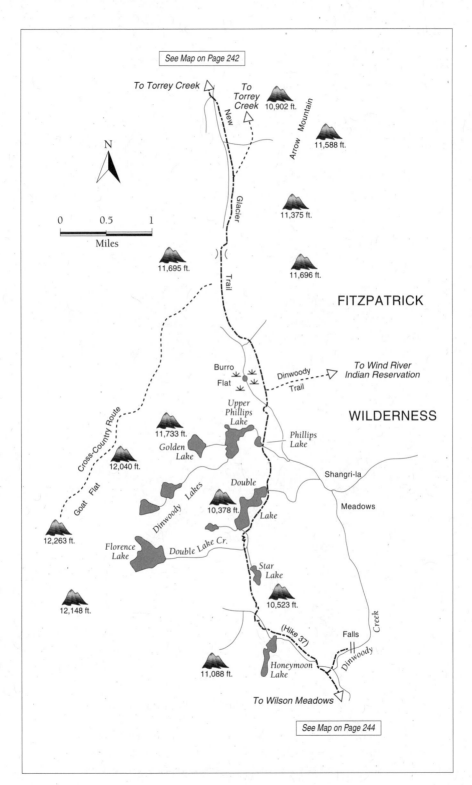

See Map on Page 242

To Torrey Creek

To Torrey Creek

10,902 ft.

Arrow Mountain

11,588 ft.

N

11,375 ft.

0   0.5   1

Miles

11,695 ft.

New

Glacier

Trail

11,696 ft.

FITZPATRICK

Burro

Flat

Dinwoody

Trail

To Wind River
Indian Reservation

WILDERNESS

Upper
Phillips
Lake

11,733 ft.

Golden
Lake

Phillips
Lake

Cross-Country Route

12,040 ft.

Double

Shangri-la

Dinwoody Lakes

10,378 ft.

Lake

Meadows

Goat Flat

12,263 ft.

Florence
Lake

Double Lake Cr.

Star
Lake

12,148 ft.

10,523 ft.

Creek

(Hike 37)

Falls

11,088 ft.

Honeymoon
Lake

Dinwoody

To Wilson Meadows

See Map on Page 244

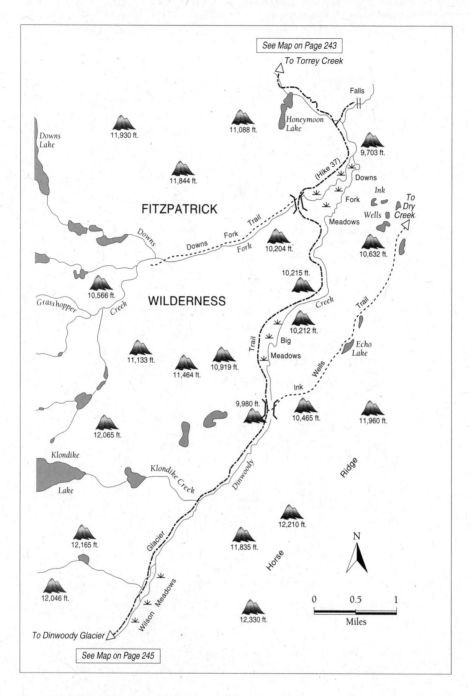

See Map on Page 243

To Torrey Creek

Falls

Honeymoon
Lake

11,930 ft.

11,088 ft.

Downs
Lake

9,703 ft.

11,844 ft.

(Hike 37)

Downs

Ink

To
Dry
Creek

Fork

FITZPATRICK

Fork

Wells

Downs   Fork   Trail

Meadows

Downs   Fork

10,204 ft.

10,632 ft.

10,215 ft.

Grasshopper   Creek

10,566 ft.

WILDERNESS

Creek   Trail

10,212 ft.

Echo
Lake

11,133 ft.

Trail

Big
Meadows

11,464 ft.   10,919 ft.

Wells

Ink

9,980 ft.

10,465 ft.

11,960 ft.

12,065 ft.

Klondike

Klondike Creek

Dinwoody

Ridge

Lake

Glacier

12,210 ft.

12,165 ft.

11,835 ft.

N

Horse

12,046 ft.

Wilson   Meadows

0   0.5   1

12,330 ft.

Miles

To Dinwoody Glacier

See Map on Page 245

the streams between Burro Flat and the site of Williamson Corrals, though
you may see moose there.

Plan on spending at least one week on the trail to get the most out of this
memorable trip. You may wish to carry supplies for a few extra days, since
you'll surely discover many worthwhile side trips that will extend your stay.

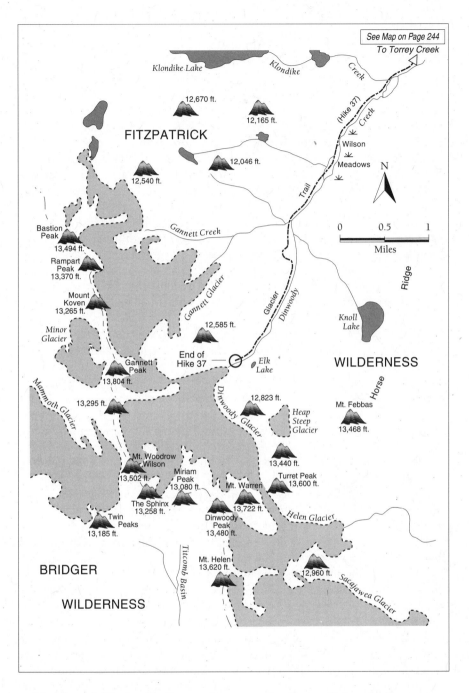

See Map on Page 244
To Torrey Creek

Klondike Lake

Klondike

Creek

12,670 ft.

12,165 ft.

FITZPATRICK

(Hike 37)

Creek

Wilson

12,046 ft.

Meadows

N

12,540 ft.

Trail

Bastion
Peak
13,494 ft.

Gannett Creek

0   0.5   1

Miles

Rampart
Peak
13,370 ft.

Mount
Koven
13,265 ft.

Gannett Glacier

Glacier

Dinwoody

Ridge

Minor
Glacier

12,585 ft.

Knoll
Lake

Gannett
Peak
13,804 ft.

End of
Hike 37

Elk
Lake

WILDERNESS

Mammoth Glacier

13,295 ft.

Dinwoody Glacier

12,823 ft.

Heap
Steep
Glacier

Mt. Febbas

Horse

13,440 ft.

13,468 ft.

Mt. Woodrow
Wilson
13,502 ft.

Miriam
Peak
13,080 ft.

Mt. Warren

Turret Peak
13,600 ft.

The Sphinx
13,258 ft.

13,722 ft.

Helen Glacier

Twin
Peaks
13,185 ft.

Dinwoody
Peak
13,480 ft.

Titcomb Basin

Mt. Helen
13,620 ft.

12,960 ft.

Sacajawea Glacier

BRIDGER

WILDERNESS

The "new" Glacier Trail, not shown on the Torrey Lake quad, was constructed after a landslide blocked the original, or "old" Glacier Trail. The new trail starts at the trailhead parking area. The old trail begins at the end of the road to Whiskey Mountain Wildlife Conservation Camp, 1.5 miles below the new trailhead. Both trails converge north of the pass, near the site of Williamson Corrals.

The new Glacier, Whiskey Mountain, and Lake Louise trails begin as one trail, leading northwest from the trailhead and ascending the lower slopes of Whiskey Mountain. Gently rising switchbacks lead across open slopes studded with sagebrush and a scattering of limber pine and Rocky Mountain juniper. The trail alternately crosses granite bedrock and the tilted sedimentary strata of Whiskey Mountain—mostly sandstone and dolomite.

After gaining 200 feet in 0.6 mile, bear left at the junction with the Whiskey Mountain Trail (see hike 40), and proceed southwest into a stand of Douglas-fir and Engelmann spruce. The trail crosses a minor bowl and, approaching the rim of Torrey Creek's gorge, meets the Lake Louise Trail (see hike 38) at 7,800 feet.

The Glacier Trail descends left from the junction to the sturdy bridge spanning Torrey Creek, which thunders below through a narrow, granite-bound gorge. Beyond the bridge ascend a minor grade over pink and gray granite, where the tread becomes rocky. The ensuing mile of trail undulates over low ice-polished domes studded with widely scattered conifers and dips into minor basins hosting sparse grasses, occasional marshes, and groves of aspen.

Good views from this sun-drenched stretch of trail reach westward up the rocky cut of West Torrey Creek to the ice-gouged flanks of Shale Mountain, and northwest to the red and gray cliff bands and ledges on the slopes of Whiskey Mountain.

Beyond the low domes the trail approaches the banks of East Torrey Creek and enters the welcome shade of a Douglas-fir, lodgepole pine, and spruce forest. A moderate ascent follows, leading into the dry lower meadow of Bomber Basin, rich with the lavender and yellow blooms of northern sweetvetch and early cinquefoil. As the trail slices through the spreading grassland look for the whitewater ribbon of Bomber Falls tumbling down its narrow chute beneath the massive boulder pile of Middle Mountain. At the meadow's southern margin, the defunct Bomber Trail joins on the left from the old Glacier Trail. Beyond that obscure juncture the trail briefly follows the banks of East Torrey Creek. It then climbs up and over a rocky knoll and drops into Bomber Basin's upper meadow, a soggy, willow-dotted spread. Broad alpine mountains streaked with snow fill the view up the canyon, beyond foaming Bomber Falls. After curving around the eastern fringes of the meadow, meet the signed Bomber Lake Trail (see hike 39), and bear left.

The Glacier Trail abandons Bomber Basin and gently ascends a shallow draw southward to the foot of a low band of cliffs. From this point, beneath a shady canopy of fir, spruce, and pine at 8,800 feet, begin a series of 29 switchbacks that gain 1,200 feet of elevation in the following 2 miles.

Midway up the ascent is an open talus slope with fine views of the surrounding alpine mountains, East Torrey Creek, and even the distant Absaroka Range. The trail then enters a timberline forest of spruce and whitebark pine, eventually leading to the shoulder of a ridge at 10,000 feet, where the grade abates. Here alpine meadows are enlivened by the blooms of cinque-

Torrey Creek cascades beneath the Glacier Trail bridge.

foil, woods forget-me-not, lupine, and American bistort. A gentle traverse ensues, leading to a rock-hop crossing of two small creeks, their banks decked with mountain bluebells and Parry's primrose.

A dense band of spruce forest lies above the crossing and hugs the bench west of the south-trending creek to timberline. If you're too exhausted to continue, or if thunderstorms are threatening, there are fair campsites and places to seek shelter in the forest, stretching south for 0.7 mile.

The trail continues uphill at a moderate grade above the east banks of the willow-bordered stream, soon entering flower-speckled tundra in a broad bowl. The grassy limestone slopes of Arrow Mountain rise above to the ·east, reaching a high point of 11,696 feet. Wildflowers such as sky pilot, cushion phlox, alpine smelowskia, Gordon's ivesia, and alpine forget-me-not herald your arrival to the alpine zone of the Wind Rivers.

The approach to the pass ahead is long and gradual. The high elevation, coupled with the day's earlier exertions, makes the approach seem longer. At length the old Glacier Trail joins in on the left. Soon the last remnants of krummholz spruces are left behind as the trail continues up the willow-studded tundra. The trail passes conical Peak 11,600, a mass of frost-shattered granite slabs, and finally attains the crest of the wide pass at 10,895 feet.

A well-deserved breather at the pass allows you to absorb the vista that unfolds before you. The deep trench of Dinwoody Creek, bounded by the alpine crest of Horse Ridge, dominates the view to the south. Crowned by 11,610-foot Dinwoody Peak in the north, and prominent Chimney Rock and 13,468-foot Mount Febbas in the south, the ridge is an 8-mile-long expanse of rock, grass, and snow.

Burro Flat and the deep cirques on the eastern flanks of Goat Flat lie closer at hand to the south. To the west, beyond the crest of Goat Flat's north ridge, are the snowy summits of Downs Mountain and Gjetetind.

Experienced hikers can easily reach Goat Flat by ascending the slopes west of the pass to a higher pass at 11,160 feet, and then following the ridge south to Goat Flat's rocky, 12,000-foot plateau.

The Glacier Trail descends a moderate grade on the south slopes of the pass, dividing into multiple paths. Stunted trees begin to appear after the grade abates and the trail skirts the willow-clad spread of Burro Flat. In early summer the tread will likely be soggy, but drier ground is found east of the meadow. A cairn marks the junction with the indistinct tread of the Dinwoody Trail, a rarely used route leading east into the Wind River Indian Reservation.

A profusion of erratic boulders dot the slopes of a minor moraine beyond the junction, and the trail becomes rocky as it descends past gnarled whitebark pines to a bridged crossing of Burro Flat's small stream. Soon after crossing the bridge, pass a grove of stunted aspens, growing far above their normal range here at 10,400 feet.

The rough, rocky trail descends steadily into timberline forest, then the grade slackens as it approaches Phillips Lake, a traditional Glacier Trail campsite. Several fair but overused campsites can be found in the spruce and whitebark forest around the lake and along its outlet stream.

The trail continues its rocky course after bridging Phillips Lake's outlet stream, then descends 200 feet while passing rocky knolls and ice-polished granite slabs to the outlet of Double Lake. There is a wide stock ford, and boulders upstream provide a dry crossing for backpackers.

Double Lake in Dinwoody Lakes basin, Glacier Trail.

At 9,960 feet Double Lake lies at the center of the broad Dinwoody Lakes cirque. Its open shoreline affords fine views of bold towers and soaring headwalls that contrast with the high plateau of Goat Flat.

Brook and cutthroat trout inhabit most of the lakes in the Dinwoody chain. Aptly named Golden Lake, tucked away in a confined bowl above Upper Phillips Lake at 10,560 feet, harbors golden trout. Ten rock-bound lakes are spread throughout the basin, and those lying off the trail are accessible via cross-country scrambles. With a little extra effort, travelers can find solitude in this shadowed, cliff-rimmed cirque.

The rocky trail follows above the southeast shore of Double Lake for 0.5 mile beyond the crossing, then crosses its inlet stream and ascends a rocky draw. The trail then gains 200 feet via switchbacks to a bridged crossing of Double Lake Creek. The ascent continues until you reach the shores of 10,272-foot Star Lake, a fine timberline lake wedged between rocky domes. Here are found several good but much-used campsites.

After cresting a minor ridge south of Star Lake, begin a rocky, 1.6-mile, 1,100-foot descent into the valley of Dinwoody Creek. The trail twice crosses the inlet stream of Honeymoon Lake, then curves east, staying above the wooded shoreline of that 9,838-foot lake (fair campsites and cutthroat fishing). From the lake the route plunges down the course of Honeymoon Creek, with the help of a few switchbacks.

Approaching the valley floor the grade slackens. Rock-hop Honeymoon

Creek and pause at a junction at 9,160 feet. The left-branching trail leads 0.4 mile to an outstanding waterfall, where large Dinwoody Creek is funneled between two prominent domes and plunges over a granite precipice.

Bearing right at that junction, begin the long, 9.7-mile trek along the course of Dinwoody Creek. The trail climbs from the canyon's forested depths to the foot of the Dinwoody Glacier, in alpine terrain at 10,800 feet.

The lower flanks of the canyon are punctuated by tree-crested domes, and the trail leads past their rounded profiles for miles ahead. The milky waters of Dinwoody Creek, opaque with glacial sediments, fluctuate with the melting and freezing of the ten large glaciers above that give life to the stream.

About 0.5 mile from the junction the trail reaches the soggy expanse of Downs Fork Meadows—the silted in remains of an ancient lakebed. Follow its margins to the junction with the dead-end Downs Fork Trail. That trail leads 2.5 miles up Downs Fork, beyond which are rewarding cross-country routes to Downs Lake and to the Grasshopper Glacier.

Bear left at this junction and drop to Downs Fork, another fluctuating, glacier-fed stream. A new bridge spans the creek, so there is no need to ford the stream.

The trail ahead winds up the forested confines of the canyon, passing beneath the rocky faces of a succession of domes for another 1.8 miles to Big Meadows at 9,600 feet, yet another ancient lakebed. Beyond the meadows, meet the northeast-bound Ink Wells Trail. That trail bridges Dinwoody Creek and ascends 800 feet in 2.6 miles to a chain of small lakes—the Ink Wells—perched on the flanks of Horse Ridge among rocky domes. These lakes offer off-the-beaten-track solitude, good campsites, and fishing for brook trout.

Beyond the Ink Wells Trail junction, the Glacier Trail curves around a bend of the valley and snow-crowned Gannett Peak finally comes into view. Here the character of the valley begins to change. A narrow band of timberline forest clings to the lower canyon walls, and above are ice-sculpted domes and glacier-clad peaks. Meadows dominate the valley floor, watered by the braided meanders of silt-laden Dinwoody Creek. Many fine campsites can be found along the following 3.5 miles of the trail.

Cross large Klondike Creek 1.6 miles from the previous junction, then continue along the meadow fringes, at times entering stands of whitebark pine and spruce. The trail crosses a channel of Dinwoody Creek in Wilson Meadows, 2.7 miles from the Ink Wells Trail, then crosses back to the west bank after 0.25 mile. Some travelers avoid the crossing by following the creek's west bank.

Wilson Meadows, at 9,800 feet, was the site of a climber's base camp operated by Floyd Wilson in the 1940s, and many travelers today use the meadows for a base camp. The tree-fringed meadows lie in a dramatic setting, with 13,804-foot Gannett Peak for an icy backdrop.

The trail ascends from Wilson Meadows to an often-difficult crossing of boulder-strewn Gannett Creek, draining the massive Gannett Glacier. From here the trail ascends into a fine alpine valley and continues climbing west of Dinwoody Creek to the fresh moraine at the snout of Dinwoody Glacier. The glacier marks the trail's end and the beginning of climbing routes to Gannett Peak and other summits.

The sprawling icefield of Dinwoody Glacier rises before you, reaching up to the Continental Divide and the snow-capped dome of Gannett Peak. Mount Woodrow Wilson (13,502 feet), The Sphinx (13,258 feet), and an array of pyramidal crags form a sawtoothed skyline above the sea of ice.

The raw moraines at the trail's end, a jumble of loose, angular rocks, represent the extent of the last major advance of the glacier, which ended in the early part of the twentieth century. Notice the tongues of rock that extend up the glacier. These either toppled from or were plucked from the flanks of the cirque and are imperceptibly riding on a giant conveyor belt of ice, destined to be dumped in a rubbly mass at the foot of the glacier.

Restrain the urge to venture out onto the ice, unless you're equipped with good judgment, experience in glacier travel, plus crampons and an ice axe.

38 LAKE LOUISE TRAIL—TORREY CREEK TO LAKE LOUISE

General description:	A day hike or easy overnight trip.
Distance:	4.6 miles, round trip.
Difficulty:	Moderately easy.
Traffic:	Heavy.
Elevation gain and loss:	800 feet.
Trailhead elevation:	7,600 feet.
Maximum elevation:	8,382 feet.
Topo maps:	USGS: Torrey Lake (trail to lake not shown on map); Earthwalk: Northern Wind River Range.

See Map on Page 242

Key points:

0.0 Torrey Creek Trailhead.
0.6 Junction with Whiskey Mountain Trail; bear left.
0.8 Junction with Lake Louise Trail; bear right.
2.3 Lake Louise.

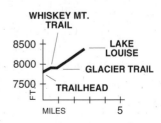

Lake Louise.

The trail: You don't have to be a dedicated, long-distance backpacker to enjoy a beautiful rock-bound lake in the Wind River backcountry. Lake Louise, just 2.3 miles from the Torrey Creek Trailhead, is accessible to anyone willing to spend a few hours walking along a scenic trail.

The trip traverses a diversity of landscapes, ranging from the desert-like trailhead area to cool forests and ice-sculpted canyon walls that rise more than 2,000 feet above the lake. Add good fishing to the inspiring setting of the lake, and you have a rewarding hike that will satisfy novice and veteran hikers alike.

Expect plenty company along this trail; it is heavily used throughout the summer.

From the trailhead follow the Glacier Trail (see hike 37) for 0.8 mile to the signed junction with the Lake Louise Trail and turn right. The trail is steep and rocky for 0.2 mile, but then the grade eases and it winds southwestward among glacier-polished knobs next to the foaming torrent of West Torrey Creek.

Rocky Mountain juniper, Douglas-fir, and groves of aspen dot the convoluted bedrock slopes of the canyon, and an array of wildflowers enliven the rocky landscape, including groundsel, stonecrop, prairie smoke, buckwheat, cinquefoil, and pussytoes. Good views reach westward up the rocky defile to the 11,401-foot north peak of Middle Mountain.

The trail leaves the banks of West Torrey Creek after 0.5 mile and ascends a draw shaded by the boughs of Douglas-fir and lodgepole pine. Beyond the head of the draw, the often-muddy trail crosses a boggy area in a shady spruce grove, then curves back to the streambanks and ascends ice-polished bedrock alongside a thundering cascade. Here the trail becomes obscure; follow ledges westward on up to the east bay of Lake Louise, where the trail ends.

Low cliffs, domes, and soaring canyon walls rise north and south of the lake, inhibiting easy travel beyond the end of the trail. A few poor campsites are situated on rocky ledges above the north shore of the 8,382-foot lake. Better campsites can be found above the south shore—if logs are in place to allow safe crossing of the outlet. Brook trout lurk in the depths of Lake Louise and fishing can be productive. But access to the shoreline is difficult, involving scrambling over rocky knolls and low cliffs.

Fine views extend westward up the deep, glacier-carved valley of West Torrey Creek to the flanks of Shale Mountain, the extensive alpine plateau on the skyline.

Douglas-fir and lodgepole and limber pine dot the bedrock around the lake, but on the flanks of the 10,000-foot ridge to the south stands a ghost forest of snags charred in a campfire-caused burn in 1976.

39   TORREY CREEK TO BOMBER FALLS

General description:	A long day hike.
Distance:	9.4 miles, round trip.
Difficulty:	Moderate.
Traffic:	Moderate.
Elevation gain and loss:	+1,650 feet, -150 feet.
Trailhead elevation:	7,600 feet.
Maximum elevation:	9,250 feet.
Topo maps:	USGS: Torrey Lake; Earthwalk: Northern Wind River Range.

See Map on Page 242

Key points:
- 0.0   Torrey Creek Trailhead.
- 0.6   Junction with Whiskey Mountain Trail; bear left.
- 0.8   Junction with Lake Louise Trail; bear left.
- 3.3   Junction with Bomber Lake Trail; bear right.
- 4.7   Brink of Bomber Falls.

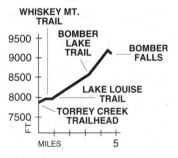

Bomber Basin spreads out in the valley below Bomber Falls, East Torrey Creek.

The trail: The unmaintained trail to Bomber Falls is one of the longer day trips from the Torrey Creek Trailhead. It leads from the meadows of Bomber Basin at the Glacier Trail junction to the whitewater ribbon of Bomber Falls. Above the falls lies the scattered wreckage of a B-17 bomber that crashed during World War II, reportedly while strafing an unidentified mammal. All crewmen lost their lives in the only crash of a military aircraft in the Wind Rivers.

Expect to encounter faint tread, a tangle of fallen trees, and steep pitches on the Bomber Lake Trail. The trail is impassable to packstock. There are a few good places to camp in Bomber Basin for travelers who wish to spend more than one day exploring the East Torrey Creek valley.

From the trailhead follow the Glacier Trail (see hike 37) 3.3 miles to the Bomber Lake Trail junction in Bomber Basin, and turn right onto that trail. This faint trail carves a swath southwest through the basin's upper meadow, soon entering lodgepole pine forest. Good camping areas can be found along the next 0.25 mile.

Hikers soon begin climbing over and detouring around a maze of fallen trees blocking the trail. The tread is often faint and careful attention is required at times to stay on track. Large Engelmann spruce begin to cast their shadows as the trail edges close to a prominent cliff rising 200 feet above the trail to the east. Then the trail briefly becomes wet and muddy, continuing its southwesterly course beneath an increasingly dense canopy of spruce and subalpine fir.

Even at close range the falls remain hidden from view behind the mantle of forest, but the thunderous roar fills the air. The trail leads to a poor campsite perched on a bench, where the tread seems to disappear. Scout around to find two paths: one leads 200 yards over slippery, boulder-covered slopes to the base of the falls, and the other climbs southward above the campsite.

That trail becomes well-defined as it marches up the exceedingly steep grade, gaining a total of 550 feet over the following 0.3 mile. Climb up and up, through shady spruce forest, to the eastern flanks of a rocky, tree-studded knob. Curving around the knob, the grade briefly abates. But soon it bends west and climbs hard once again to the crest of the knob, just above the valley of East Fork Torrey Creek.

Here a fine view unfolds, reaching west to the rubbly mass of Middle Mountain and up-canyon to soaring canyon walls and rocky alpine plateaus. Carefully scan the lower western slopes of the canyon, opposite this viewpoint, to spot some of the bomber wreckage. Or wade across the creek to reach it.

The Bomber Lake Trail continues up the canyon, ultimately leading to Bomber Lake (3.3 miles ahead), via a demanding and obscure route. But to reach the brink of the falls, follow the trail as it descends toward the canyon floor, then leave the trail and head north, following the course of the creek downstream. A path follows the streambanks, leading to a boulder field at the brink of the falls—exercise extreme caution here.

Although only the upper cascades of the falls can be seen from here, the chute carved by the large creek here frames a fine view that reaches down to Bomber Basin, past the alpine slopes of Arrow Mountain, and to the distant Absaroka Range on the northern skyline.

General description:	A rigorous day-long or multi-day trip.
Distance:	12 miles, round trip.
Difficulty:	Strenuous.
Traffic:	Moderate.
Elevation gain and loss:	+ 2,850 feet, -900 feet.
Trailhead elevation:	7,600 feet.
Maximum elevation:	10,240 feet.
Topo maps:	USGS: Torrey Lake, Simpson Lake; Earthwalk: Northern Wind River Range.

See Map on Page 242

Key points:

0.0 Torrey Creek Trailhead.

0.6 Junction with Whiskey Mountain Trail; bear right.

3.0 Junction on south slopes of Whiskey Mountain; bear left to Ross Lake (or right to Whiskey Mountain).

4.9 Unsigned junction with faint Ross Lake Trail; turn left and head south.

6.0 Ross Lake.

Best day hike destination: A 6-mile round trip to the trail junction on the slopes of Whiskey Mountain is a strenuous but rewarding day hike, offering expansive vistas and a rich assortment of colorful alpine wildflowers.

Strong hikers and those on horseback will enjoy the 7.2-mile round trip to the crest of Whiskey Mountain, which offers even better wildflower displays and far-ranging vistas.

The hike: When viewed from the Wind River Valley near Dubois, Whiskey Mountain is not especially attractive. Its broad slopes rise from the high desert to an alpine crown of tundra, with a narrow band of forest cloaking its middle flanks. Farther south rises similar Arrow Mountain, and together these massive sedimentary peaks block from view the ice-chiseled high country of the Wind River Range.

But Whiskey Mountain is far from being the drab, lifeless mountain it appears to be from below. Its alpine slopes host expansive grasslands and a wide variety of alpine cushion plants and their fragrant, colorful blossoms. And views from its crest are far-reaching, encompassing a broad stretch of mountainous northwest Wyoming.

Most noteworthy, however, is the mountain's importance as exceptional bighorn sheep range. Approximately 1,000 Rocky Mountain bighorns winter on the lower flanks of Whiskey Mountain, comprising the largest bighorn sheep herd on Earth. This herd is the seed stock for bighorn sheep transplants throughout the western United States.

During summer, many of the bighorns travel south to the high, cliff-edged plateaus east of the Continental Divide, but some remain behind on Whiskey Mountain. If you are fortunate enough to spot bighorn sheep while on the mountain, please observe them from a distance; they are very sensitive to human intrusion.

The National Bighorn Sheep Interpretive Center in Dubois is well worth a visit. The center offers information on bighorn sheep, on the Whiskey Mountain herd, and on the management of the herd through the cooperative efforts of various state and federal agencies and private landowners.

From the trailhead, follow the Glacier Trail (see hike 37) as it ascends sagebrush-clad slopes for 0.6 mile to the signed Whiskey Mountain Trail, and turn right onto that trail. This trail continues the ascent of Whiskey Mountain's south slopes via steep switchbacks. The tread along the following 2.4 miles is derived from limestone, and the trail can be very slippery and sticky during and shortly after rainfall.

These sun-baked, south-facing slopes are covered in sagebrush, and a scattering of limber pines and Rocky Mountain junipers reflect the trees' competition for scant moisture. Enlivening the drab trailside slopes are the brilliant reds and yellows of Indian paintbrush and groundsel.

Looming above the trail the tilted sedimentary strata of Whiskey Mountain are exposed in graphic cross-section. Red, tan, and gray cliff bands of sandstone, dolomite, and limestone comprise the mountain's flanks, clearly showing the sedimentary materials that accumulated in the region between 600 and 250 million years ago. Following uplift of the Wind Rivers, those rocks were tilted upward along the flanks of the fault block, and much of that rocky veneer has since been stripped away by erosion.

When you pause to catch your breath on the relentless ascent, enjoy the fine views that stretch eastward across the colorful Dubois Badlands to the Owl Creek Mountains, and south across Torrey Creek canyon to the broad slopes of Arrow Mountain and the rubbly mass of Middle Mountain. Even from the heights of the trail, Torrey Creek can still be heard rumbling far below.

At 8,500 feet, 1.2 miles from the trailhead, the switchbacks end and a steeply rising traverse ensues. Douglas-firs now begin to supplant the junipers and limber pines. With further elevation gains, Engelmann spruce appear in sheltered draws, and lodgepole pine and aspen make an occasional appearance. But the limber pines persist in the forest, high above the trees' normal range. Their gnarled, spreading forms reach greater dimension here, where greater moisture and shade is available.

At 9,200 feet the grade briefly slackens as it enters a small meadow with

Ross Lake, with Ram Flat, Downs Mountain, and Gjetetind in the background.

a good view of the high alpine slopes of Whiskey Mountain. From this meadow to the trail junction on the mountain ahead a few camping areas are found near the trail, and three small springs provide water.

The steep grade of the trail moderates beyond the meadow but continues to lead steadily uphill. Spruce dominates the forest in a draw above the meadow, which hosts a trickling, early season stream. Near the head of the draw, at 9,880 feet, the tread becomes muddy where it crosses the runoff from the seeping spring shown on the topo map.

Above the spring the grade moderates further and soon crosses the runoff from two more springs. The trail then opens up in timberline meadows cradled by groves of stunted spruce and whitebark pine. Wildflowers begin to splash their colors across trailside slopes, including the blooms of shooting star, alpine forget-me-not, pasqueflower, goldflower, dandelion, leafy aster, and mountain bluebells.

Eventually the trail reaches the junction high on the slopes of Whiskey Mountain, at 10,240 feet, just beyond the highest grove of timberline trees. The grand panorama that unfolds from here easily justifies the effort required to enjoy it and is surpassed only by the vista from the crest of Whiskey Mountain.

To the southeast lie the smooth, green tundra slopes of Arrow Mountain, looming 4,000 feet above the ice-scoured defile of Torrey Creek. To the southwest lies difficult-to-reach Hidden Lake, and above it rises Middle

Mountain. On the western skyline is the broad alpine plateau of Shale Mountain, its flanks scalloped by snowy cirques. And on the southwest horizon are the snowy cones of 13,349-foot Downs Mountain, and Peak 13,202, dubbed Gjetetind (Goat Mountain) by climbers.

Alpine cushion plants reflect the arctic-like conditions that prevail on the mountain. Within several yards of the junction look for rock jasmine, arctic sandwort, yellow-flowered cushion draba, alpine cinquefoil, mat milkvetch, cushion phlox, and cliff anemone.

If Whiskey Mountain is your goal, turn right at the junction (see description below). To reach Ross Lake, bear left and begin a west-bound traverse, crossing alpine meadows at first. Then enter a timberline stand of spruce and whitebark pine. When the trail reaches terrain dominated by granitic rocks, the tread becomes rough and rocky.

The trail, with minor ups and downs, leads westward, at times passing through stands of charred and sun-burnished snags. In 1976, a fire that began at Lake Louise burned itself out here at timberline. In early season, the tread may be wet and muddy in places. About 1 mile from the junction enter a broad meadow at 10,200 feet, its rock-studded expanse adorned with the blooms of subalpine buttercup, woods forget-me-not, cutleaf daisy, and American bistort. Boulder-heaped knobs and ridges encircle the spread, and a prominent granite spire punctuates the southwest skyline, pointing the way to Ross Lake.

Hop across the small stream draining a pond in the meadow, then follow its southern margin, flanked by an open forest of whitebark pines. Some travelers use this meadow area as a base camp and take day trips to Ross Lake. Look for good places to camp in the forest both north and south of the meadow.

At the southwest corner of the meadow a cairn marks the junction with the obscure, seldom-trod Ross Lake Trail, heading north. Here the main trail bends south, crests a minor rise, then begins a steep and rocky, 300-foot descent via switchbacks into West Torrey Creek canyon. Enjoy glimpses of Hidden and Ross lakes on the descent into the realm of glacier-polished domes and knolls.

The descent ends alongside a willow-clad opening, beyond which the trail rises slightly to a saddle, then descends once again, losing another 350 feet of elevation and dropping into an increasingly heavy forest. Pass west of a tarn-dotted notch; a final descent leads to the northern arm of Ross Lake, where the trail ends.

There are places to camp above the east shore, and fishing for cutthroats and rainbows makes the lake an attractive destination for anglers. Lakeshore travel is restricted to the east shore, where paths forged by anglers are found. The west shore is impassable due to steep talus slopes, huge boulders, and soaring cliffs. Some anglers pack in inflatable rafts or float tubes for better access to the lake's deep waters.

Two-mile-long Ross Lake is the largest backcountry lake in the Wind Rivers, and it lies in a grand setting befitting that distinction. Although the lake lies at a modest elevation—9,675 feet—timberline here is much lower than it is in other parts of the range. Here timberline is influenced by an abundance of bedrock that inhibits the establishment of trees, and by deep, lingering snows.

The flanks of Shale Mountain, jutting skyward more than 2,000 feet from Ross Lake's west shore, provide an exciting backdrop of cliffs, talus fields, buttresses, and hanging cirques. Ram Flat and its nearly level, 12,000-foot expanse looms as a rim above the southwest shore of the lake. Rising at the head of West Torrey Creek to the south is the 12,234-foot crag of Spider Peak.

WHISKEY MOUNTAIN

To reach the crest of Whiskey Mountain and enjoy far-flung vistas, bear right at the junction 3 miles from the trailhead. There is no trail here, but cairns lead the way up the steep tundra. Watch for bighorn sheep; they are often observed on the slopes of the mountain. The views enjoyed at the junction continue to expand as the trail gains elevation. The vista includes the long crest of Horse Ridge to the southeast and the bold crag of Spider Peak to the southwest.

Even more colorful and fragrant wildflowers bedeck the grassy slopes above the junction. In addition to the blooms listed above, amateur botanists may also notice alpine bluebells, cous biscuitroot, silky phacelia, shooting star, alpine sunflower, cutleaf daisy, beautiful paintbrush, plus the striking purple blossoms of the prostrate Jones columbine.

The cairned route crests Whiskey Mountain at 10,960 feet, on a broad saddle separating the east and west summits, 1.1 miles from the junction. Here an unforgettable vista unfolds. To the north lies the rugged south wall of the Absaroka Range, rising beyond the colorful badlands in the Wind River Valley. The Tetons form the sawtoothed horizon in the northwest, and eastern peaks of the Gros Ventre Range can be seen in the west, framed by a low notch in the Wind Rivers' crest.

On the crest of the range west of this viewpoint, you can see where progressively lower alpine mountains finally give way to tree-crested summits that march northwestward toward Togwotee Pass, where the Wind River Range merges with the volcanic peaks of the Absarokas.

BACKCOUNTRY CHECKLIST

To be sure you haven't forgotten an essential piece of equipment, always prepare a checklist before leaving home. No one will take everything on the following list, but it may help ensure that you've packed all the necessary gear for your trip.

- [ ] Day pack and/or backpack
- [ ] Sleeping bag
- [ ] Foam pad or air mattress
- [ ] Ground sheet and/or tarp
- [ ] Dependable tent
- [ ] Sturdy footwear
- [ ] Lightweight camp shoes or sandals
- [ ] Sunglasses
- [ ] Sunscreen
- [ ] Lip balm
- [ ] Insect repellent
- [ ] Mosquito headnet
- [ ] Maps and compass
- [ ] Matches in waterproof container
- [ ] Toilet paper
- [ ] Lightweight plastic trowel
- [ ] Pocket knife
- [ ] First-aid kit
- [ ] Survival kit
- [ ] Flashlight with fresh batteries and spare bulb
- [ ] Candle
- [ ] 50 feet of nylon parachute cord
- [ ] Extra stuffsacks for bear-bagging food
- [ ] Water filter
- [ ] One-quart water container(s)
- [ ] One-gallon water container (collapsible) for camp use
- [ ] Plastic bags (for trash)
- [ ] Biodegradable soap
- [ ] Towel
- [ ] Toothbrush
- [ ] Cookware
- [ ] Spoon and fork
- [ ] Camp stove and extra fuel
- [ ] Pot scrubber
- [ ] Enough food, plus a little extra
- [ ] Fishing license
- [ ] Fishing rod, reel, flies, lures, etc.
- [ ] Camera, film, lenses, filters, tripod

- ☐ Binoculars
- ☐ Waterproof cover for pack
- ☐ Dependable rain parka
- ☐ Windproof parka
- ☐ Thermal underwear (polypropylene is best)
- ☐ Shorts and/or long pants
- ☐ Wool cap or balaclava
- ☐ Wool shirt and/or sweater
- ☐ Jacket or parka (synthetic pile is best)
- ☐ Extra socks
- ☐ Underwear
- ☐ Mittens or gloves
- ☐ Watch
- ☐ Sewing kit
- ☐ Hat
- ☐ Field guidebooks
